THE MAID OF ORLÉANS

SVEN STOLPE

THE MAID OF ORLÉANS

The Life and Mysticism
of Joan of Arc

Translated from the Swedish by
ERIC LEWENHAUPT

IGNATIUS PRESS   SAN FRANCISCO

Original edition © 1956 by Pantheon Books, New York

Front cover image:
© Shutterstock.com/Remy Musser

Cover design by Davin Carlson

Introduction © 2014 by Ignatius Press, San Francisco
Published in 2014 by Ignatius Press by arrangement with
Bloomsbury Publishing Plc.
All rights reserved
ISBN 978-1-58617-152-0
Library of Congress Control Number 2006939360
Printed in the United States of America ♾

CONTENTS

INTRODUCTION

On the morning of May 30, 1431, in the city of Rouen in northern France, Joan of Arc was burned at the stake as a relapsed heretic. Her enemies certainly hoped that this event had conclusively settled the matter of her spiritual legitimacy and had permanently shattered her reputation. Just to be sure, the English dumped the ashes of her body into the Seine River. And yet, their efforts to consign Joan to the dustbin of history (via the currents of the Seine) proved immensely futile, as nearly six centuries later she remains one of the most widely known figures of the Middle Ages. Part of this is due to the fact that, on account of her various trials, the Maid (*la Pucelle*) is one of the best documented people of the pre-modern era. This abundance of documentation has undeniably boosted the myriad of books about her, but it is her feats, her resolve, and her virtue that have made so many want to study Joan. Sven Stolpe, the author of this book, speaks for many when he describes her as "a figure unlike any hitherto known to history" (p. 22 below). Her story is a truly remarkable one: an illiterate peasant girl claims a divine military mission and succeeds in reversing her country's fortune during the Hundred Years' War. Indeed, even those disinterested in the past or who have the vaguest recollection of their high school or college history courses tend to be aware of the French heroine. But for many others, from the fifteenth century to the present, Joan is not some hazy historical recollection. The mountain of books about her reflects a fascination with the Maid of Orléans that has been a constant since she burst like a supernova into the popular consciousness in 1428.

Since that time many have laid claim to Joan. The Catholic Church rehabilitated her in 1456 (via her posthumous retrial) and canonized her in 1920. Over the centuries, French nationalists have regularly recalled her memory when defying various invaders, while French politicians have shamelessly invoked her to boost their electoral prospects.[1] She

---

[1] One need only look at the 2012 presidential elections in France for evidence of how politicians of various leanings still try to appropriate Joan's image and reputation to enhance their own electoral pedigree.

has been subjected to various labels and categorizations. The English called her a witch—a sentiment that seemed to still have some traction in the Elizabethan era as evidenced by Shakespeare's *Henry VI, Part 1*, in which Joan is described as the "foul fiend of France".[2] In George Bernard Shaw's play, *Saint Joan*, she is depicted as a type of proto-Protestant, with her disregard for ecclesiastical authority. Feminist scholars, such as Marina Warner, have thrust upon the Maid the mantle of a gender-challenging, patriarchy-defying rebel.[3] More recently, some have even attempted to cast her as merely the protégé—or even pawn—of a Spanish queen.[4] For Mark Twain, Joan was "perhaps the only entirely unselfish person whose name has a place in profane history."[5]

Sven Stolpe certainly lacks the renown of Shaw, Shakespeare, Twain, or some of the other famous writers who have weighed in on the subject of Joan of Arc. A Swedish writer who converted to Catholicism in 1947, he was most widely known during the 1940s and 1950s for his novels and essays, though he made the occasional foray into the genre of historical biography. Indeed, his book on Queen Christina of Sweden, who abdicated the throne following her own conversion to Catholicism in 1654, was very well received upon its publication.[6] While this Scandinavian queen was a fitting topic for an author who mirrored Christina in both his ethnicity and his own Catholic conversion, his decision to take on Joan of Arc seems a more surprising choice at first glance. He did spend some time studying in Paris, which may have contributed to his interest in Joan. Clearly, as the ample references throughout this book attest, Jacques Cordier's controversial 1948 study on Joan of Arc played a major role in propelling Stolpe toward this topic.[7] Cordier's book offers an extremely contrarian view on Joan, arguing that most of what we

[2] The vitriol aimed at Joan in the play has resulted in some Shakespeare scholars arguing that the work was the result of collaboration and that this mysterious co-author is responsible for the anti-Joan components. For more on this see Charles Boyce, *Shakespeare A to Z* (New York: Roundtable Press, 1990), p. 274.

[3] Marina Warner, *Joan of Arc: The Image of Female Heroism* (New York: Knopf, 1981).

[4] Nancy Goldstone, *The Maid and the Queen: The Secret History of Joan of Arc* (New York: Viking, 2012).

[5] Mark Twain, *The Personal Recollections of Joan of Arc* (San Francisco: Ignatius Press, 1989), p. 20.

[6] Sven Stolpe, *Christina of Sweden*, trans. Alec Randall and Ruth Mary Bethell (New York: Macmillan, 1966).

[7] Jacques Cordier, *Jeanne d'Arc, sa personnalité, son rôle* (Paris: Éditions de la Table Ronde, 1948).

know about her is legend, that her military contributions were minimal, and that her revelations were personal hallucinations. As Stolpe notes in the postscript, "To a great extent, I have agreed with this treatment of the material for a biography of Joan, but I differ radically from Cordier concerning the basic view of Joan's person" (p. 274 below).

Stolpe, though, overstates his similarity to Cordier—especially since he more or less rejects the notion that Joan's voices were hysterical phenomena. However, he does take a very skeptical view of some oft-repeated stories about the Maid, particularly when the information comes from later sources, such as the *Chronique de la Pucelle*. His rejection of the famous episode where Joan, without ever having seen him before, correctly identifies the Dauphin while he is standing amid his courtiers at Chinon, is indicative of his tendency to debunk stories that do not come from (or at least mirror) information recorded in Joan's various trials and examinations. And frankly, his skepticism concerning some of these stories is often persuasive. Occasionally, his tendency to debunk or downplay is off the mark. A glaring instance of this is his disregard for Joan's military contributions, a position which has been undone by more recent scholarship on this topic.[8]

More importantly, Stolpe's desire to prune the foliage of legend that has become entangled in the biography of the historical Joan is not mere mimicry of Cordier's pseudo-scientific skepticism. Rather, this demythologizing of the Maid serves his primary aim of elevating an underappreciated aspect of Joan: her mysticism. Ultimately, it is this dimension of Joan that inspired Stolpe to add to the already overcrowded stacks of Maid-related tomes. As he opined with some frustration, "The great fault with nearly all previous accounts of Joan's life is that they have ignored or minimized the fact that her spiritual development was that of a typical mystic" (p. 50 below).

Because of this approach, *The Maid of Orleans* has a freshness to it in spite of being more than sixty years old.[9] Granted there are some dated elements, such as the frequent Cordier references or the occasional World War II–related analogies (though I for one was quite amused with his likening fifteenth-century Normandy to Vichy France). Nevertheless,

[8] The best work on this subject is Kelly DeVries, *Joan of Arc: A Military Leader* (Stroud: Sutton Publishing, 1999).

[9] The book was first published in Swedish in 1949, *Jeanne d'Arc* (Stockholm: Bonnier, 1949), with a subsequent English edition appearing in 1956.

the emphasis on the spirituality of the Maid makes the work very relevant to the current debates about Joan, which tend to center around the credibility of her revelations. A recent scholarly biography that posits the voices were concocted by Joan as "an excuse for her to leave her home and go to the king" embodies an increasingly typical disregard for her spiritual claims.[10] It should be noted that Stolpe's consideration of Joan's mysticism is not fixated on her revelations; indeed, the author emphasizes that at her canonization the voices were not even mentioned. Thus, the examination of her mysticism takes a much wider lens in ascertaining the aspects of her life as a whole that embody this spiritual dynamic.

For those reading Stolpe's book for the first time, the reaction might be akin to the reception of the Danish film director Carl Theodor Dreyer's silent film *The Passion of Joan of Arc* during the 1980s. First released in 1928, the original negative (as well as a second version reconstructed by the director) was destroyed in a fire. All that remained for many decades was a heavily edited, inferior version of the film. But serendipitously, in 1981, in the closet of a Norwegian mental institution, a janitor stumbled upon some canisters that turned out to hold an original cut of the film. Upon its re-release, the film was showered with praise. In spite of being a silent film, it remains—even in the age of progressing technology and ubiquitous social media—a powerful, intense, and draining cinematic experience. Books and films are obviously very different mediums, but Stolpe's monograph reminded me of the Dreyer film in this sense of how something clearly old and forgotten (or in this case, long out-of-print) could convey such a fresh pertinence. These two projects are also similar in the shared Scandinavian heritage of both the author and the director. But most concretely, *The Maid of Orleans* and *The Passion of Joan of Arc* are united in a shared appreciation for Joan's faith. Or, as Dreyer put it in an essay he wrote for the Danish Film Institute about his movie: "realized mysticism".

—Vincent Ryan
Assistant Professor of History
Aquinas College, Nashville

[10] Larissa Taylor, *The Virgin Warrior: The Life and Death of Joan of Arc* (New Haven: Yale University Press, 2009), p. 134. An especially extreme example of the modern rejection of Joan's revelations can be seen in the execrable 1998 film *The Messenger*, which presents Joan's voices as a hysteria rooted in some type of post-traumatic stress disorder she suffers after supposedly witnessing the rape of her sister by enemy troops.

CHAPTER I

The Hundred Years' War: Louis of Orléans Is Murdered in Paris and John the Fearless on the Bridge of Montereau

Like a pack of young wolves the English hurled themselves on France.

Edward III had already assumed the title King of France, and he easily vanquished the French king, Philip VI, who had placed the Valois dynasty on the throne of France. But the decision came only with the first naval battle off Sluys on June 24, 1340, and afterward, on land, with the battle of Crécy on August 26, 1346, which was to prove one of the worst catastrophes in French military history.

The English had an enormous military superiority, due partly to their bowmen and their use of gunpowder, but also to a system of tactics that took the French by surprise. The Black Prince, son of Edward III, contributed greatly to the victory, and poets and chroniclers sang his praise. The forces engaged were considerable for those times; twenty-five thousand Englishmen fought at Crécy, and, according to contemporary reports that are not fully authenticated, defeated seventy thousand Frenchmen, of whom about half fell in battle, while the English casualties were insignificant. A great part of the French nobility were among the fallen.

Edward captured Calais, and from this port, which remained in English hands for two centuries, was able to continue his attacks on France.

After this disaster came another, perhaps more serious—the Black Death. Death required no help from battling armies and straggling marauders; it carried on its work with enthusiasm and success.

The two nations had hardly recovered from this horror when the war blazed up anew. The decisive battle was this time at Poitiers, where the Black Prince won another glorious victory. The French king, John II, surnamed the Good, was captured in humiliating circumstances, together with his son Philip. By the Treaty of Bretigny, 1360, the French were compelled to pay an enormous ransom for the captive king, and a number of important provinces were ceded to the English.

France's fate seemed now to have been sealed, especially since after his liberation John took a measure that was to prove disastrous for his country. He conferred the fief of Burgundy on his younger son, Philip, thereby causing an inner division that took centuries to bridge. John's son, Charles V, the Sage, possessed many excellent qualities as Regent, but if for a short while it seemed as if France might regain her position, this was due less to him than to his collaborator, the legendary High Constable Bertrand du Guesclin. A cleverly camouflaged loophole in the Treaty of 1360 enabled him to make use of an opportune moment, when the State finances had become stabilized. The High Constable had carefully studied the English tactics and discovered how to counter them. The English king, Richard II, was driven step by step from his conquests and soon held in France only Calais, Bordeaux, and Bayonne.

But Charles V's son, Charles VI, was never favored by fortune. When he came to the throne he was only a young boy, and his Regency Council quickly dissipated what had been gained. Before long, in 1393, it was discovered that he was feeble-minded. With short intervals, his mind remained clouded until his death in 1422. The country was ruled by his brother, Duke Louis of Orléans, who also became the lover of the Queen, the notorious Isabeau of Bavaria. This, however, did not prevent the Duke of Orléans from boasting of his success with the Duchess of Burgundy, the wife of Philip the Bold.

During this period, the opposition between the Crown and Burgundy grew in strength. At this time too, unexpected economic crises made their appearance; taxes could not be collected, the State's finances became disordered. Subterranean social forces rose from the depth of the nation. At regular intervals ruthless leaders appeared who remind one of the French Revolution.[1]

---

[1] It should be mentioned that the military and "heroic" side of the Hundred Years' War is rather overemphasized in contemporary English and French documents. The economic or, if one prefers, the strategic-geographic side has been more clearly discerned by, for example, the Belgian historian Pirenne. Thus from the very beginning the war can be seen as part of the eternal struggle for the Southern Low Countries, where at that time English wool was converted into precious and useful Flemish cloth. English and French interests had been in conflict in Flanders since the end of the 1320s. The coming war was being prepared here.

In these circumstances an improvement in the relations between the Crown and Burgundy was a necessity. However, when the Burgundian duke died and his son, John the Fearless, succeeded him, France's real ruler, Louis of Orléans, found a bitter and more dangerous adversary.

John the Fearless, whom we know from Jan van Eyck's portrait in Antwerp, was an astute and ambitious politician, who saw no reason why the country should be ruled by the mentally defective French king and the immoral regent, the Duke of Orléans. "A short, dark man with blue eyes, full face, unwavering gaze and strong chin", virile, ugly, lacking in charm and sensibility, but a man of action, dangerous as an eagle, such was John the Fearless. *"Je ay desir de moy avancer"* was one of his famous sayings, summarizing his ambitions and aspirations. Had John the Fearless succeeded in his policy, the fate of France, and perhaps even that of Europe, would have been very different. As one visits the ducal palace in Dijon and gazes at the portraits and art treasures—the works of the sculptor Claus Sluter and of Jean de la Huertas, and the magnificent monument on the tomb of Philip the Bold by Antoine le Moituriers—one is aware of a curiously independent atmosphere, a new direction in French history, which was interrupted but which might just as easily have continued toward the realization of the Burgundian dream: a great Franco-Flemish empire under the leadership of Burgundy.

John the Fearless was not squeamish about the means he employed to reach his ends. On November 23, 1407, he murdered his mother's lover and his own rival, Duke Louis of Orléans, in Paris. The two dukes had met in order to be reconciled. A few days before, they had been to Holy Communion together. On November 22, they sat together at a magnificent banquet.

Louis was staying in the Hotel Barbette in the Marais quarter with his mistress, Queen Isabeau. John the Fearless had bribed his valet, Thomas Courteheuse. In the course of the evening, the valet entered the Duke's room and found the Queen with him. Bowing, he said, "Monseigneur, the King requests you to come to him on a matter of great importance for him and for you."

A strange message from the mad monarch! And a strange hour for a rendezvous, half past nine in the evening!

But the Duke mounted his mule and rode off, accompanied by two men on horseback and five or six servants on foot. *"Se faisait assez brun ceste nuit"* (It was rather dark that night), relates the chronicler.

Some twenty men suddenly appeared in the darkness.

"I am the Duke of Orléans", cried Louis.

The answer came immediately:

"Good. It is him we want...."

The Duke's companions were cut down or scattered. The Duke himself fell from his mule with his skull smashed, one arm broken, and his left hand severed by a sword blow. Then came a sharp command in the darkness:

"*Eteignez tout! Allons-nous-en! Il est mort! Ayez coeur d'homme!*" (All lights out! Away with us! He's dead! Courage!)

The following day John the Fearless, swarthy and tight-lipped, stood sorrowing at his cousin's grave.

The investigation ordered by the Court soon drew the right conclusions, and John found it wise to depart from Paris in great haste and ride back to Flanders. Later he confessed his part in this tragedy to the Dukes of Anjou and Berry. He said that he had instigated this murder "through the intervention of the devil". The deed does not appear to have weighed heavily on his conscience.

A full-scale civil war now broke out.

The leader was Charles of Orléans, son of the murdered man, and he found a capable collaborator in the Duke of Armagnac, father-in-law of the murdered duke.

But John the Fearless had foreseen everything. He knew how to gain the confidence of the Parisians. He appeared as the friend of the people, and at the same time took care to flatter the brains of France, in the first place the powerful University of Paris. By his immoral life and his severe taxations, the murdered duke had made himself thoroughly hated in the French capital, and there were terrible revolutionary risings. In many of its incidents, the period recalls the great French Revolution. During the month of May 1413, the venerable churches and religious houses of Paris were to witness unparalleled scenes of bloodshed. The Duke of Armagnac crushed the rebellion with a hand of iron—from that time loyal Frenchmen were always referred to as "Armagnacs" in Burgundian and English propaganda.

While the Gregorian chants rose with poignant sweetness into the spring nights, the streets and alleys of Paris echoed with shrieks.

The civil war was followed with pleasurable attention in London. Both sides, it turned out, appealed for English intervention.

It was only their own internal troubles that had compelled the English to discontinue the war in France. Social disturbances almost like those of our own day[2] had prevented Richard II from continuing his war of conquest. As soon as England was again at peace, after the Duke of Lancaster had assumed the crown under the name of Henry IV, her interest in France revived. In Shakespeare's drama, we find realistic pictures of these events. It was Henry IV's son, Henry V, who led the English armies over to France. He was a king of great ability, a ruthless man equally at home in politics and war. His great aim was clear—to be "King of France and England". Suddenly it seemed possible to realize Edward III's ancient dream. In the background, other grandiose plans were laid—a crusade, the conquest of Constantinople and Jerusalem—but before this the two countries must be united into a great empire.

Though the sympathies of Henry IV had been more on the side of the Armagnacs, that is, of the French crown, the young King Henry V made approaches to the Duke of Burgundy. Harfleur was captured in 1413, and in 1415 the great battle of Agincourt was fought. While the Duke of Burgundy watched inactive, the French crown, determined to wipe out the disgrace of Crécy and Poitiers, sent a great army against the English. But the battle resulted in an English victory of such magnitude and glory that it was to live as an inspiration in English consciousness for centuries to come. Seven or eight thousand French soldiers fell, and a far greater number were butchered as captives—against the rules of war even of those days—for the number of prisoners was so enormous that the victors were unable to guard them. Only fifteen hundred Frenchmen survived, among whom was Duke Charles of Orléans, who from now on was an English prisoner. This was the poet Charles of Orléans who was loved by Joan of Arc with such touching loyalty, though she was never to meet her hero.

France now lay open to invasion. The whole of Normandy was conquered and was to remain a pro-English province for many decades. The abbots of the mighty Norman monasteries were for the most part convinced from now on that France would never again rise except under English leadership. It was this "Vichy policy" that culminated in the trial of Joan of Arc in Rouen.

[2] The first edition was published in 1956.

In 1416, a younger son of Charles VI, later Charles VII, Joan of Arc's king, became heir to the throne, or "Dauphin", at the age of thirteen. The Duke of Armagnac became the real ruler. Thanks to his efforts a breach occurred between the heir and his mother, Isabeau, who was banished from court. The Queen fled to John the Fearless and became the mistress of the man who had killed her brother-in-law and former lover. From this time she was the irreconcilable enemy of the Dauphin. Whether he was really the King's son has long been debated.

Paris sided with Burgundy. In May 1418, there was a new rising, accompanied by an incredible massacre. The Duke of Armagnac himself was murdered, and so intensely were those loyal to the monarchy hated in Paris that, according to a chronicler, the words "He is an Armagnac" were enough for the person in question to be immediately run through. More than 3,500 Armagnacs were murdered. The bishops of Lisieux, Évreux, Senlis, and Coutances were all murdered, as well as the abbot of Saint-Denis, known as *"un très faulx papelard"* (an out-and-out hypocrite). Three hundred intellectuals, professors, and students of the University were butchered. The young heir to the throne was saved by a pure chance and taken south to the loyal Loire country.

A month later, John the Fearless entered Paris. His entry took the form of a magnificent military display. He rode into Paris on the 14th of July at the head of five thousand armed men. First came 1,500 knights, *"bien joins et bien serrés ensemble"* (in close formation); then one thousand men from Picardy in five squadrons led by Jean de Luxembourg; then came the Burgundians, who formed the main force of 1,500 lancers. The parade ended with a rearguard of five hundred. John was welcomed by two papal cardinal-legates and by representatives of the city. The sick King still remained in Paris. In the Louvre, he received the Duke, in whose company was his own wife. The poor muddled King kissed the Queen, who loathed him, twice, and said to the Duke of Burgundy: "Beau cousin, you are very welcome. I thank you for all you have done for the Queen."

However, when later wine and food were served, the Queen and the Duke refused them. But if one is to believe the Burgundian chronicler, many of those present found the scene so elevating that they shed copious tears of emotion.

John the Fearless took up residence in the Hôtel d'Artois and set about cleaning up the town. Capeluche, the executioner of Paris, a figure of terror who had adopted princely modes of life, was immediately liquidated. His last sadistic deed had been to murder a young pregnant woman for no reason whatsoever. He was arrested and sentenced to death. At the block he gave his successor in the profession expert advice as to the best technique, and followed his own execution for as long as he was able with cold professional interest.

The advisers of the Dauphin now recommended a conciliatory meeting with the triumphant John. With the English preparing for new attacks at any moment, an understanding between the Crown and the Duke of Burgundy was the only hope.

The meeting was preceded by the most solemn promises of personal security for both parties. John the Fearless and the heir to the French throne met on September 10, 1419, on the bridge at Montereau, south of Paris, which spans the river Yonne. They advanced slowly toward each other and grasped one another's hands in the middle of the bridge. At a fitting distance behind the two principals were ranged their staffs. It was not long before a violent altercation began. The Duke of Burgundy exclaimed contemptuously that in any case the Dauphin could decide nothing without the approval of his mad father and was about to turn his back upon him. Charles, distressed and frightened, was on the point of leaving the bridge when he heard behind him sounds of violence and clamor. It is uncertain what really happened, but it is believed that one of Charles' men had rushed in fury at John the Fearless and buried his battle-axe in his skull.

Henry VI, Philip the Good, and Charles VII

The son of John the Fearless, later Duke Philip the Good, was at Charolais when he received the news. A Burgundian chronicler describes his reaction:

"Philip uttered a loud cry. One could see how his face blanched and then was convulsively contorted. He clenched his teeth, his lips were dry, he looked like a dead man. His clothes had to be torn off him and his mouth opened by force. He fainted, while many of the onlookers wept. His wife, Michelle, fell to the floor as if dead."

The room was filled with "cries of woe and sobbings".

Philip, the new Duke of Burgundy, was a fine-looking, vigorous man, whose personal conduct belies the devout impression he makes in contemporary portraits or in the portrait sculpture that stands behind the ducal palace at Dijon. We know of some thirty of his mistresses, and he had seventeen recognized bastards, two of whom were successively Bishop of Utrecht. But it was not without reason that he was given the appellation "the Good". He had a warm heart and in contrast to his pitiless father was capable of being moved by a single humble word. And with all his excesses he possessed a considerable measure of self-control; another of his surnames is *"l'asseuré"*, "the Controlled".

It has been debated whether it was he himself or his chancellor, Nicolas Rollin, who directed the Burgundian policy after the murder of John the Fearless, but it remains a fact that the assassination on the bridge at Montereau gave his policy quite a new ruthlessness and strength. Where John the Fearless had made a secret treaty with Henry V, his son made a cynically frank one. The assassination of his father had roused general indignation. "The false and most illoyal treacherousness of this dreadful and detestable murder" was a universal subject of conversation and greatly strengthened the Burgundian cause throughout the country.

In the Treaty of Troyes with the English in 1420, no further account was taken of Charles, the heir to the throne. Even his mother ignored him.

The Queen of France and the Duke of Burgundy now formed an open alliance with the enemy of France, and the English king, Henry V, married Catherine, sister to the Dauphin. He made it clear that he held the Dauphin responsible for the assassination—probably without any good reason. Henry V was now called Regent of France in anticipation of the death of the mad King Charles VI; he entered Paris and continued his war of conquest in northern France.

But the English king was to die before the old, sick King of France, who, however, followed him to the grave later that year, 1422. The new English king, Henry VI, bore the title "King of France and England". But Charles VII also assumed the royal title. His own mother spoke of him as "the so-called Dauphin from the Viennois".

Although Charles VII was repudiated by the parliament of Paris and declared to be unworthy of the succession, and although public opinion was indignant over the murder of the Duke of Burgundy, and the English, more or less supported by the Burgundians, were gaining great victories, strangely enough there was growing up in France at that time a strong loyalist movement that gave the weak Charles VII considerable support. True, it was whispered that he was not the legitimate son of his father, but there had to be a limit to what is permissible and reasonable; the English should not be allowed to conquer the whole country with the help of a rebellious prince of Burgundy and a Bavarian queen who had betrayed her husband. The University of Paris solemnly gave its approval to the Treaty of Troyes, but not so the burghers of the cities south of Paris nor the tortured peasants of France.

Henry VI, the English king, was a year old when he succeeded to the throne. His interests were promoted with great skill by his uncle, the Duke of Bedford. Under his direction the English continued the war with success, and Charles VII did not venture north of the Loire. His counselors did not compare favorably with either the Duke of Burgundy or the Duke of Bedford, and sometimes they were actually fighting each other. France seemed weaker than ever.

The France of the last Capets was a rich country, but the long-drawn-out wars soon ruined even the richest of her provinces. Now began the *"grande pitié"* of which Joan of Arc speaks. The war was especially cruel to the peasants. Year after year they were plundered not only by the combatants but also by innumerable bands of *condottieri* and brigands. Complete lawlessness reigned throughout the whole country. Agriculture became paralyzed, and many starved even of those who had formerly been well-to-do. Whole districts were turned into wildernesses. The Bishop of Lisieux tells us that the cattle, sheep, and pigs became so accustomed to alarm signals and the ringing of church bells that they ran to safety of their own free wills when they heard them. Another contemporary writer said: "The country was silent, neither cock nor hen was heard."

Only recently has modern research been able to present this decline in its proper light.

The value of money sank catastrophically, and the circulation of counterfeit currency assumed enormous dimensions; the cost of living rose steeply, savings became valueless, and there was an unprecedented wave of speculation. What is now called the "black market" flourished, and a new class of ruthless new-rich made its appearance. The agricultural workers put forward desperate demands, of a type familiar to us, for such things as the limitation of working hours. But the war industry flourished, that is to say, the armorers, and they could ask any price they pleased. The manufacturers of textiles also made astronomical profits, so that in the midst of a starving population there was a new class of wealthy, unscrupulous adventurers who could afford everything. In the midst of so much impoverishment there were those who were "*trop doux nourris*" (overfed), the mild comment of the court chaplain, Jean Courtecuisse.

The value of the monetary unit sank by twelve thousand percent. A chicken, which in normal times would have cost four francs, now cost forty thousand francs. It is not necessary to give further examples to make clear that we see here an exact parallel to, say, the German economic collapse after the First World War. The authorities tried to establish a "price ceiling", but were unable to do so. Crime increased to an unbelievable extent, and the number of suicides grew continually.

With this material poverty and suffering went a corresponding spiritual decline. It was as if all fixed norms had vanished. Justice no longer functioned; no firm lines were drawn. Whom was one to back? Charles VII called himself King of France, and was, of course, the son of mad Charles VI, but was he a legitimate son? On the other hand, the Englishman, Henry VI, was the undoubted son of the French Princess Catherine and legitimately elected.

On the night of All Saints, 1428, the unfortunate Charles VII knelt in his chapel and asked a despairing question of God. Was he of legitimate birth or not? Should he continue his fight or not?

He received no answer.

The English continued the war with icy determination and efficiency. In one invaluable source for the history of this period, the *Journal d'un Bourgeois de Paris*, it is said laconically: "At this time, the English took one fortress from the Armagnacs in the morning, and if they lost one, they took two more by the evening. So the war went on, cursed by God."

During the minority of Henry VI, the Duke of Bedford, who was married to a sister of the Duke of Burgundy, called himself Regent of France. The Duke of Brittany and his brother, Arthur de Richemont, opposed Charles VII. For a time, the royal army was able to hold its own against the English, but it was crushed in the Battle of Verneuil on August 17, 1424. This defeat can rank with the catastrophes of Crécy, Poitiers, and Agincourt. A bright spot was the sudden defection of Richemont, brother of the Duke of Brittany, who went over to Charles, but before he could make any useful contribution he was eliminated by the intrigues of one of the King's most fatal counselors, La Trémoille. Charles lost heart and withdrew to Brittany.

In spite of all, there were still towns and districts that clung obstinately to Charles VII and refused to give in to the English and Burgundians. Among these were Beauvais and Tournai in the north, where the Treaty of Troyes had never been recognized; and among these also was the holy city of Reims. There were "resistance groups" working energetically all over the country who interfered considerably with the operations of the English. And in the west lay Mont-Saint-Michel, unconquered and defiant.

The Duke of Bedford recognized all these difficulties. He was determined to make use of the friendship of the Burgundians as long as it was useful to him. The Burgundian policy at this time was strikingly similar to that of Pétain after the fall of France in 1940. In the summer and autumn of 1427, it looked as if the English could force a decision. In the east, English troops conquered Champagne and in the west Pontorson. Another force advanced southward and surrounded Orléans.

The capture of Orléans would probably decide the war, if only because of its strategic situation—it was the key to the territory loyal to the King. Duke Charles of Orléans, son of the murdered Louis of Orléans, was still a captive in England, busy with his poetry. This fact was to assume a strange significance, because even in a lawless world certain laws still hold good. For instance, it was not permissible to conquer a country whose ruler was in captivity. The English could, therefore, not undertake the storming of Orléans until they had given the Duke his freedom. But he was never given his freedom, and it was largely on this account that the investment of Orléans produced such extraordinary bitterness throughout the country. This event can be compared with the brutal military methods of the Nazis in the Second World War, for the reaction was almost the same.

Dunois, "the Bastard of Orléans", brother of the imprisoned Duke, led the defense and became the hero of France. All eyes were directed on the city. If Orléans fell, all would be lost.

Charles VII tried his best. The information reached him that a great column with provisions for the English army before Orléans was advancing southward, led by Sir John Fastolf. Troops from the Auvergne were dispatched to halt Fastolf, but the King's men were not capable even of this modest task. On February 12, 1429, Fastolf thoroughly defeated his adversaries.

This little battle has gone down in history as "The Battle of Herrings" (*la journée des harengs*), because the English provisions consisted largely of salted herrings.

With this slightly farcical new defeat, it looked to the surrounding country as if all hope had to be abandoned.

But the citizens of Orléans were determined never to surrender. Charles VII meanwhile sat apathetically pondering over his fate. If he were the true heir to the crown of France, why then did he not have the help of God and the saints?

At that moment came an unexpected happening.

A figure unlike any hitherto known to history entered the arena.

CHAPTER 2

Queen Isabeau and the Prophecy

That Charles VI's queen, Isabeau, was little loved by French historians was not due only to her Bavarian extraction. When she came to France she did not know a word of French. She was presented to the court in 1384 and at the age of fifteen was a pink-cheeked, plump German girl without noticeable charm. The chronicler, Froissart, described her thus: "The young girl remained completely silent with no movement of either eyes or lips. At that time she did not know a word of French."

However, it was not long before she acquired at any rate the vices of the French court. She was so fat that even official documents gave this as a reason for her not taking part in affairs of state, which seems to indicate an extreme obesity. The invaluable observations of the monks of Saint-Denis show that the Queen caused considerable consternation. After her husband had become definitely deranged, she threw herself into the arms of lovers, some of them men in subordinate positions at the court. She seems to have had no love for her children. When the King, her husband, in a relatively lucid moment, questioned his eldest son, the latter told him that it was three months since his mother had kissed him. A courageous monk gave her a piece of his mind: "The goddess Venus is an absolute ruler at your court; drunkenness and immorality are her attendants and make the night into day in a world of abandoned dancing. If you do not believe my words, O Queen, then go into the town dressed as a plain woman and you will hear what everybody says."

In outwardly virtuous England, the French court was regarded as a veritable Babylon, and we must remember this fact when we consider the English attempts to create a new order in France. A few days before the Duke of Orléans was murdered, the Queen gave birth to a still-born child whose father was probably the murdered duke. She did not grieve long over her dead lover, but consoled herself by increasing the intimacy of her relations with the Burgundian party and with the Duke of Burgundy personally, while preserving the greatest possible contempt for her own son, the future Charles VII. She did not object to the English king occupying her country and made no protest when he called himself King of France. In return, she received two thousand *écui* a month for her private amusements. Not unnaturally, she never felt herself to be a Frenchwoman. In the chronicles of the monks, we find references to the large fortunes she smuggled out of the country. "The Queen had dispatched six horses loaded with minted gold to Germany. This convoy was stopped by the burghers of Metz, who were informed by the men in charge that they had several times before been sent on similar missions to Germany. There was great amazement when it was learned that the Queen allowed France to be impoverished in order that Germany be made rich."

Another thing which did not find favor with the French historians was her delight in a dish described as *compote de choux,* or in modern French *Choucroute.* This seems to have upset the first modern historian of Joan of Arc, Siméon Luce, more even than the incredible sums she spent on animals and birds: in her still extant accounts we find entries for the purchase of sheep to feed her pet leopard. This, Siméon Luce remarks angrily, can be seen as a symbol of her deliverance of the lamb of France to the leopard, Henry V of England.

Queen Isabeau's immorality and political treachery seem to have evoked deep emotional repercussions. It is possible to prove that, even before the appearance of Joan of Arc, a belief existed that only a pure virgin would be able to obliterate the evils caused by this unclean and conscienceless queen.

During the trial at Rouen, Catherine le Royer stated in evidence in Vaucouleurs that Joan had said she intended to go to the heir to the throne and ask him if he did not know the prophecy that France should be destroyed by one woman and reborn through a virgin from Lorraine.

Several other witnesses also testified to this.

One need not be very familiar with modern psychology in regard to evidence to feel skeptical about such retrospective statements, since there are always individuals who after great events claim to have heard them prophesied. But even if a great part of the legends surrounding Joan of Arc can be disregarded on these grounds, much remains that cannot have arisen retrospectively.

Throughout France, sayings and prophecies of the magician Merlin played a great part. Merlin, a figure of the Arthurian romances, is supposed to have lived in Scotland in the fifth century. To him is attributed the saying: *Descendet Virgo dorsum sagittarii et flores virgineos obscurabit.*

The French translated the prophecy in their own way: "A virgin shall descend on the back of the (English) bowmen and with her shadow protect the (French) lilies." It was through their dreaded bowmen with their six-foot bows that the English so easily defeated the French knights. Now these dangerous robbers were to be conquered by a French virgin.

Merlin, the magician and visionary, was believed to have prophesied that France would be saved by a virgin in male attire. Not only that, but it was said that he prophesied that this young woman would come from Lorraine. One of the witnesses at the trial, the prior Pierre Miget, claimed to have read in an ancient book about Merlin's prophecies that this virgin was to come from an oak forest in Lorraine. The fact that Merlin was referring to quite another country does not matter. What is important is to realize the beliefs that were prevalent in France before the appearance of Joan of Arc.

More remarkable than these distortions and interpretations of Merlin's prophecies is a statement of Marie d'Avignon, a pious woman who had such remarkable revelations that she felt it her duty to go to Charles VI and tell them to him. Her visions always concerned the terrible sufferings of France. A voice had told her that France would suffer even greater disasters. In her visions she saw a suit of armor and was terrified at the thought that it might be for her; but the voice told her that it would be worn by a maid who was to come after her, and who would conquer the enemy and free the monarchy in France.

Even that sober soldier Dunois, the Bastard of Orléans, stated in evidence during the Trial of Rehabilitation that at that time a ballad about the Maid was often heard in France and was well known to the English officers. When the commission in Poitiers, to which I shall return later, made its investigations concerning Joan of Arc, before the liberation of Orléans, these rumors and prophecies were considered, and the commission ruled that they had now come true. It is significant that Joan of Arc herself, who was extremely well balanced, accepted these prophecies. Her entourage gave definite and clear evidence that she had spoken of the rumors that France should be saved by a virgin and believed that they would be verified by her own deeds.

There is an error based on a naïve theory of evolution that often appears in arguments against Christianity. It is observed that certain ceremonies and tenets of belief in the Christian faith can be found also in earlier religions or civilizations: from this it is concluded that Christianity must in some way be compromised.

The conception of the Trinity, or something similar to it, is discovered in an earlier religion; sacrifices reminiscent of those of the Jews are found, and conceptions of a god or the son of a god who must sacrifice his life for man, and conceptions of a mother of god.[1] There are also ceremonies of baptism and prayers that are reminiscent of Christian ceremonies and prayers; the conclusion is drawn that Christianity, with its assertive claims, is only a link in a development that, it is believed, will continue through and after Christianity just as it existed before Christianity.

But this easily proven historical connection can and should be interpreted in quite a different manner. It does not constitute any indictment of the Christian Faith, nor an argument against it. On the contrary, it is in perfect harmony with this faith, which has always claimed to be a continuation and realization of the noblest dreams of earlier centuries.

This is most clearly illustrated in the *figura* concept.

The characters of the Old Testament are prefigurations of those of the New Testament: they proclaim their coming. It is not here a question of symbols, which involve a quite different conception. When Christianity says that Joshua who leads the Jews to the Promised Land is a *figura* for Jesus who leads humanity to Paradise, this does not mean that Joshua is a symbol of Jesus. Joshua had a historical existence that became a moment in history like every other. But in addition to this is his particular attribute as a *figura* for Jesus.

A *figura* is a historical reality that at the same time anticipates another and greater historical event. Moses is not a mythical character because he is the *figura* of Christ. An illustration can be used that is realistic from the point of view of Christian interpretation of history: a *figura* casts its shadow before it in history. Noah's ark is a *figura* for the Church; the

---

[1]Up to the time of the Revolution there was preserved in the crypt of the Cathedral of Chartres a *virgo paritura*, a pregnant virgin god-mother, from the time of the Druids. A replica of it is still in the crypt.

priesthood of Aaron is *umbra et figura aeterni sacerdotii*; the slave Hagar is the *figura* of the Old Testament, and Sarah that of the New.

As one studies the wealth of figures on the porches and portals of the Gothic cathedrals, one realizes the dominating role exercised by this interpretation of history. At the time of Joan of Arc, nothing was known of the theory of evolution. Nothing was known of historical causality in our sense, or at any rate the little that was known was of no significance. History was divided into two parts both orientated toward the same point, the period before and the period after God became man. Nothing occurred in history after the Resurrection of Christ that did not have a visible or invisible connection with the mission of the Son of God. Joan's view of the French king as the Vice-Regent of Christ and her judgment of the political conflicts reveal this same idea that the true meaning of history is to be found in its relation to the divine mission of salvation. In the same way, the period before Christ was one of strivings and confusion, of gropings and hopes and inhibitions and longings, in which one could everywhere distinguish events and figures that in a mysterious manner foreshadowed and designated what would one day become a historical reality. When the peasant gazed up at the portal of the cathedral in Chartres and saw Abraham with his knife raised preparing to sacrifice his son, he knew, first, that this was a historical happening with its own inner meaning, and secondly that this historical fact foreshadowed God's sacrifice of his own Son. At a time when there were no reviews, newspapers, or books, the ordinary man received no other visual education than that of the picture language of the cathedral. Here this interpretation of human life and history was clearly and distinctly displayed.

It is against the background of this world view, so infinitely more realistic than the historical view of the Marxist, where purely metaphysical conceptions like "the classes" and their "interests" create their own history, that we must consider the problem of Joan and the prophecies that preceded her appearance.

Mary, the Mother of God, was filled with a willingness and longing for sacrifice to which the most inspired men and women of the Old Testament had given expression, for she was the incarnation of what generations of Jewish mothers had dreamed. For centuries, this accumulation of longing and hope had grown till the time was ripe. Through the grace of God, a young woman without original sin was found willing and capable of her superhuman task.

Of course this is first and foremost a mystery, but the importance of the mystery is not diminished by examining the historical background.

In the same way, Joan had, consciously or unconsciously, been nourished by the hopes and aspirations of her time. What one sees around her in primitive, often magical, forms are variations of the same longing; purity shall one day conquer uncleanliness, or, in a more concrete form, a pure maiden from the untouched countryside of France shall destroy the spirit that had emanated from the vicious Queen Isabeau. Joan's judges in Rouen made the same mistake as modern skeptics; they see the strange portents and think that the cause itself is compromised by them. Joan's deed is not lessened by the hopes she heroically realized, even though those hopes found expression in a magical form as superstition and witchcraft. She lives her life influenced only by the Church, by the legends, to which I shall return, and by the naïve prophecies. All this material converges in herself. She rejects what is unclean; the magical and the trivial are cast aside when they come into contact with her pure will, and only the great fact remains that a maid shall give her life to God, shall live pure and spotless, and willingly follow his inspiration. And from this will emerges the salvation of the country.

Jacques d'Arc and La Romée

We possess an almost unique mass of evidence about Joan of Arc, thanks to the three separate investigations regarding her person, her spiritual experiences, and her faith that were instituted during her lifetime and immediately after her death. Nor is it difficult to obtain a true picture of her childhood and youth, since we possess all the necessary documents for a reconstruction.

Domrémy is the name of a village in the valley of the Meuse on the border of Champagne and Lorraine. Opposite the village is another, Greux, and sometimes the two village names are combined into one. On the other side of the river in Lorraine is the village Maxey. Though Joan of Arc always called herself "La Lorraine",[2] these facts suggest that she would have been named more correctly "La Champenoise". The river that flowed between the two villages Domrémy and Greux has since

[2] The family name was really Darc. It was only in 1576 that a poet of Orléans, to commemorate her being raised to the rank of nobility, referred to her as Jeanne d'Arc, a form retained ever since.

28

changed its course several times, and we have no certain knowledge of its position at the time.

The house in which Joan was born still remains, though it has been altered and extended. What is important is that it stood, and still stands, quite close to the village church, which had been dedicated to Saint Rémi, the apostle of the Gauls. The basic fact of Joan's life is that she grew up close to a church in a period of tremendous political convulsions. Born in 1410, or possibly in 1412, she had two elder brothers, Jacques and Jean, and a sister, Catherine. A third brother was born later.

She never went to school. In common with the peasant children of that time, she could not read, though there was a school on the other side of the river. However, her mother taught her the most essential objects of learning, that is, the Paternoster, the Credo, and the Ave Maria, besides which, of course, she had heard a great deal of the lives of the saints.

Curiously enough, this part of France sided almost solidly, not with the Burgundians, but with the Armagnacs. Here the people were for the King of France against Burgundy and England—very unlike the other part of Champagne, especially Reims, where there was strong sympathy for Burgundy. Research has shown that Domrémy was not an isolated backwater; an important road led past the village, and it was continually visited by pilgrims, refugees, and merchants. We may therefore assume that all the most salient events of the war were discussed, in a more or less distorted form, in the marketplace and in the kitchens of Domrémy. Largely under the direction of Joan's father, who seems to have possessed qualities of leadership and who enjoyed a certain degree of prosperity, the peasants adopted various measures to protect themselves from the ceaseless attacks of the regular troops and the marauding bands of robbers. Thus the peasants of Domrémy had combined to rent an abandoned castle on an island in the river. The negotiations for this leasing were conducted by Joan's father. When warned of an impending attack, the peasants could seek refuge in the large courtyard of the castle with their families and cattle. It may be supposed that provisions were stored there.

In Maxey, on the other side of the river, the children, like their parents, were Burgundians, which led to many fights between the children of the two villages. Domrémy itself more than once suffered plunderings and disaster. Joan's sister was married to a man who, probably, fell in one of these battles. Her childhood must have been filled with tales of violence and murder, attacks and plunderings, and her youth spent in a condition of tension and anxiety.

The King's representative in the district was at that time Robert de Baudricourt, commandant in Vaucouleurs. We shall meet him later in close contact with Joan herself. He fought manfully against the Burgundians and seems to have enjoyed great esteem as a soldier.

In 1424, his position, and that of Domrémy, became very difficult. The enemy this time was Jean de Vergy. The greater part of the district had been devastated, and the population of Domrémy lived in a state of unrelieved tension, for at any moment the church bells might issue their warning for flight. In the summer of 1425, a marauding knight named Henry d'Orly descended on the villages of Domrémy and Greux. Evidently there was no time to gather the cattle into the safety of the castle, for they were all driven off to the castle of the robber-baron some twenty leagues away. Valuable furniture and other household goods were also carried off in such quantities that some of them had to be deposited in the courtyard of another castle in the neighborhood. No doubt many of the villagers lost their lives in this fray. Fortunately for the peasants, a wealthy and influential lady, la Dame d'Ogivillier, who among others bore the title of "Dame de Greux et Domrémy", resided in the neighborhood. She reported the happenings to her neighbor, the Count de Vaudemont at Joinville, and he immediately dispatched a troop of soldiers with orders to return the stolen cattle. At that time, Joan of Arc was thirteen. The event is here related to show in what kind of a world she grew up.

Nothing is known of Joan's father beyond what has been mentioned, but there have been many discussions concerning her mother, Isabelle Romée. According to enthusiastic earlier investigators, she was believed to have been the main inspiration of her daughter's religious life, and they even attempted to define the nature and orientation of her mother's religion. But modern scholars, well represented by the careful Jacques Cordier, have asserted definitely that beyond a few purely external data nothing is known about Joan's parents. The question is, however, of some importance and ought therefore to be briefly touched upon; for it is not a matter of indifference whether Joan of Arc's parents were ordinary French peasants or whether the mother may be said to have been a strongly developed religious personality of whose life something at least is known.

The question hinges on the correct interpretation of a single text, a testimony given by the Augustinian Pasquerel, who was for a long time Joan's confessor. This is as follows: he first heard of Joan and learned how she had gone to the King, when he was in the town of Le Puy, at a time when Joan's mother and a few of those who had accompanied her to the King were also there. He became acquainted with them, and they suggested that it would be an excellent thing if he were to go with them to Joan and said that they would not part from him until they had brought him to her. So he accompanied them to Chinon and afterward to Tours, where he was a reader in a monastery. At that time Joan was quartered in the same town in the house of Jean Dupuy, and the people who had conducted him there said to her: "Joan, we have brought with us this good Father, and when you have come to know him you will like him very much." Joan replied that she was very glad to meet him as she had already heard of him, and that she would make her confession to him the next day.

The following day he heard her confession and said Mass in her presence, and he accompanied her from then on until she was taken prisoner at Compiègne.

This is undoubtedly an important document, for it is Joan's mother who sends to her a monk who stays with her until her captivity.

The matter becomes of still greater consequence if we consider the importance of the town of Le Puy at that time. It has been shown that Le Puy, with its famous "Black Madonna", was influential in the religious life of Charles VII, who repeatedly visited it. Thus at the same time that Joan of Arc starts off on her first expedition, her mother, the unknown peasant woman from Champagne, begins her pilgrimage to Notre Dame du Puy. We may imagine that it came about in the following manner:

1. Joan of Arc's mother is not only a person of strong religious feeling, but is to a lesser or greater degree influenced by the particular religious atmosphere and revelation of Le Puy.
2. Perhaps this revelation was also connected with Joan's own orientation.
3. The mother sends to Joan an Augustinian, who therefore must have her entire confidence. That Joan of Arc immediately accepted him as her confessor may mean that the mother possessed a strong authority over her child, and also that Joan was

to some extent under the influence of the mother's particular religious conception, which must have been the same as that of the Augustinian.

Siméon Luce was the first scholar who, in the eighties, studied the case, and his conclusions were rather arbitrary. The problem was taken up again by Gabriel Hanotaux, who developed these views in a brilliant manner. He discovered that there was more to it than the mystical connection between the pilgrimage of the mother and the daughter's ride to the King, pointed out by Luce. He gave an analysis of the particular religious atmosphere of Le Puy and thought it probable that this had a close connection with Joan's own conception of her task. According to this scholar, Joan's public mission cannot be explained without this independent religious activity of her mother, who clearly intervened in later stages of her child's spiritual life, just as she had earlier, in Joan's own words, been her only teacher.

Who was this "Black Madonna" ("*nigra sed Formosa*"—black but of lovely form) of Le Puy?

According to tradition she originated in a time before the Virgin Mary's earthly life, and was believed to have been sculptured by the prophet Jeremiah. She was supposed to have been treasured for a long time by the masters of Babylon and later brought to Le Puy by Saint Louis himself.

Mighty trains of pilgrims came to Le Puy to visit this Madonna, and also to visit a holy stone which was there. These pilgrims numbered hundreds of thousands a year, and their enthusiasm was so great that documents still extant indicate the anxiety of the ecclesiastical authorities lest the feebler pilgrims be trampled or squeezed to death by the advancing masses of the faithful. Those who wished to kiss the veils covering the holy images carried before the processions literally risked their lives. Abbot Suger, the creator of the church of Saint Denis, north of Paris, has given a vivid description of how the people, particularly women, were trampled to death with shrill cries by the excited pilgrims. Morbid aberrations, such as preachers (like Vincent Ferrer) surrounded by hordes of flagellants, belong to the picture of these times.

But the religious passion of Le Puy had also another significance. Le Puy became the center of a specific type of mystical religion, whose core was the cult of our Lady as the pure virgin. It was in Le Puy that the *Salve Regina* was composed. According to tradition, it was there that Saint

Dominic introduced the Rosary. The period resounded with clamor for a reform of the Church. The mendicant orders especially, and the masses influenced by them, fought for a pure, genuine religiosity with poverty as its ideal. When the towering Vincent Ferrer came to Le Puy in 1416, he thundered against the rich and worldly higher clergy. It was particularly in France that this popular religious feeling inspired by the new orders appeared. Dominic was a Spaniard, but he came to France, as Thomas had come from Italy, Anthony of Padua from Portugal, and Vincent Ferrer from Spain; Saint Francis sang his canticles in praise of the Lord in French. What we now regard as the Babylonian captivity of the Popes in Avignon was considered as the right and proper state of things by contemporary France (and is so to this day by the guardian of the papal palace in Avignon); for France was the only kingdom able and willing to protect the Church.

It is against this background that, according to Hanotaux, Joan's actions must be viewed. Through her mother, she had been brought into contact with some of the most important contemporary currents of thought: the Christian royalism that had its citadel in Le Puy, to which Charles VII often came on pilgrimage; the Christian mysticism that was concentrated on the immaculate Virgin Mother; and the upsurge of popular religious feeling in opposition to the higher clergy and the dead formalism of the Church, which sprang up in the footsteps of the mendicant orders.

Joan probably did not know Bridget or Catherine of Siena, but she was a child of the same epoch and found it natural and reasonable that God should have chosen a weak and unknown woman for the defense of the country and the Church. If Joan was accepted with relative ease by the entourage of Charles VII, this was because there had been recent living examples such as Bridget and Catherine—women standing alone who had prophetically warned Popes and cardinals and had cast themselves fearlessly into the political maelstrom.

Another light was thrown on the matter by Jacques Cordier, who reexamined the problem in 1948. Everything depended on whether Pasquerel had actually spoken of Le Puy, though that town undoubtedly was an important religious center. In Latin it says in the text *"in villa Aniciensi"*, which in actual fact means "in the town of Le Puy". But Quicherat, the man who first published the trial of Joan of Arc, had already denied that there was any connection with Le Puy. Cordier himself suspects that the words should have been "*villa Anceiensi*", which means "Anché", a community between Chinon and Île-Bouchard, in the neighborhood of the place where Joan was at that time stopping. Another scholar (Le Brun de Charmettes) further believes that "mother" was written in error instead of "brother". We know a good deal about Joan's brothers and their participation in the war, but nothing about her mother at that time.

Cordier does not wish to take issue over this last question, but he believes that he can prove that Joan's relatives—whoever they were—could not possibly have taken part in a pilgrimage to Le Puy in the south of France. His arguments, however, do not appear to me to be wholly convincing.[3] On the other hand, it is rather incredible that an event of such importance as Joan's mother's pilgrimage to distant Le Puy should not have been mentioned in any other place in the records.

But this question may remain in suspense for the present. What is certain, however, is that the mother could travel, that her journey had some connection with her daughter's mission, and that she herself took an initiative of a spiritual nature, in this case to bring about the contact with an excellent religious guide. Even if, therefore, the mother was without personal contact with the particular nationalist-religious mysticism that flourished round the Black Madonna in Le Puy, one can see here glimpses of her true self. If the father must have been a sober, sensible man, held in high esteem by his fellow villagers, it is clear that the mother was deeply religious and full of initiative, a rather exceptional peasant woman.

[3] Cordier's reasoning is as follows: The festivities in Le Puy began on March 25. In order to reach the place in time, Joan's relations and friends would have had to ride from Touraine at the latest on March 17. But at this time she was at Chinon, and the King had not yet decided to let the commission in Poitiers examine her claims, and still less to give her a kind of command. Cordier thinks that Joan's relations and friends could not on March 17 have acted with knowledge about matters that only became a reality about April 13. It was only during the week of April 15 to 21 that Joan found herself in Tours and could have met the monk and her friends.

This argument is not convincing, for why should not Joan's mother and her friends have ridden to Le Puy without knowledge of her daughter's later fate, only knowing that she had reached the King? Why should her friends have required exact knowledge of her "appointment" before making her acquainted with a monk whom they themselves highly esteemed and who had influenced them greatly? Why should not this little group of friends, as the monk stated, have searched for her first in Chinon and later in Tours, ignorant as they were of all the events that had overtaken her?

34

CHAPTER 3

At Domrémy

During the many examinations of Joan of Arc, numerous incidents from her childhood were brought out, which give a fairly clear picture of the early part of her life. She called herself a shepherdess, but she often said that she preferred to sit at home while others looked after the animals.[1] She probably did both in turn. Many reports speak of her fine physical condition, and her playmates were said to have seen her run so fast that her feet hardly seemed to touch the ground. It is certain that she gave a general impression of strength and vigor, which qualities were strikingly confirmed later by her long rides and martial deeds. She had a special friend, a neighboring girl named Hauviette, who, when questioned by the magistrate about Joan, said touchingly, "She is wonderfully kind." Another little friend of her childhood was Mengette, who was to marry young and who lost her husband in the disturbances. Joan did everything to console her. When a small son of a neighbor fell ill, Joan nursed him like a mother.

Joan preferred household duties to tending the flocks and proudly told her judges that there was no woman in Rouen whom she could not equal in needlecraft. She never used bad language, confining herself to such exclamations as "*sans faute*", and during her short military career would use the equally harmless expression "*par mon martin*". When the church bells sounded, she knelt and made the sign of the cross. On Saturday evening, the day of our Lady, she often climbed the small hill that rises above the village of Greux. From this, a rivulet trickled down, and above it stood a small chapel dedicated to Our Lady of Bermont. In it was a statue of our Lady with the Child Jesus that was believed to have

---

[1] "*Aadens quod, dum esset in domo patris, vacabat circa negotia familiaria domus, nec ibat ad campos cum ovibus et aliis animalibus*" (She added that, when still in her father's house, she busied herself with domestic duties and did not go to pasture with sheep or other animals) were the words in the proceedings.

miraculous powers. Joan often visited this chapel, alone or in the company of her elder sister Catherine and, when she could afford it, would light a candle in honor of our Lady.

A short distance from Domrémy there was a wooded hill that could be seen from her home. This was the oak grove that in the proceedings was described as "*le bois chesnu*" and was to play a sinister part in Joan's life. Here was the spring that Joan, according to one report, used to call "*La Fontaine-aux-bonnes-Fées-Notre-Seigneur*", a name indicating that the spring in an earlier age was believed to have magical powers and to be the abode of nature spirits, but which had since been exorcised and blessed. These fairies (*fatales*) were to have an important part in the trial, and were well known to Joan, as she herself admitted. On the other hand, she always insisted that she had never believed in the stories of their powers nor thought it right to invoke them. Not far from there was a great tree, an enormous beech, whose mighty branches, which nobody dared to touch, bent down until they touched the ground. Nowhere else were there such beautiful flowers. It was generally believed, and must have been known to Joan, that it was under this tree that the fairies had their abode. Joan's godmother related that she had heard that in the olden days the fairies were seen under this tree, but because of their sins they no longer came there—meaning that after the place had been blessed by the priest the nature spirits dared not reveal themselves. Especially on the day before Ascension Day, it was the custom for the priests to visit the spot in procession and there to read a passage from the Gospel of Saint John, which was supposed to be particularly effective against evil spirits. Another of Joan's godmothers said that she had with her own eyes seen these fairies around the tree, although she was a quiet and unhysterical woman whose word carried great authority. She had spoken of this to Joan.

Joan admitted that all these occurrences were known to her, but denied that they had influenced her in any way. On Laetare Sunday in Lent, the peasants celebrated a special feast when they gathered around the great beech tree and the spring. Boys and girls went in procession to the tree and hung wreaths and garlands of flowers on its branches; then they sat down under the tree and consumed the good things they had brought from home. They then drank water from the spring and performed their dances until darkness fell. Joan had also heard it said that the sick could be cured if they drank the waters of the spring or walked around the great tree. Under a hazel bush, there was a mandrake, and anyone who would dare to pull it out of the ground could be certain to become rich. The neighborhood was naturally still familiar with many forms of ancient magic. One witness asserted during the trial that it was known for its witchcraft, but it can probably be assumed that in this respect, as in others, it was not different from other villages.

The "Voices"

This was the setting where Joan of Arc at the age of thirteen suddenly heard "a voice". She listened and was gradually able to grasp the message of the voice better and better, but she waited five years before she heard the voice order her to arise and save France. Since the story of Israel, history has scarcely recorded a similar phenomenon.

Man will always argue about the nature of such experiences. The rationalist will always claim that it is a case of hallucination, but he will have to face the problem of explaining why this should happen to a girl of such unshakable common sense and so devoid of hysteria. But those familiar with the history of the Church and the saints and with the psychology of revelations recognize a phenomenon that is well known to them and scarcely sensational; for to them it is self-evident that certain purified and blessed individuals can receive messages from a spiritual sphere that others less spiritually advanced cannot apprehend.

What was it that Joan heard and experienced, and under what circumstances?

On February 21, the first day of the trial at Rouen, she refused to speak. She said that she had not revealed the revelations she had received from God to anyone except to Charles, as she called her king. These were matters to which she would not refer, even if they were to sever her head from her body, because she knew that she had received them through visions or through her secret counselors. But she added, which indicates her hesitation, that she would know within eight days if she could reveal them or not.

But the next day already, when again pressed with questions, she made her "confession". She first asserted that everything she had done had been due to revelations. According to the record of proceedings, she stated in reply to a series of questions regarding her religious life that at the age of thirteen she had heard a voice of God that would help and lead her. At first she had been very frightened. She had heard this voice about noon in the summer in her father's garden, and she had not fasted the previous day. She had heard the voice on her right from the direction of the church. She seldom heard the voice without also seeing the light. The light was always seen on the side from which the voice came and was generally very strong. When she later came to France she often heard the voice.

This is the conclusive document, for this, in Joan's own words, which she never withdrew, describes the way in which her revelations began. It is on this that the psychologists have fastened, and, according to Charcot especially, many hysterics have had hallucinations accompanied by light phenomena from one side, like those of Joan.

The judges continued their interrogation. How was it possible that she could perceive a light that was always on the side? But Joan preferred to ignore this question, though she added some interesting details.

She said that if she found herself in the forest, she often heard the voices coming toward her. She said she thought that the voice was a noble one and believed that it had been sent to her from God; after hearing it three times she realized that it was the voice of an angel. She also said that this voice always protected her and that she well understood what it said.

It can be seen how this contact with the supernatural arose from Joan's desire for solitude and love of praying in the forest. The judges listened eagerly to her statements, believing as they did that she was a witch, and they continued their interrogations with the most detailed questions. Posterity must be grateful to them for their thoroughness.

It became evident that what the voices first told her was to take good care of herself and attend church frequently. This was the beginning. Those who have studied revelations in modern times, for example at La Salette in 1846, at Lourdes in 1858, and at Fatima in 1917, will recognize the phenomenon. It is usually a case of simple peasant children accustomed to great solitude whose entire learning is the catechism. They do not suffer the inhibitions and prejudices of learning. They are not disturbed by the noise and clamor of a great city, but, kneeling in church or listening to nature, they have learned to look inward. In the beginning, they perceive a voice, a light, or a luminous figure, and when the message reaches their psychic senses it takes the form of simple, moral advice.

Immediately after these statements Joan relates how the voice came back two or three times a week. How it had told her that she must journey to France, that she must not remain in Domrémy, that she must raise the siege of Orléans, that she must go to the commandant, Robert de Baudricourt, and so on. All this was true and confirmed both by other utterances and by what she actually did, but quite clearly belongs to a later period. It is of importance to keep in mind the picture of Joan's first revelation, the deep silence in her father's garden, a voice, a light, and some general moral advice. Nothing else.

The voice was "good and noble", this is all she would say at first, but on February 27, she added some fresh details. She told of her meetings with Saint Catherine and Saint Margaret, but in reply to a formal question stated that the first to reveal himself to her was Saint Michael, the Archangel Michael. She saw and heard him at the age of thirteen; he was not alone, however, but surrounded by the celestial host mentioned in the liturgy.

The judges asked her if she had really seen Saint Michael and the angels with her own eyes, but she replied, "I saw them with my own eyes as clearly as I see you. And when they disappeared I wept and wished that they had taken me away with them."

The Archangel Michael

Historical research has shown that for special reasons the Archangel Michael was very much in evidence at that time in those parts of France that were loyal to the King.

Each dynasty had its favorite saint. The Merovingians and to a certain extent the Carolingians had Saint Martin. The Capets favored Saint Denis. Saint Michael became the patron saint of the House of Valois and in the fifteenth century was popularly regarded as the special protector of the country and the monarchy. Mont-Saint-Michel in Brittany, which since the end of the fourteenth century had been a place of pilgrimage, played a great part in this cult. As an example, it may be mentioned that from August 1368 to July 1369 the hostel of Saint Jacques in Paris gave shelter to no less than 16,690 pilgrims, of whom the majority were on their way to or from Mont-Saint-Michel. Twenty-four years later, the youth of Montpellier on the Mediterranean left the town in great numbers for the same destination. Large bodies of boys from all over

France made their way to the Norman coast. When Charles VI in 1394 had his first mental disturbance, he made a journey to the monastery and returned temporarily improved in health. He himself attributed this to the holiness of the place and the influence of the Archangel, who commanded the heavenly hosts in the battle against Satan.

When the English invoked Saint George, the French, during the Hundred Years' War, more and more eagerly turned to the Archangel, especially after that great national catastrophe, the capture of the monastery of Saint-Denis by Henry V in 1419, when the standard of France, the sacred Oriflamme, fell into the hands of the hated *"godons"*, those English devils who in the popular imagination were often believed to be equipped with tails. Joan of Arc was asked during the trial if she had ever seen Saint Denis and immediately replied in the negative, apparently not realizing the importance of the question. What lay behind the question was the belief that Saint Denis, after the conquest of the monastery, no longer helped the cause of France. It is true that Joan of Arc in 1429 had deposited her suit of armor in the monastery of Saint-Denis, but when asked why she had done so only replied: *"Parce que c'est le cri de France"*, for the battle cry of France had long been "God and Saint Denis".

Charles VII had quite clearly adopted Saint Michael as his patron saint after the fall of the monastery of Saint-Denis. When he took up the fight against his mother and the Duke of Burgundy, he had the Archangel's portrait painted on his banners, and one of the most important aims of his policy was to protect the city of Mont-Saint-Michel, which had for decades defended itself with magnificent bravery against the English, and which was for a long time the only fortress in the west that did not surrender.

Ten days before the death of Charles VI, there occurred an event which was regarded by all the royal party as a miracle and attributed to the direct intervention of the Archangel.

On October 11, 1422, the Dauphin was in La Rochelle when the floor collapsed in the banqueting hall, which was on the first floor, carrying all the guests with it. Many French noblemen lost their lives, and a great number were seriously injured, and the Dauphin, in spite of his physical frailty, was almost the only one who suffered no injury. He attributed this to the intervention of Saint Michael and six months later gave orders that a special Saint Michael Mass should be celebrated every year on October 11 in commemoration of, among other things, the miracle of La Rochelle. One can be certain that all this became known before long in Domrémy.

This belief was kept alive by the furious efforts of the English to capture Mont-Saint-Michel and the remarkably energetic efforts of Charles VII to relieve the town. In August 1424, the Duke of Bedford decided to make a determined attempt to crush the stubborn garrison of the rock fortress. There was violent fighting, but the garrison remained unconquered. The English then gathered a powerful fleet to blockade the town from the sea. Mont-Saint-Michel appealed for help to the famous seafarers of Saint Malo, who, inspired by their bishop, equipped a fleet that was placed under the command of Briand de Chateaubriand, the admiral of Brittany. In June 1425, this fleet attacked the blockading English fleet, which lay at anchor before the town. The English ships were larger, but the Bretons soon boarded them and after a violent battle were able to capture the whole English fleet except for a few units. This glorious naval victory was enthusiastically fêted all over France, and naturally the victory was attributed to the intervention of the Archangel.

This occurred toward the beginning of the summer in which for the first time Joan of Arc heard the voice of the Archangel and saw him in her father's garden.

Saint Catherine

It was this mighty angel who revealed himself to the young girl. It was in his presence that she first heard the divine voice.

We shall now return to the trial in Rouen.

Cross-examined, Joan replied to all questions with great frankness and said that everything that she had done—and from a human point of view her deeds are nearly inexplicable—was by the order of God.

"*Tout ce que j'ai fait, est par commandement de Dieu!*"

Quite naturally the judges wanted further details and also wished to know why Joan could be so certain that the voices which spoke to her were of God and not of the devil.

At first she only speaks of one voice, which had led her step by step, but pressed hard by the prosecution she admits that there were several voices. By the side of the Archangel, Saint Catherine and Saint Margaret had also revealed themselves to her with crowns on their heads and robed in beautiful garments. The Archangel had also told her that these two saints would reveal themselves to her and that she was to follow their advice, because it all came from the will of our Savior.

She encountered these two saints more and more often. They appeared before her daily, sometimes several times a day. They bore themselves like queens, and Joan greeted them with great reverence, kissing their knees and the hems of their dresses, distinctly aware of the fragrance emanating from them. They addressed her as "Daughter of God", and their first orders seem to have been very simple—to be good and attend church. Very soon, however, the young girl received a clear message that was to be of decisive importance for her development and that made it possible for her to carry out her whole mission. She promised the saints that her entire life would be one of chastity and thereby vowed to pay the first price demanded that she may become the repository of high secrets; for no one who does not sacrifice himself can serve as a tool of God.

This vow of chastity, however, cannot be understood unless one can realize what these saints represented to the thirteen-year-old girl. Her own mental picture of Saint Catherine was derived from a statue in her own church, preserved to this day, and she must also have known of the legends concerning this saint. It may be assumed that what Joan remembered about Saint Catherine would be roughly as follows:

Saint Catherine was the patron saint of young girls, especially of those engaged in needlework, and Joan's own sister was named Catherine after the saint, who had her own church in Maxey.

Catherine was the daughter of a king. She devoted her time to needlework and erudite studies. She was of exceptional beauty, and though wooed by many a knight had always declined with the words: "Find me a husband who is wise, handsome, noble, and rich."

But one night she saw in her dreams the Holy Virgin with the Child Jesus in her arms, who asked her: "Catherine, wilt thou take him for thy bridegroom? And thou, my dear Son, wilt thou take this maiden for thy bride?" The Child Jesus replied, "No." He refused to accept Catherine, who was not a Christian, but added that if she would allow herself to be baptized he would place the ring on her finger. Catherine consented to be baptized and shortly after in her room saw Christ appear with a host of angels and saints. He placed the ring upon her finger.

At that time, Maxentius was Emperor of Rome. He commanded the people of Alexandria to offer sacrifices to the gods, and from the room in which she was praying, Catherine could hear the chants of the pagan priests and the lowing of animals about to be sacrificed. She went out into the square and in front of the temple encountered the Emperor, to whom she said: "How can you be so foolish as to order these people to worship idols? You admire this temple because it is built by the hands of workmen. You admire these precious ornaments, which are nothing but dust that will be swept away by the wind. Instead you should admire the heaven and the earth and the sea and everything that is there, and when you have learned all that, you should ask yourself who is its Creator. It is our God. The God of Hosts and the God of Gods."

The Emperor had her brought to his palace, for he admired her both for her learning and for her beauty. He summoned no fewer than fifty learned men and said to them: "A daughter of a mysterious spirit tells me that our gods are nothing but demons. I could have forced her to sacrifice or I could have punished her, but I found it better that she should bend before the strength of your arguments. If you can triumph over her, you can return home loaded with honors."

Before the disputation took place, the Archangel Michael appeared to Catherine and told her that she would emerge victorious and receive from Christ the hope and the crown he confers upon those who fight for him.

The learned doctors were defeated by her learning and eloquence, and the first of them informed the Emperor that they saw no alternative but to become Christians themselves. Whereupon the Emperor flew into a rage and had all the fifty learned men thrown into a fire. He then turned to Catherine with great benevolence and told her that if she would sacrifice to the gods he would give her the first place in his palace after that of the Empress, and that her image would be erected in the city and worshipped as that of a goddess.

Catherine replied, "Let there be an end to such talk. It is a crime even to think thus. Jesus Christ has taken me for his bride, and he is my whole love, my whole honor, my whole joy."

When the Emperor sentenced her to death, she said, "Jesus Christ sacrificed himself for me. It is a great happiness for me to be permitted to be sacrificed as an acceptable burnt offering for the honor of his name."

The Emperor ordered that she should be flogged with rods and cast into a dark dungeon without food. He then left on a voyage, but the Empress, who was also a pagan, had a vision in which she saw Catherine standing before her surrounded by a brilliant light. Angels clad in white stood at her side, but because of the dazzling light that emanated from them she could not distinguish their faces. Catherine told the Empress to approach. She took a crown from the hands of one of the angels and placed it upon the head of the Empress, saying: "This is a crown sent to you from heaven in the name of Jesus Christ, my God and Lord."

When the Emperor returned, he let Catherine choose between death and sacrifice to the pagan gods. Catherine replied, "I wish nothing more than to sacrifice my flesh and blood for Christ."

The Emperor ordered an instrument of torture to be constructed. Four grazing animals were to tear Catherine's body to pieces. But an angel crushed this instrument with such force that splinters killed many of those standing around. The Empress, who had watched the preparations from her tower, came down and reproached the Emperor for his cruelty, whereupon he ordered her to make sacrifice to the gods. She refused, and he punished her by having her breasts torn off and her head severed. Before the Empress was led away by the executioner, Catherine encouraged her, "Rejoice, O Queen, beloved of God, for today you shall exchange a perishable kingdom for an eternal one and a mortal bridegroom for an immortal one."

After the execution, the Emperor went to Catherine and said that if she now repented having caused the downfall of the Empress by her magic she could be the first in his palace. But she must choose between sacrificing to the gods and death.

She answered, "Do what you have decided so that I may take my place among the maidens who accompany the Lamb of God."

She was led away to execution and raised her eyes to heaven saying, "Jesus, the hope of salvation of the faithful, the maiden's honor and beauty, I pray to thee that everyone who appeals to thee in memory of my martyrdom may have their prayers answered at the hour of their death and in all danger."

A voice was heard from heaven, "Come, my beloved bride. The gate of heaven stands open for thee. From above I promise help to all those who appeal to me through thee."

Faced by such a classical legend concerning a saint, we must remember that it was accepted quite literally by the Christians of the Middle Ages. In order to grasp the effect of these legends the people met with in the sermons of the priests, in the decorations of churches and cathedrals, and in the stories related by wandering monks, one should consider the part played in the lives of simple girls of all classes today by film stars and their private lives. It is the dress and appearance of the beauties of Hollywood that awkward peasant girls imitate as far as they can. It is the film star's naïve experiences in love and romance, in wealth, luxury, and travel at the side of a handsome and wealthy businessman, that nourishes the dreams of young girls nowadays.

One can more easily understand the mentality of the Middle Ages if one attempts to realize that this role was filled, only in an even more intense degree, by the saints and their legends. Few people at that time could read, and in any case there were no books or newspapers. The only form of propaganda that reached the ordinary man came to him through the images seen in the churches. The conception of hell was nourished not only by the sermons of the priest, but also by the sinister gargoyles and figures in the cathedrals. The personalities of the Bible were given life by the sculptures on columns and altar furnishings. Joan of Arc doubtless dreamed her sentimental dreams about Saint Catherine in the same childlike manner as a peasant girl from Lorraine today dreams about her favorite American film star. In modern times, there are, of course, other factors of suggestion; the images engendered by the Church still live a vigorous life, especially in Catholic countries. During the Middle Ages, however, there was nothing else that could compete. Obviously, it was unusual for a girl of thirteen to devote herself so systematically to prayer and contemplation as did Joan of Arc. But it was impossible for anyone to avoid this world of images from the Bible and the holy legends.

Strangely enough, most modern people regard it as cultural progress that the personalities of the Bible and the saintly legends have been replaced, as examples and ideal images, by the heroes and heroines of films and "comics".

Saint Margaret

Thus one of the saints who captured the imagination of the youthful Joan was a woman who had guarded her chastity and never forsaken her faith. These two facts, and also the fact that she had been especially encouraged by the Archangel Michael, penetrated very deeply into the young girl's consciousness.

With Joan's later experiences in mind it is strange to reflect on the other side of the legend, one to which the girl probably did not at first attach much importance—Catherine's successful disputations with fifty learned men and her subsequent martyrdom for her faith. Here, too, Joan was to follow in the footsteps of the saint.

The other saint whom Joan said she had seen and from whom she had received guidance was Saint Margaret. She had seen a full-length painting of her in the church, holding in her hand an aspergillum, her foot placed on the head of a dragon. She knew that Saint Margaret was the patron saint of women in childbirth and of peasants, and that she helped ordinary simple folk who had difficulties in their daily tasks.

There is a legend about Saint Margaret that was probably known to Joan. According to this legend she was born in Antioch, where her father was a pagan priest. She was, however, secretly baptized. One day when she was out minding the sheep, the Governor, Olibrius, saw her and was impressed with her beauty. He ordered his servants to bring her to him. If she was a freed woman he would marry her, if a slave he would take her into his service and make her his mistress.

When she was brought before him, he asked who she was, her name, and to what faith she belonged. She replied that she was called Margaret and was a Christian. Olibrius answered, "How can such a noble and beautiful young woman as you worship the crucified Jesus?"

She answered that Jesus Christ lived an eternal life. His reply was to cast her into prison.

The following day he had her brought before his tribunal and told her that if she persisted in her blindness he would have her decapitated. Margaret replied, "Jesus died for me. I wish to die for him."

The Governor then ordered that she be flogged and her body torn to pieces.

Those present wept when the order was carried out and the blood streamed from her body. The Governor himself hid his face in his hands so that he should not see her blood and ordered her to be taken back to the prison.

She was there tempted by the devil and prayed to God that she be permitted to see the enemy whom she was to combat. A gigantic dragon appeared and threatened to devour her, but she made the sign of the cross and the dragon vanished. The devil then appeared in another guise and approached her as a man. He came quietly up to her and taking her hand said, "Margaret, you have suffered enough."

But she seized his hair, hurled him to the ground, and placing her foot on his head, exclaimed, "Tremble, great enemy. You now lie under the foot of a woman."

The following day she was led before the judge, who told her that she must make sacrifice to the pagan images. She refused to do this and was burned with torches, but did not appear to feel any pain. Olibrius became afraid that the people seeing this miracle would be seized with terror and allow themselves to be baptized, and he ordered her to be beheaded.

She said to the executioner, "Brother, take your sword and strike."

In one blow her head was severed, and her soul rose toward heaven in the form of a dove.

This legend was extremely well known and the theme of many ballads and mysteries. The name of the Governor was so familiar that any unusually stupid and evil-minded person was described as an "Olibrius".

This naïve legend acquires a strange and deep significance if read against the background of Joan's later life. Here, too, we are concerned with a young woman who guarded her chastity and preferred to die rather than deny her faith.

It is impossible to ascertain with any degree of certainty by what steps these revelations came to influence Joan more and more, but this much can be established: the first thing she was told was that she must be a good girl and pray frequently.

She obeyed this order with great zeal. We have much evidence to prove that without revealing her secret to her friends or her parents she accepted the words of the saints with complete seriousness. It has been disputed whether she took counsel with a priest. Cordier regards this as unlikely, but a modern historian, Joseph Calmette, who in a brief but uniquely excellent work has compressed all the known facts about Joan of Arc, regards it as self-evident that Joan had confided in a priest and also gives his name. It was her father confessor, the priest of Greux, Guillaume Front, to whose parish Domrémy belonged. Calmette goes so far as to characterize Guillaume Front as an austere man, with the typical traits of a Franciscan. (At that time the Dominicans were in the main supporters of Burgundy, while the Franciscans supported the Valois.) It is quite probable, though it cannot be definitely proved, that Calmette's

47

opinion is correct and that this priest bears the responsibility for Joan's moral and spiritual education, although she told the judges that she had had no other education than that which her mother gave her and had not confided her visions to anybody else.[2] For it is improbable that a girl who was deeply religious, who lived close to a church and had many priests in her family, should keep these remarkable experiences to herself during confession. And it also seems improbable that a religious attitude of such marked clarity and consistency as that of Joan should develop spontaneously in a primitive consciousness without the guidance of a priest.

What probably happened is that the girl went to her confessor and told him first about the mysterious voice, which the third time proved to be that of the Archangel Michael, and afterward about the two female saints whom the priest probably helped her to identify, and about whom he no doubt gave her a detailed account. It is reasonable to suppose that he listened to her talk, helped her to understand her revelations, gave her directives for her moral life, and in the end loyally accepted her definite mission, which must certainly have far exceeded what he had originally thought possible.

What was the life of Joan of Arc during the first period of the five years that passed before she set out, never to return?

A priest, Henri Arnolin, relates that Joan confessed three times during the same fast. He also relates that, later, she prayed in the churches with such fervor that she was close to ecstasy. "She sometimes knelt before the crucifix with her face touching the floor and at other times sat there motionless, with her hands folded and her face and eyes fixed on the crucifix or on the Blessed Virgin."

The people of Domrémy made fun of her because of her piety, so that she blushed. Hauviette, Joan's playmate, relates that the parish priest himself was a little worried about her fervor: "I once heard the priest say that she confessed too often."

These small incidents hidden away in the testimonies of the trial—otherwise generally rather monotonous—are of the greatest importance. Here we have a close-up of how a priest guides Joan and even has the

---

[2]Lucien Fabre accepts this literally: "Joan never mentioned her vision to her confessor." The actual words in the proceedings were, "Asked if she had mentioned her visions to her parish priest or any other priest, her answer was 'No'." This was undoubtedly the answer the judges desired.

common sense to warn her against excessive zeal despite her marvelous revelations. It makes it possible to assume that Joan's notably unhysterical disposition and her spiritual soundness, which have so often been spoken of, had some connection with a mature and wise religious guidance during the five years of waiting.

We also know that Joan took much care of the poor, that she had to be prevented from giving up her own bed to the sick and sleeping on the floor, that she nursed the sick, and that, altogether, in the words of her little playmate, she was "so wonderfully kind".

Joan often heard the voices in her parents' garden, but she also heard them at the spring and in the forest. Later, in an unforgettable passage, she relates that she sometimes waited in vain for the "voices", but they returned when she heard the church bells and blended with the chimes, which cleansed her soul and made her deaf to the clamor and noises of the day and to her own doubts. This was, she supposed, what the chimes were for. It is said that she so eagerly longed for Compline, the evening prayer of the Church, that she at once noticed if the verger rang too late or forgot it. Once she even promised him some nice cakes if only he would be kind enough to attend to his duty and sound the bells at the exact hour. This last incident belonged to the small touches that make the portrait of the young Joan of Arc so alive and fascinating. We also hear that she began to withdraw from the games of the other young people and would no longer dance under the oak except when she played with small children. It appears that from this time on she no longer found the same pleasure in wandering about the fields with the cattle, but remained at home and cheerfully busied herself with simple household duties.

If the priest was satisfied, it may be assumed that her father was less so, and I will later produce evidence to show that he despaired about Joan's mission, of which, strangely enough, he became aware even before she had mentioned it by word.

The village boys teased her—she who before had been so gay and had raced with them and was now so appallingly pious. We know that this caused her unhappiness, but she bravely continued her way of life. When they left her, she sometimes wept and wished that she could have gone with them. It is clear that during these years she was going through a schooling necessary for the great and exacting tasks that awaited her. It was only when she was so hardened that she obeyed and blindly believed in her "voices", never raising objections or letting herself be affected by the criticism and ridicule of her fellow men, that she was ready for her mission.

The soldierly and unhysterical qualities of Joan of Arc have been emphasized. There is nothing unhealthy or morbid in this strong and fresh personality. Everything in her is, on the contrary, wholesome and pure, as if she had sprung straight from the best soil of France. But to say this is not to deny her mysticism. The great fault with nearly all previous accounts of Joan's life is that they have ignored or minimized the fact that her spiritual development was that of a typical mystic. Through hard moral schooling, through listening to the inner voice, and through asceticism, she advances to the supreme sacrifice, martyrdom. Behind such a life there must be an inner spiritual development that in its main features is the same in Joan of Arc as in other great mystics of a less active type.

We may therefore assume with fair certainty that a young girl living in a village where the ancient nature mysticism still existed, who had undoubtedly long been attracted by what has been called the mysticism of eternity, entered step by step into personal mysticism, thanks to a succession of revelations and skillful guidance. We can see her clearly in imagination, physically healthy and strong, running on winged feet, active and infinitely helpful, shaken and horrified by what she heard said by her father and neighbors about the sufferings of France, about the shameful Burgundians and the cruel English, and about the poor Dauphin and his criminal mother—but also frequently seeking solitude, binding garlands around her beloved saints or lingering in the beechwood, listening to marvelous, though still vague and indistinct, voices from her innermost being, ripening for a wonderful mission which she could not yet distinguish.

A spectacle as rare as it is beautiful—that of a young human being humbly preparing for the mission of her life.

For a writer like Anatole France, Joan's vow of chastity was unimportant and induced by the magical significance that chastity was supposed to possess in earlier times. For those who can realize that Joan's life was that of a mystic, this promise in the years of her youth is of fundamental importance. The romanticism of modern life is largely connected with sex. The men and women of the Middle Ages were without doubt as vulnerable to the temptations of the flesh as those of our own times, and they knew from the teachings of the Church that this instinct is implanted in us by God, and that an honorable marriage is not only permitted but is a holy sacrament, and is therefore looked on with favor by God. But the young women of the Middle Ages also saw another road intended not for everyone, or even for many, but for a blessed few—the road of chastity. They had in their community no clergy in comfortable vicarages with wives and children, but unmarried priests who in this respect too followed our Lord.

They saw nuns and monks, the majority of whom at any rate had forsworn the world not from fear of it but to render all to God. They knew that it is easier for one who is not tied to a single individual to love all mankind. In the ideals and dreams of women, marriage naturally played a great part, but by its side virginity was a second ideal, an ideal wreathed by the finest poetry and exalted in beautiful Latin hymns and conventual chants.

Like all normal girls, Joan must have had dreams about men and marriage, and I will return later to her normal and healthy view of her own body and of her male friends. But she also listened to the legends of Saint Margaret and Saint Catherine, beautiful, desirable women who could have possessed all the glories of the world if they had given themselves to the men who wanted them, and who nevertheless did not yield to the temptation. Why? Because they could not be satisfied by anything but the highest, the love of Christ. Can a married woman then not reach the love of Christ? Undoubtedly, but there is another path reserved for a minority, for the few human beings who are consumed by such an overwhelming love for Christ that they wish to follow him in everything, to share his sacrifice and take part in his sufferings in a world where passions otherwise have free play, and where all men demand and desire, and greedily fight for pleasures and enjoyment like wild animals for food. For these the Church insists uncompromisingly, century after century, that true peace is only gained by him who conquers himself. There is another world than the one that now dazzles us with its promises. What is highest in the life of man is the love that does not demand but gives; the saints are those who have loved most on earth.

This was the call that echoed in the young girl's mind.

It took concrete form in the images of the two beautiful women saints, and we may suppose that during many solitary hours in church or in the forest Joan contemplated their destinies with inner vision. There was then no literature to confuse her with naïve theories about indulging one's desires to obtain freedom, no silly wishful dreams of elopement with rich youths. The only destinies known to her outside the material plane were those of the Bible and the legends. And these high destinies spoke a single unequivocal language. Man has a great task, a great calling. "Adhere to thy Church and listen to thy inner voice, and thou shalt one day know which calling is thine, and woe to thee if thou failest."

It was for this reason that Joan, facing the two chaste saints, promised God not to give herself to any man. She knew well what this meant. She knew what was demanded of a nun, and though she never stated this herself she must have believed, long before her summons to political action, that her spontaneous vow of chastity meant life in a convent. However, we have no certainty about this.

One thing, however, is quite certain, and that is the profound significance of Joan's vow. Through her revelations she was completely convinced that the reality she encountered in sermons, legends, and religious imagery was true and tangible. She knew that it applied to her also. She does not say that the vow of chastity was demanded of her, although she gave it spontaneously because her heart longed for that life of obedience, sacrifice, and love which the saints had lived. More than this she probably did not know herself at first—we may say the same of her confessor, whom she may have consulted.

We come to another matter that has been touched on earlier but that now becomes of great significance. We know that Joan of Arc was aware of the prophecies that had spread through the land foretelling that France, now ravaged by a wicked woman, would be saved by another woman who (it was even stated) would come from Lorraine and must be a virgin.[3] Celibacy was here the first step toward an extraordinary summons. One need not believe that Joan was consciously influenced by dreams of becoming the Maid through whom the country was awaiting its salvation. In any case, not at the age of thirteen when she was still a child. But her decision was not unconnected with these rumors, which in their turn were rooted in the early Christian belief that personal sacrifice, particularly the sacrifice of sexual happiness, was necessary for a human being destined by God to great deeds.

[3] In connection with all these prophecies one should remember the opinion of the sober Cordier. He thought it probable that these alleged prophecies, which for the most part were derived ultimately from the works of the Venerable Bede and from legends about the magician Merlin, were first mentioned in connection with Joan about the time of the examination in Poitiers in March 1429 in order to create an atmosphere favorable to the prosecution.

CHAPTER 4

The Summons

Nobody but herself knows when the "voices" ceased to speak to Joan about herself and began to speak about France. In any case, a day came when the "voices" spoke a quite different language from that to which she had become accustomed.

"*Fille de Dieu,* you must leave your village and set out for France!"

We may assume that at this moment Joan became frightened. The thought seemed to her beyond all reason, and according to her own account she answered, "But I am only a poor girl, and I can neither ride nor fight!"

But the voices persisted. Day after day they repeated their summons, though the phraseology varied. Once they said to her, "Receive your banner from the King of Heaven. Take it bravely, and God will help you."

Joan had heard of a banner from heaven in another connection. She knew that the Oriflamme of the monastery of Saint-Denis had fallen into the hands of *les godons,* the English invaders. It is evident that she was more than once tempted to join the other village children in a fight to punish the children from the other side of the river who were friendly to the Burgundians, but according to her own statement she never took part in these childish battles. She took care never to allow herself to hate the English or the Burgundians. But she knew where her sympathies lay.

The "voices" continued their exhortation, and their orders finally became definite. "*Fille de Dieu,* you must lead the Dauphin to Reims, so that he may be crowned in the right manner."

These words awakened many memories in Joan's mind, memories of legends and tales she had heard told. It was at Reims that the great miracle had occurred when the pagan King Clovis was about to be baptized by Saint Rémi, the saint who had given his name to Domrémy. The legend relates that when the procession reached the chapel containing the font, the priest who bore the holy oil was unable to make his way through the closely packed spectators, so that it seemed as if the ceremony of blessing the baptismal water could not take place. The bishop then raised his eyes to heaven and prayed silently and in tears. At that moment, a white dove descended from heaven holding the amphora in its beak. The fragrance filled the whole church, the bishop seized the amphora and poured a drop of the holy oil into the baptismal water, whereupon the dove disappeared. The amphora that had descended from heaven was still in the town.

Now Joan understood. The Dauphin, the unhappy, persecuted Charles, had not been anointed. It was her task to lead him to Reims.

Whatever comments one may wish to make concerning this revelation, against whatever background one wishes to see it—traditions, legends, rumors, suggestions, priestly influence—nothing of this explains what was the heart of the matter, that the girl regarded it as a celestial order and was immediately willing to obey. Anatole France, who when not blinded by anti-clericalism is a master in giving life to historical traditions, expresses it beautifully:

> The girl listened. The mists cleared, and the shining light spread in her soul. So it was for this that she had been chosen by God! Through her the Dauphin, Charles, would be crowned in Reims. The white dove which had once been sent to Saint Rémi would now again in answer to the prayer of a maiden descend to the earth. God who loves the French marks their king with his sign, and if this sign is absent his kingly power does not exist. It is only by the anointing that he becomes king, and *messire* Charles Valois is not anointed. His father rests in the basilica of Saint Denis in France with the crown on his head and the sceptre in his hand, but his son is only the Dauphin and cannot come into his whole inheritance until the day when the holy oil touches his forehead. And it is she, the young ignorant peasant girl, whom God has chosen to lead him through his enemies to Reims, where he will receive the same anointment as Saint Louis.

But how was this to come about? Humanly considered, it was an impossible task, which she could not discuss even with her brothers and parents, for they would only have ridiculed her. She kept the celestial command to herself, probably mentioning it only to the parish priest, Guillaume Front, of whose reaction nothing is known.

54

But her "voices" persisted. They also indicated to her the man who would make her mission possible. But a long time was to elapse before Joan obeyed, in agony we must assume, and with misgivings and despair.

She had only the celestial "voices", which she heard daily, to keep up her strength.

Hallucinations?

I have already indicated that no agreement on the subject of Joan's revelations is likely to be reached between rationalists and atheists on the one side and Christian critics on the other. What the former regard as imagination and wishful thinking is for the latter obvious and impressive reality. Perhaps we should here allow both parties to plead their own cause; in this manner the picture of Joan and her relation to the "voices" may become clearer. The reader will then be able to take his own stand over the question of illusion or reality.

Cordier thinks that at the outset Joan had only certain visual and oral sensations that she was unable to interpret. Gradually, however, she complemented these sensations with a tangible content drawn from the two sources at her disposal, that is, from her own subconscious and from the general world of imagination of that period. To Cordier, the saints and angels she sees are, of course, nothing but hallucinations.

Cordier wants to prove that Joan's revelations agree with modern psychological views about the phenomena of hallucination, and for this purpose he arranges his material in a series of short paragraphs, which he compares in turn with modern psychological conclusions based on the observation of a number of cases.

1. *Joan is absolutely certain that her "voices" are genuine.*

EXAMPLE:

"I have seen them [Saint Michael and Saint Gabriel] with my own eyes, and I believe that it was they as surely as I believe in God's existence."

"She knows this through revelation as surely as she knows that we stand before her."

"As regards the angels, she has seen them with her own eyes."

PSYCHOLOGIST:

What distinguishes the genuine hallucination is that the individual in question is firmly convinced of the reality of his false imaginings.

The imagined words are distinct. They are whispered into the ear or uttered in a loud voice such as another person would use.

2. Joan obeys her orders exactly.

EXAMPLE:

"She answered that she obeyed with all her strength the orders she received from God through her 'voices' as she understood them."

PSYCHOLOGIST:

The hallucinatory commands are often executed spontaneously and without the slightest hesitation. This is an argument in favor of the opinion maintaining that hallucination is only an expression in words of subconscious tendencies.

3. The "voices" gave her permanent help.

EXAMPLE:

"She also said that she would be dead were it not that the revelation gave her renewed strength every day."

"When she had said her prayer to God, she heard a 'voice' which said to her: '*Fille de Dé, va, va, va, je serai à ton aide, va.*' (Daughter of God, go, go, go, I will help you; go.)"

"And the 'voice' said to her that she should answer courageously [during the trial] and that God would give her strength."

PSYCHOLOGIST:

In many cases the invisible powers give support and strength.

"Go, my son. I will defend thee." (Example from a modern case.)

4. She hears, sees, touches, and feels her "voices".

EXAMPLE:

"She answered that she had touched Saint Catherine, who was visible before her, and that she had kissed both Saint Catherine and Saint

Margaret. Asked if they had a fragrant odor, she replied, 'It is good to know that they have a fragrant odor'."

PSYCHOLOGIST:

Different mental hallucinations, particularly sensitive and oral, are often combined with the imagined outer form.

5. Joan's "voices" are above all oral.

She always hears them but sometimes doesn't see them. When she sees them, she can only distinguish their faces and hair.

EXAMPLE:

"Asked if the voice was really in her room, she replied that she didn't know, but that it was in the castle."

"They always have the same appearance, and their heads are richly crowned. She does not speak about their clothing. Questioned if their hair was worn long and hanging down, she replied, 'I don't know.' She also said that she did not know if there were arms and other limbs."

PSYCHOLOGIST:

In those cases where different sensations occur, mental impressions of a certain kind always dominate.

6. She sometimes sees her "voices" surrounded by a number of small figures.

EXAMPLE:

"She said that it was Saint Michael whom she saw with her own eyes, but he was not alone but surrounded by the angels of heaven."

"Asked about the number of angels that accompanied him, she replied that they appeared before her in the shape of a kind of very small figure."

"The same Joan said that she had had revelations that came to her sometimes in great numbers, at other times in the shape of very small figures."

PSYCHOLOGIST:

Lilliputian hallucinations are not rare. Figures appear like dolls, sometimes in bright colors; sometimes animals pass by.

An English doctor relates that after an illness his mental impressions had been disturbed, and he thought that he saw "a row of small manikins who retreated step by step like a row of medallions".

7. *Joan has real conversations with her "voices".*

EXAMPLE:

"She said that Saint Catherine and Saint Margaret willingly allow her to confess, sometimes to the one and sometimes to the other, on different occasions."

PSYCHOLOGIST:

It is not unusual for such patients to hear three, four, and even up to ten voices, and often the patients even answer their questions and have long conversations with them. A typical example is Luther's conversation with the devil.

8. *Joan can distinguish one voice from the other.*

EXAMPLE:

"She recognized them by their manner of greeting her, and because they themselves gave her their names."

PSYCHOLOGIST:

The mentally sick can distinguish different imaginary persons by the sound of their voices.

9. *Joan hears her "voices" when she needs them.*

EXAMPLE:

"Asked if she calls on Saint Catherine and Saint Margaret, or if they appear without being summoned, she replies, 'They often come without being summoned; and sometimes if they do not come at once I pray to God to send them.'"

"Asked if it had ever happened that the saints did not appear when she called on them, she said that she had never had need of them without their also appearing."

PSYCHOLOGIST:

There are cases when people believe that they can on their own initiative cause the "voices" to come.

There are cases where the hallucinations appear to be called forth by
their own will. The mentally sick will talk to his unseen friends when it
pleases him, and if he is asked to put a question to them he listens for a
while and then repeats the reply.

10. *Of Joan's counselors, who are three, one, namely Saint Michael, ceases to
visit her.*

EXAMPLE:

"She also said that she had not seen Saint Michael since she left the
castle of Le Crotoy."

PSYCHOLOGIST:

Changes in the number of voices are usual. A person who for several
months asserted that he could distinctly distinguish three voices, one day
reported that he could now only hear two. In another case the reverse
occurred.

11. *Joan is sometimes awakened by her "voices" when she sleeps.*

EXAMPLE:

"Asked what she did yesterday when the 'voices' came to her, she
replied that she slept and that the 'voice' aroused her. When she awakened, she asked the 'voice' to advise her as to what she should answer,
and told the 'voice' that she wanted God's guidance on this point."

PSYCHOLOGIST:

It is usual that hypnagogic illusions occur at night just before falling
asleep or before awakening in the morning.

Hallucinations may begin during sleep and continue after awakening.

This is Cordier's summary. He concludes that there is nothing in Joan's
revelations that does not correspond to the results of modern study of
hallucinatory cases. Cordier shows, using among others the case of Saint
Teresa of Avila, that hallucinations of this nature can easily occur in a
person who in other respects is completely normal. He assumes that Joan

had a certain pathological disposition, but he believes this to have been isolated and to have had no influence on the rest of her spiritual life. His examination gives us a picture of a thoroughly healthy, sober-minded, sensible, vital young girl, who displays the single peculiarity that the stirrings of her subconscious, nourished partly by her warm personal desires, partly by suggestions derived from contemporary ideas, appear in her as hallucinations, which to her own senses are completely real. Or, to use the actual words of this scholar, "Joan's 'voices' are Joan herself." Thus, if we are to approach closely to truth, when Joan speaks of her "voices" we must translate the expression "the voice said" into "I wish".

According to this approach, Joan of Arc's case is simply the following: an emotional motive, felt for a long time, was strengthened by horrifying political experiences and rumors and by the recent news of the siege of Orléans. In Joan there was already at an early stage an exceptional urge to intervene personally and to act, unusual in a young woman. "Nothing would be more human, nothing more natural for a generous person." Joan's fighting spirit is the only unusual feature of the case, for with women this particular hallucinatory disposition as a rule disposes to prophetic manifestations only.

Or a Meeting with Spiritual Reality?

The historian Joseph Calmette, in the foreword to his short book on Joan of Arc, takes a firm stand regarding the question of the authenticity of her revelations.

> A historian who knows what he owes to his science, which by its very nature is objective, can never permit himself to be influenced by purely subjective feelings on religion and philosophy. A truly methodical historical scholar seeks nothing but to recognize the elements of truth contained in records. These can only give facts, and the impression these facts made on their times. More cannot be asked of them. Joan believed in her heavenly mission. Some of her contemporaries believed, others did not. These convictions, which in certain cases were hesitant and fluctuating, helped to decide the course of events. It is quite meaningless to ask medical science to explain Joan's case. One psychiatrist will say that she is mad, another that she is hysterical—both vain attempts at diagnosis without real contact with historical records. These give every impartial observer the impression of an unusually well-balanced disposition. Whether Joan

was a saint who performed miracles or merely an instrument for a purely human patriotism, even if she were mentally afflicted, it does not alter in the least degree the historical sequence of her life and the process which led to the salvation of France. In the same way the history of Christianity is not altered in the smallest detail by the acceptance or denial of the divinity of Christ.

It is therefore the task of the historian to tell to the best of his ability what actually happened, to tell what Joan believed she heard and the impression this made on herself and her times. But there is something more that he can do. He can, as is emphasized by Calmette, seek to determine whether this young woman, whose revelations were to be of decisive importance for the whole history of France, was an hysteric or a normal, healthy-minded woman. And he can compare her with other women who have had similar revelations.

In psychological literature, Joan's case has often been included among cases of mental disorder and hysteria. It is strange that such a clear-sighted man as Cordier, to whom we have already referred, does not recognize the importance of the one really interesting fact—namely, that Joan, in contradistinction to most of the other cases with which he compares her, does not display passive delusions but intervenes actively and creates history. All the commands of her "voices" are obeyed, their promises kept.

When we consider a poet of genius, we are not much concerned as to how far his inspirations are related to those of hysterics and visionaries. The one important fact that distinguishes the poet from the others is that where the latter create nothing but confusion, the former builds and creates values.

It is the same with great religious personalities. Like most other geniuses they display characteristics that have a certain relationship with the abnormal. They often work under an abnormal strain and take greater risks than so-called normal people. They give more, they stake more of their life energy, they are under greater pressure and become more sensitive, more vulnerable. For a superficial observer all this seems unnatural, unhealthy. But a genius must be measured by that which he achieves.

There is another way of approach that seems to provide greater clarity.

Calmette and Cordier were both struck by the balance, strength, and simplicity of Joan's character. She seems completely unhysterical. Is this unusual among mystics? Even such a writer as Lucien Fabre seems to think so. He writes: "Joan was in the original and correct meaning of the word 'transported' by her visions but never to the point of ecstasy. She never appears to have exhibited symptoms of catatonia or depersonization. Her playmates saw her sometimes withdraw herself, and it seemed to them as if she were 'speaking about God'. This is all that witnesses could observe. A great gulf separates Joan from the mystics...."

The last sentence quoted does not seem justified. It suggests a false view of mystics as having diseased and abnormal minds. There are certainly mystics who display symptoms of an abnormal nature, just as there are poets who are in many respects pathological cases. But what characterizes the great mystics is, on the contrary, their normality.

Gabriel Hanotaux, in his book on Joan of Arc, says with great authority: "Such psychological phenomena as visions and revelations do not occur with frequency and strength in the case of feeble and uncertain individuals, but in strong, complete, purposeful, dominating natures." One can agree with this author in his other theses; the structure of Joan's spiritual life is identical with what we know of the great mystics.

In the period nearest to the appearance of Joan there were two female saints, Saint Catherine of Siena and Saint Bridget of Sweden. The former had revelations even when she was a child. She went out into the world as a young woman and became the spiritual leader of churchmen and monks; she brought the Pope back to Rome from Avignon, thereby making an important contribution to world history. At an age when the interests of most women did not extend beyond the family circle, she played a leading part in politics. She had a great knowledge of human nature and, though she could be stern when the situation called for it, she was full of gentleness and motherly love, and yet could solve the most complicated practical problems with sovereign ease. Everything about her suggests health, purposefulness, strength. She left for posterity a literary work, her "dialogue", which has a place among the classics of mysticism and gives evidence of spiritual experiences of the highest order. Though this young woman did not hear what Joan of Arc called "voices", she continually had visions and frequently went into a state of ecstasy. She lived a long life, often under abnormal conditions; a number of witnesses (of unshakable authenticity) have testified that she lived for long periods without eating—she would consume only the host of the Holy Communion. The "suburban Voltaire", whom T. S. Eliot has made the representative of modern, superficial, rationalist ignorance, may shrug his shoulders at such a phenomenon, just as he may deny the Resurrection and miracles of Christ, but the conscientious historian cannot do so. Catherine of Siena certainly had supernatural experiences, but the spheres she entered are not accessible to such persons as have allowed their spiritual body to wither away and make their spiritual poverty into an arrogant omniscience, denying all that in their spiritual blindness they cannot see, in their cowardice do not dare to believe, in their egoism have not the strength to love. Who is the sound, the normal human being: this daughter of a dyer who sacrificed everything to place herself in the hands of God and transformed herself into an obedient instrument for the spiritual world—or a superficial, empty, modern robot moved only by his desires?

Immediately before Catherine of Siena—and probably in a historical connection with her—appears Bridget of Sweden, the greatest religious figure of Swedish history. In the vulgar tradition, Bridget is a hysteric, and some writers have tried to explain her revelations by reference to the fact that she was a (sex-starved) widow. But Bridget was a woman who had been married for decades, she was a most realistic, purposeful, and energetic woman, and her most notable characteristics were moral balance, severity with herself and others, and a complete absence of sentimentality and hysteria. Nevertheless, she had visions and revelations that, in a normal way, entered into and dominated her spiritual life. It is unfruitful to compare Catherine of Siena and Bridget of Sweden with hysterics and unusual pathological cases. It would be more reasonable to compare them with Saint Paul.

When Joan of Arc was canonized, the Church wisely refrained from any reference to her "voices". Joan of Arc was declared to be a saint on quite different grounds. This means that these experiences and visions, like most other similar ones, cannot be adequately formulated, because contact with supernatural spheres is *ex definitione* a miracle and cannot be analyzed.

It does not mean that Joan's voices are suspect, a strange side-issue that must be accepted for the sake of her real services. On the contrary, Joan of Arc is a healthy, sound human being who acts differently from us because she is the object of higher grace, and who makes herself deserving of this grace by greater fidelity and bravery than we are capable of.

Our modern time is a period of spiritual withering away, the final episode of naturalistic decadence. The attitude of superstitious positivism with which most historians and psychologists now regard the real peaks of history is anything but normal. From the point of view of a frog, the peaks are invisible, but this does not mean that the peaks no longer exist or that the frog represents what is normal. From such a low point of vision, spiritual life necessarily appears to be an illusion, miracles superstitions, and revelation a hallucination.

Unless we are prepared to recognize that our own experience is as limited as a child's, that our knowledge is partial, and that the normal way of looking at things today is a distorted and unsound one, we shall never understand the case of Joan of Arc.

With Robert de Baudricourt at Vaucouleurs

We have said that Joan of Arc was told not only what her mission was, but how it was to be carried out. What the "voices" told her was this: "*Fille de Dieu,* you will go to the captain, Robert de Baudricourt, in the town of Vaucouleurs. He will provide you with soldiers who can take you to the Dauphin."

This takes us to the heart of the actual situation of Joan and her neighbors.

In 1427–1428, the English and Burgundians began a campaign against the fortified loyalist strongholds in the valley of the Meuse, and particularly against the town of Vaucouleurs. In the middle of 1427, the Duke of Bedford decided to crush finally such places as Mouzon, Passavant, Beaumont-en-Argonne, and Vaucouleurs. These strongholds constituted a permanent threat to the English left wing, which operated in Champagne. Bishop Pierre Cauchon, whom we shall later meet as Joan's judge and implacable enemy, was given the task of collecting stores and materials for the campaign in Reims, Laon, Soissons, Nyon, Saint-Quentin, and Châlons. Jean de Luxembourg was appointed commander of the forces assembled to mop up the valley of the Meuse. In April 1428, he stood before Beaumont.

These events must have been followed with the greatest excitement and anxiety in the little village of Domrémy. In May 1428, just as the siege of Beaumont entered into a serious stage, Durand Laxart, a friend and relative of the d'Arc family, arrived in Domrémy. It was really his wife who was related to Joan's mother, but Joan always called him uncle. He was a man of about thirty, who seems always to have felt a special sympathy for Joan. Apart from the parish priest, he was the first person who really understood Joan's mission and believed in it.

In the record of the trial it says baldly:

> She further confessed that the "voices" told her two or three times a week that she must set off and journey to France, and that she must not remain where she was. The "voice" also told her that she should raise the siege of Orléans. She also said that the "voice" told her that she must go to Robert de Baudricourt in Vaucouleurs, where he was the commander, and that he would provide her with soldiers who would accompany her. And the said Joan answered that she was a poor girl who could not ride or wage war. She also said that she went to her uncle and told him that she wished to remain with him for a time. She stayed about eight days and said to her uncle that she must go to Vaucouleurs, and he guided her there.

The uncle, Durand Laxart, lived just outside Vaucouleurs. He induced the parents to let the girl go, and to him Joan opened her heart. She told him that she was chosen by God, that she was the Maid awaited by the country, and that she alone could liberate France. When he hesitated, she asked him, "Has it not been once said that a woman shall devastate the kingdom of France and that another woman shall resurrect it?"

The astonishing thing is that the uncle took her seriously and promised to lead her to the commander in Vaucouleurs. It is probable that, like the rest of the people of the neighborhood, he was in terror of the advancing English troops and clutched at the possibility that presented itself. Before Joan left his home she said to Durand's wife, Aveline, who was soon to give birth to a child: "If your baby should be a girl, call her Catherine after my dead sister." Her sister had recently died. This suggests that at that decisive moment Joan dwelt more than ever on Saint Catherine and her miracles.

Robert de Baudricourt was a good and rough soldier who defended his city with great energy and was a credit to his king, but he was not always over-delicate in his methods. A few years before, he had captured the emissaries of a cardinal and not released them until they had paid heavy ransom. Later he did not fare so well; he ravaged territories belonging to the bishopric of Toul, and for this was excommunicated. His reaction was to burst into a roar of laughter, but he was soon captured and thrown into prison, where according to one report he ended his days. But at the time with which we are concerned he was at the height of his power and commanded his garrison with a strong hand, fearing neither God nor the devil, but unswervingly loyal to his king.

We know that Joan came to Vaucouleurs clad in a patched red dress. She reached the commander's headquarters without difficulty, hesitated a moment, doubtful which one was he among the many present, and then, guided by her "voice", went up to the commander. "I have come", she said, "by the order of my Master [*Messire*] so that you shall tell the Dauphin to wait and not begin to fight his enemies."

She announced that before the celebration of mid-Lent *Messire* would bring help to the Dauphin, and added: "The kingdom does not yet belong to the Dauphin, but *Messire* wishes that the Dauphin shall become king, and that he shall rule the country under his guidance. Despite his enemies, the Dauphin shall become king, and it is I who will lead him to be crowned."

It is not surprising that the commander became irritated as well as astounded. Even the word *Messire* appeared strange to him. "What *Messire* is it you are speaking of?" he asked.

"The King of Heaven", replied Joan simply.

This was enough foolery for the soldier. "Take the wench back to her father", he said, "and tell him to give her a good spanking."

As far as he was concerned that was the end of the matter.

The attempt had failed completely. One report suggests that the commander had threatened for a moment to turn the girl over to the soldiers for their amusement, but the good uncle was able to bring her home unmolested to Domrémy after a week. It can be guessed what her state of mind must have been. Her "voices", however, never ceased their exhortations, and it is curious that at this time she was not always able to keep her secret. To a youth of her acquaintance, she is believed to have said, "Between Coussey and Vaucouleurs there is a girl who within a year shall crown the King of France."

And to another neighbor, Gérardin d'Épinal, she said, "If you were not a Burgundian I would tell you something."

Perhaps these remarks reached her father's ears, perhaps he drew his own conclusions. However the matter may be, there is a record of a curious remark made by him at this period. He had been having strange dreams. In the course of the trial, Joan was questioned about her father's dreams. She said that while she was still living with her parents she was several times told by her mother that her father had said that soldiers had set out with his daughter Joan. She also said that her father and mother took great care of her and showed her great consideration, but that she obeyed them in everything. She also said that her mother had related that her father had said to her brothers, "If I thought that that would happen to her which I have dreamed, I would rather you drowned her, and if you would not do it I would do so with my own hands." And they were nearly in despair when she set out for Vaucouleurs.

We can guess that the father was thinking of the great risks a young girl would run traveling without protection in those disturbed times. The commander's threats showed that his fears were justified. Rather than see his only surviving daughter raped, he would see her dead—that is probably the real meaning of his brutal words.

The English offensive continued, and one loyalist stronghold after another fell in the Meuse valley, until only Vaucouleurs remained. For months, the Duke of Bedford made preparations for its siege. On July 20, the investment began. Domrémy was seized by panic and the inhabitants prepared to evacuate their village. Men and women, the aged and the children, left their homes, driving their cattle before them and carrying as much as they could of their possessions. Joan accompanied her fleeing friends to Neufchâteau, six or seven miles from Domrémy. There the owner of an inn, popularly called "La Rousse", let her have a room. During the trial, it was stated that Joan had been in the service of the innkeeper during the fortnight she was there and got into bad company. In the speech for the prosecution it was stated:

> The said Joan in her fifteenth year without her parents' consent came to the town of Neufchâteau in Lorraine and served for a time with a certain woman called "La Rousse", where a number of young women of no reputation resided and where also a great many soldiers were quartered. During the time she was employed in this inn, she spent part of the time with these women and part of the time looking after the animals in the field and leading horses to be watered. It was here that she learned riding and the use of arms.

The judges were insinuating that Joan had been living and perhaps taking an active part in a soldiers' brothel. She rejected the accusation with contempt. The testimony of a large number of witnesses confirms that

67

she was never there alone, and we know that she was not happy at the inn, also that at that time she confessed three times to Franciscan friars.

The inhabitants of Domrémy soon returned home, to find their village pillaged and burned to the ground. Even the church was burned down. At this difficult time, Joan's parents seem to have considered whether she ought not to be married. At any rate, we know of a young man who asserted that Joan had consented to marry him.

In the accusation, this was distorted into the following episode: "Joan was supposed to have brought an action against the youth in question because he was not willing to marry her, while his defense was that he could not accept as his wife one who had lived with these fallen women."

The young man died during the examination.

Joan denied this version and maintained that the truth was the exact opposite. It was the youth who had wished to marry her, while she had refused. Her "voices" had assured her that she would win her case in court. Joan stated that her conduct on that occasion was one of the rare cases when she consciously acted against her father's will. When one knows of her vow of chastity and understands its connection with her supernatural mission, her attitude seems natural.

The political situation became more and more grave. In October 1428, the siege of Orléans began in earnest. It became ever clearer to Joan that she must at all cost obey her "voices". The whole future of France depended on her. "As God ordered, so it had to be, she told her judges. Even had she had a hundred fathers and a hundred mothers, even had she been the daughter of the King, she would have departed."

Again it was her uncle, Durand Laxart, who helped her. Madame Laxart was finding it difficult to manage her household without help after the birth of her child, and this gave Joan a good pretext to visit her uncle's home again. In January 1429, Joan left Domrémy never to return.

When her friends came to say good-bye, she said quietly, "Farewell, I am going to Vaucouleurs."

However, she could not bear to bid her best friend, Hauviette, farewell.

She was just eighteen.

Very soon she left the Laxart home and appeared before the commander Robert de Baudricourt as she had done nine months earlier. She repeated what she had said on the previous occasion, adding that she would raise the siege of Orléans. We do not know much about the commander's reaction. One report says that Joan uttered these words of prophecy: "When I have one day accomplished the great things *Messire* has ordered, I will marry and have three sons, one of whom will be a pope, one an emperor, and one a king." According to the story, the commander coarsely enquired if he could not be of service, to which Joan replied that the time had not yet come but that the Holy Ghost would intervene.

These words should perhaps be rejected as unreasonable, but attempts have been made to interpret them symbolically, so that Joan by the three sons had in mind different aspects of the celestial kingdom that should be established after her victory. The whole thing sounds improbable.

In Vaucouleurs Joan lodged with friends of the Laxart family. Joan would go to Mass with the wife and assist her in her domestic chores. She often went to the Chapel of Sainte-Marie-de-Vaucouleurs to pray. To her hostess she spoke openly about her mission. "Don't you know that it has been prophesied that France which has been ravaged by a woman shall be saved by a maiden from Lorraine?"

She spoke to many others about her aim to make her way to the Dauphin and always added that she was acting on the orders of God.

She does not seem to have had any success until she met a young man by the name of Jean de Metz to whom she confided her failures with the commander. She added that she must arrive before mid-Lent "even if she should have to crawl on her knees". She insisted that she was the only hope of salvation of the country. In some way, she succeeded in gaining the confidence of the young soldier. "I promise and swear that with God's help I shall lead thee to the King", he said, and added, "When do we depart?"

Joan replied, "Better immediately than tomorrow, and better tomorrow than later."

Jean de Metz, twenty-seven years later, related that he discussed the journey with her and pointed out how difficult it would be for her to travel dressed as a woman. She replied that she would like to dress as a man. Jean de Metz was doubtless affected by the girl's enthusiasm and faith, but nevertheless felt disturbed, and to be on the safe side asked the priest for advice—was Joan inspired by God or the devil?

This led to the priest's visiting Joan; asking her hostess to leave the room, he proceeded to read prayers of exorcism over her. Joan appears at first not to have understood the meaning of these rites and afterward confided her disappointment to her friend—the priest should not have done this, had she not confessed to him and did he not know her?

This part of Joan's life has often been described in romantic terms. Here was a noble, innocent girl, misunderstood and mocked by the mighty, only one or two faithful Frenchmen understanding her great task; only after many insults and trials was she able to overcome all opposition and reach the King. Instinctively one feels that there is something not quite right here. Joan's adversaries are made a little too like the evil giants in the fairy-tales to be quite credible. One usually gets nearest to the truth if one sets out from the premise that more often than not historical figures are led by their own selfish interests. In the study of Joan of Arc, it is Calmette and Cordier who have done most to provide us with a new view of her history. Cordier rejected the idea that Joan visited Vaucouleurs twice—according to him there is no evidence of more than one visit—but his arguments do not appear entirely convincing, and we have therefore adhered to tradition up to now. However, Cordier's views are probably correct concerning the next phase of Joan's life, that is, concerning all that followed her contact with Baudricourt. Here we obtain an entirely new picture of what happened.

In December 1428 Joan was an unknown peasant girl.

Four and a half months later she entered Orléans at the side of the Bastard of Orléans, *grand chambellan de France et lieutenant de monseigneur le roi sur fait de guerre, ès duché d'Orléans, comtés de Blois et de Dunois* (Great Chamberlain of France, Lieutenant of Monseigneur the King and royal Marshal, Duke of Orléans, Count of Blois and Dunois), mounted on a noble charger in full armor, carrying her own standard and greeted with indescribable enthusiasm by the population of the town.

What had happened in the interval?

Evidently what happened was that Robert de Baudricourt sent a report to the King's staff stating that he had been visited by a strange girl. He was himself in doubt but dared not turn her away. In all probability, it was he who sent the priest to visit Joan in her quarters and to exorcise the evil spirits that might be there. Here, therefore, it is not a question of an isolated episode, but of a link in a logical sequence.

The only evidence touching this matter was given by Catherine Le Royer to the effect that "she saw Robert de Baudricourt, who was commandant of Vaucouleurs, and the priest, Jean Fournier, enter her house, and Joan had told her that the priest in question had come equipped with his stole and that he had read exorcisms over her in the presence of the commandant. And Joan had also said that she had crept on her knees to the feet of the priest and added that he had acted badly as he had heard her confession."

The witness added that in spite of the favorable outcome of the examination Joan did not receive the commandant's permission to set out, and therefore she planned to leave without it. She said Joan was as anxious as a pregnant woman who expects her child to be born at any moment. A number of theories have been built on these statements suggesting that Joan really departed in the company of some faithful friends, but had turned back and returned to Vaucouleurs because, according to Père Petitot among others, she did not wish to start on so important an expedition in such a manner. Probably the story can be dismissed as legendary.

What is probable is that the commandant took further steps to ascertain what Joan really represented. Here again we must throw doubts on a legend accepted for centuries. According to this legend, Joan was summoned to the aged sensualist, Duke Charles II of Lorraine, in Nancy, who for a long time had been close to the Burgundians. He had long lived with Alison-du-Mai, a former florist, "as beautiful as she was grasping". He now believed that Joan would be able to cure him and had her summoned to his court. This postulates something that seems improbable, that is, that she was then already well known and enjoyed great authority. He asked her if she could cure his ills, but she replied that she had no revelation concerning this. She added that he "behaved very badly and would never be cured unless he took back his legitimate wife". Joan is also supposed to have promised to pray for him and asked him to give her his son and some soldiers who could conduct her to the King. The Duke answered her evasively but presented her with a gift of money. According to *La Chronique de Lorraine*, a highly romanticized literary work written forty years after Joan's death, Joan was presented with a horse by the Duke and sprang into the saddle without touching the stirrup. These details alone relegate the reports to the sphere of legend.

But there is some kernel of truth in the legend of this meeting. It may be assumed that Robert de Baudricourt asked the Duke if he would have a look at the girl and advise him as to what action to take. According to Cordier, Joan was at this period kept under supervision by the commandant, and it is hardly likely that she was even known outside a very limited circle. All that had happened so far was that she had uttered a few presumptuous words to a very small number of people. On the other hand, the commandant was a close friend of René d'Anjou, a relative of the King and married to the daughter of Duke Charles II. We know that on January 24, René d'Anjou wrote a letter to his father-in-law; on January 29 he wrote another letter to Baudricourt, and on February 9 a third to the King; but we do not know the contents of the letters. We also know that René d'Anjou journeyed to Nancy and left that town on February 24. It is possible that it was René who in the legend is described as the Duke's son, whom Joan had asked if she might "borrow". In any case it seems reasonable to think that the commandant had something to do with the exorcising, and that Joan visited the two nobles in Nancy so that they could judge her qualifications. It is natural that nothing became known about these investigations, and thus legend was given free play. It is also possible that Joan herself never understood the reason for the visit.

According to legend, it was Jean de Metz and Bertrand de Poulengy who accepted the responsibility for the journey to the King. It is not necessary to minimize their interest and grasp of the situation, but it is important not to forget that both were subordinate to the commandant and hardly in a position to take important decisions without consulting him. The probability is that the commandant, after his two experiments and after having received a favorable reply from the court, simply dispatched Joan. One can also with Cordier go a step further and assume that it was the court that had initiated the two experiments. A difficulty here is, however, the disinclination of the court to receive Joan once she had arrived in Chinon. News of the "Battle of Herrings" also reached Vaucouleurs at about that time and may have influenced the commandant's decision.

In any case, on February 12, 1429, Joan was ready to depart. She had cut her hair short, wore male clothing and armor, and the commandant himself presented her with a sword and a charger, and made her escort swear on oath to protect her.[1]

---

[1] Joan's own words during the trial were that the said Robert de Baudricourt made those who were to accompany her swear to protect her carefully. And Robert said to Joan as she was about to set out, "Depart. It is time to go."

In the records of the prosecution, Joan's equipment is carefully specified. It says first that the commandant was very unwilling to agree to her wish to wear male attire, and then: "*Ces*

Her companions were Jean de Metz, the leader of the expedition, Bertrand de Poulengy, the archer Richard, two servants, and Colet de Vienne. The last-named was of a certain importance, a kind of liaison officer who traveled about the country as the King's courier. Even the existence of such a "courier from the King's stables" among Joan's following indicates that the King's staff probably had some connection with the expedition.

Thus do the preparations for the journey appear when seen in the sharp light of research. The enterprise may have lost something of its romantic coloring, but it has certainly retained its character of adventure.

Without the consent of her parents, a girl of eighteen rides out into the world surrounded by a guard that is to lead her through enemy-occupied territory to the King. We may assume that after years of doubts and obstacles she felt a great joy in her heart as she spurred her horse, felt the sword at her side and the wind sweeping over her forehead, and knew that before her lay the great mission God had given her.

---

vêtements et ces armes etant fabriqués, ajusté et confectionnés, ladite Jeanne rejeta et abondanna entière- ment le costume féminin: les cheveux taillés en rond à la façon des pages, elle prit chemise, braies, gippon, chausses joignant ensemble, longues et liées audit gippon par vingt aiguilettes, souliers hauts, lacés en de- hors et robe courte jusqu'au genou ou environ, chaperon découpé, bottes ou houseaux serrés, longs étriers, épee, dague, haubert, lance et autres armures." (As soon as these clothes and weapons were made, fitted and finished, Joan threw off and completely abandoned feminine attire: she had her hair cut round the head like a page, took shirt, trousers, underdrawers, and stockings combined, which were long and tied to the drawers by twenty strings, trousers, shoes tied on the outside and a short tunic down to about the knees, a tight-fitting cap, boots or leather gaiters, long stirrups, sword, dagger, hauberk, lance, and other weapons.)

CHAPTER 5

The Ride to Chinon

Joan rode out through the Porte de France in Vaucouleurs accompanied by her six new friends.[1] It was winter, and perhaps the mists lay heavy over the Meuse, as is so often the case at that season. The small party had to avoid the most frequented roads. Probably several of them were familiar with such expeditions; certainly the King's courier must have been. I think all romantic reports about Joan taking the lead with divinely inspired self-confidence can be relegated to legend, since she did not know a foot of the country through which they passed.

One writer has attempted to describe the ride, with the hooves of the horses wrapped in cloth to prevent their being heard on the hard frozen ground. It might have been so, though we have no details about it. But there is reason to dwell for a moment on the fact that Joan for eleven days and eleven nights rode alone with six men.

We know that during the night she slept between her two closest friends, Jean de Metz and Bertrand de Poulengy. They have both testified that they felt no carnal desire. Jean de Metz said Joan lay close to him on the ground, well sheltered, but that he never dreamed of making her any proposal, nor did he have the least sexual desire. Bertrand de Poulengy said the same—he "had no physical desire for her".

Joan, whose salient characteristic, according to Michelet, was her sound common sense, was well aware that here was a real problem. On one occasion, she said that male and female attire were equally suitable to a maiden. "If God told me to wear a man's clothes, it is because I shall carry men's arms."

Another time she says realistically that it was best for both her and her companions that she were not dressed as a woman: "If I am dressed as a man among men, they will not feel any physical desire for me, and I

[1] According to more recent research, it has been established that the journey lasted eleven days and did not begin, but ended, on February 23.

74

believe that I myself will be able better to preserve my virginity, both in thoughts and acts."

She was thus not so naïve as to neglect the possibility of temptation. She was an attractive and well-built young woman, and the customs of the time were not delicate. Nevertheless, she compelled the unquestioning respect of her companions and never found herself in any difficulties, although several men were to be very close to her.

Jean d'Aulon, who was later to fill the post of her master of the horse or chief of staff, has given us a realistic report. He said that Joan was young and shapely and that on several occasions he had seen her breasts and legs but had never felt any sexual attraction to her, and he believed that the same was the case with all those who were closest to her.

The Duke of Alençon has given a plain-spoken, though admittedly respectful, picture of Joan. Looking at her with the eyes of a man, he found that she had shapely breasts, but he was never tempted by her. (In this connection, it may be mentioned that Joan, who has often been represented as fair, really had black or dark brown hair.)

Dunois, who was to stand very close to her, has testified that he did not think "any woman could be more chaste than la Pucelle". This so impressed the young soldier that he felt it must be due to divine intervention.

Several students of Joan of Arc have thought that she may have been completely lacking in physical attraction. Nothing definite can be said concerning this question, but we have shown that there is ample testimony by young men who have spoken in emphatic terms of her shapely body. The probability is that, without being a beauty—her face is never mentioned—she was a fresh and pretty young woman whom men regarded with pleasure, but who kept them at a distance through the majesty and gravity that emanated from her. Bertrand de Poulengy, who accompanied her on her long ride, says, "I would never have dared to make her an improper proposal because of the virtue I felt she possessed."

This is putting into very simple language the fact that Joan possessed a spiritual quality which impressed even rough soldiers and checked their natural impulses toward her as a woman.[2]

---

[2]But Joan surprised her entourage in more than one way. Simon Charles relates: "*Dicit insuper ipse loquens quod dum erat in armis, nunquam descendebat de equo pro necessariis naturae.*" And Jean d'Aulon: "*Dit encores plus qu'il a oy dire à plusieurs femmes, qui ladicte Pucelle ont veue par plusieurs fois nue et sceu de ses secrets, que oncques n'avoit eu la secrete maladie des femmes et que jamais nul n'en peut rien cognoistre ou appercevoir par ses habillemens, ne aultrement.*"

This purity and majesty form part of the picture of Joan still unknown and untried, riding day and night over the hard frozen ground, through a country she had never seen before, without a trace of fear—as we know from the testimony of several witnesses—at the obvious dangers that faced the expedition. We need hardly believe the legends and later chronicles that tell us that her followers lost heart and had to be encouraged by Joan, for they were doubtless good and experienced soldiers. But other words attributed to her have an authentic ring. On one occasion she is reported to have said, "If we could, we would be wise to attend Mass."

This was not so easy, as they were riding mainly through occupied country and wanted to avoid notice as much as possible. The first evening, after riding the whole day, the expedition found quarters for the night in a monastery, the abbey of Saint-Urbain, whose abbot, Arnoult d'Aulnoy, was a relation of Robert de Baudricourt. The church of the monastery contained relics of Pope Urban. The next day Joan attended High Mass, whereupon the expedition continued on its way over the Marne. They crossed the Aube at Bar-sur-Aube, the Seine near Bar-sur-Seine, and the Yonne near Auxerre. In this last town, they took the risk of entering mounted, and Joan went to the church unnoticed in male attire and heard Mass in the side chapel without anyone suspecting her of not being a youth of the town.

Two days later the Loire was crossed, and they arrived at Gien, the first loyalist town on their way. Danger was thus passed, and there was no longer any need to conceal their identities. Had Joan adopted male attire only for the ride, she would have exchanged it now for woman's clothing, and the fact that she did not do so but from then on continued to dress as a man shows clearly that for her it had a symbolic meaning. She was no longer a woman, but a maiden who had sworn chastity and whose mission was of a warlike nature.

Her next stop was Sainte-Catherine-de-Fierbois, nineteen miles from Chinon where the King resided. From this place, Joan addressed a letter to the King. While Colet de Vienne bore the letter to the King to announce her coming, Joan and the remainder of the small party stayed behind, and Joan used the occasion to visit and pray in the church, which must have been of special interest to her, for it was here that Charles Martel himself laid down his sword. No other church in France had a more important part in the cult of the saint who by her life and work had so inspired Joan—Saint Catherine.

Forty years before, the church had become a ruin, but it had been rebuilt through a miracle. In 1375, Saint Catherine appeared to a blind paralytic, Jean Godefroy, and promised that he should be healed if he would make a novena on the spot where Charles Martel had laid down his sword. Jean Godefroy had himself carried to the spot, but the nave of the church was so overgrown with vegetation that a path had to be cut through it. The saint performed the miracle she had promised, and Jean Godefroy regained his sight and his health, which made such an impression on the people of the neighborhood that the church was rebuilt. Since then many miracles had occurred there, and the saint had played a great part in the war, for when the French fell into the hands of the English they often prayed for her assistance, and not in vain. In 1424 a soldier from Saumur, Jean Ducoudray, who was imprisoned in the castle in Bellême, confiding himself to the hands of Saint Catherine, leapt from the window, overpowered the guard, and threw himself from a wall the height of two lances without being injured.

Another story that was probably told to Joan while she was there was the following:

Jean du Chastel had escaped from the English officer who had taken him prisoner. The Englishman charged him with having broken his parole, and they then fought a duel in which the Frenchman was the victor. He attributed his victory to the intervention of Saint Catherine, and in the presence of many notable persons, among them the Bastard of Orléans and La Hire, known from the later part of Joan's history, presented the church with the Englishman's armor, which Joan may well have admired when she visited the church.

In this church Joan heard three Masses in succession, spending most of the morning in prayer.

In the evening Colet de Vienne returned from the King, from whom he had obtained permission for the party to enter Chinon. The same evening, according to legend, bandits were on the point of attacking the little party but at the last moment retreated. This may or may not be true.

At noon the following day Joan reached Chinon. To her judges she said simply that after her dinner she had gone to him whom she called her king, who lived in the castle.

Joan's father confessor related that in Chinon she was saluted by a soldier who recognized her and realized that she was the much-discussed "la Pucelle".

"Isn't that that maid? If I could only get hold of her for a night, by God, she wouldn't be a virgin much longer."

Joan heard these words of greeting. She looked sternly at him, "You mock God," she said, "and yet you shall soon die."

Less than one hour later the man fell into the river and was drowned.

Joan and Charles VII

Joan had lodged in a little hostelry in Chinon for some time before she was received by the King. Why was this?

The most trustworthy account relating to those days is that of Simon Charles, *Président de la Chambre des Comptes*, who on his return from a journey to Venice in March heard how she had been received by the King. He says that when Joan came to Chinon the Council debated whether the King should receive her or not. At first she was asked why she had come and what her intentions were. Though she did not want to speak to anyone but the King himself, she was compelled to give the reasons for her journey. She said that she had two commands from the King of Heaven—one to raise the siege of Orléans, the other to lead the King to Reims to be anointed and crowned. Some of the King's counselors then said that the King should not attach any belief to Joan, and others said that as she claimed to be sent by God and had a message for the King, he should at least give her an audience. It was decided, though after some difficulty, that the King should receive her.

When Joan arrived in the castle of Chinon, the King, influenced by some prominent persons at the court, hesitated to speak to her until he received Robert de Baudricourt's letter saying that he was sending him this woman and learned that she had been brought through country occupied by the King's enemies and had crossed rivers in an almost miraculous way to reach him. This made the King decide to grant her an audience.

Even this first audience has been described by legend with an almost nauseating sentimentality.

On reading the ordinary accounts of the life of Joan, one has the same feeling as when one comes to Lisieux, the town of Saint Thérèse of the Child Jesus. One may grieve for the town of Lisieux, which was so terribly bombed during the last war, but one cannot sufficiently regret that no bombs struck the appalling basilica erected in honor of the saint, and all the small shops with their mendacious, sugary representations, medallions, portraits, and souvenir mugs. Thérèse, whose whole being emanated strength, will, and purity, has been buried under an almost impenetrable layer of sickly sentimentality and aesthetic horrors. The picture of this simple and crystal-clear soul has had to be falsified and dragged down to the nineteenth-century bourgeois sentimentality that is the only level upon which most of her worshippers seem able to exist. To come to Lisieux from a chaste and severe, warm and motherly Romanesque cathedral is in truth to recognize that aesthetic and spiritual decadence accompany and complement each other. Even prints of photographs of Saint Thérèse are touched up by the convent that is there to preserve her memory.

When I first read the story of how Joan of Arc entered the King's chamber and with supernatural inspiration turned her pure gaze on the King, recognizing him immediately, and then drew him into an anteroom where she revealed to him the secret of his life, after which the radiant King placed her at the head of his army, I guessed that this could not be the true story. Modern research has shown us that most of this is pure legend—invented, and invented with bad taste. Those of a later era who cannot see the great religious personalities as they really were, but who wish at any price to see them as persons on a level with themselves, can only solve the problem by distorting truth, turning spirit and fire into plaster of Paris and sugar, and transforming passion and suffering into sentimentality.

We were taught at school that through a miracle Joan of Arc identified Charles VII among all his courtiers. This is, of course, nonsense. If there was anybody in the country easily recognized it was the King, about whom Joan must have learned all there was to know. He did not look like an ordinary man. The eleventh child of a madman and his completely amoral wife, he was the picture of degeneration and timidity. His face, with its long nose and watery eyes, was without eyebrows and almost without eyelashes, while his knees were abnormally large, and he had spindly, bowed legs. He went about in a state of constant fear, especially since the day when he had witnessed the murder of the Duke of Burgundy on the bridge at Montereau. He was extremely pious and attended Mass three times a day, but also dabbled in astrology and magic, and still trembled with anxiety lest the floor should give way under him as happened at La Rochelle. He failed in everything he undertook. He knew that there were people in his entourage who deceived him and took advantage of the desperate situation of the country to lend him money at usurer's rates.

Is it likely that he should not be recognized immediately by this keen-eyed, healthy girl when she entered the audience chamber, ninety feet in length and forty-five in breadth? Admittedly she may have been momentarily dazzled by the three hundred knights, the fifty servants bearing torches ranged along the walls, by the glitter of swords and the magnificent colors of the clothing. But who can believe seriously that she could for a moment fail to recognize who was the King among the dashing, handsome, and arrogant nobles? The whole story of her identifying the King is suspect and derives from persons who were not themselves present at Chinon, Simon Charles and Jean Moreau; it was later embroidered by busy chroniclers and pious gossips. Cordier, who was not, perhaps, capable of understanding Joan's spirituality but who possessed an excellent critical training, writes simply and clearly, "It is a simple fact that neither Joan herself, nor Gaucourt, or Dunois and Regnault Thierry, who were the only witnesses present at the time, allude to the incident."

This in no way lessens the poetry and fascination of the scene. It still remains one of the great moments in French history. It turns our thoughts to another scene when another young, solitary woman, perhaps of a very different spiritual schooling and of a far greater genius, entered into the great hall of a castle and told the truth to one of the great men of the earth—Catherine of Siena, before Gregory XI in the papal palace at Avignon.

Among all the embroidering and later traditions, among all the silly talk of inspirations and marvels, there is found here and there a reliable piece of evidence of how Joan really behaved on this occasion. Those who love her recognize the ring of authenticity in these documents. Here is Gaucourt's simple and unambiguous account: "He was present at Chinon when she arrived and saw how she went up to the King with great humility and simplicity like a poor little shepherd girl."

This is Joan of Arc. If one has been affected by these simple words, then one reads with eagerness her first words as remembered by Gaucourt: "Most illustrious Sir Dauphin," she began, and we must believe that her voice at first trembled, "I have come and have been sent from God to bring help to the kingdom and yourself...." It was as simple as that.

80

That first Louis de Bourbon and later the King himself should have tried to deceive her is not confirmed by reliable sources.

If one goes further in one's investigations, one comes upon another legend that is more difficult to unmask, and which may after all contain a mystery.

It belongs to the current tradition about Joan of Arc that the King took her aside into an anteroom and that she showed him there that she knew of his great sorrow and could release him from it. The poor prince was still brooding about whether he was really the son of his father, and Joan is supposed to have convinced him that he was the legitimate heir to the throne.

In the *Abbréviateur du Procès* (Abstract of the Trial), we find that Joan had asked the King if he would believe her if she could tell him certain secrets known only to himself. When he replied in the affirmative, Joan is supposed to have told him that the King on an occasion in the chapel of the castle of Loches had prayed to God for three things. In Joan's words:

> The first prayer was that God deign to deprive you of your courage when the time came to reconquer France if you were not the legitimate heir, so that you be no longer the cause of continuing a war which brought with it so much suffering. The second prayer was that you alone should suffer punishment by death or by other means if all the unhappiness and suffering with which the unfortunate French people have so long been afflicted were caused by your own sins. The third prayer was that the people should be forgiven and God's anger appeased if their sins were the reason for their sufferings.

Even a trained historian, such as Calmette, accepts on the whole this tradition, but it seems more probable that it is pure fiction, and very bad fiction, too. Of course, Joan uttered words implying that she regarded Charles as the legitimate French king—about this there can be no doubt—but that her confident demeanor should have suddenly swept away the King's troubles seems unlikely. He was still unconvinced of her qualifications. He, the ever-hesitant and compromising, was to wait for weeks while learned experts examined and cross-examined her before he dared to believe that she had been sent by God.

Let us examine the rumors. There were early ones that Joan had confided a secret to the King or that she had shown that she knew his secret. It is clear that in their conversation some secret was touched upon into which few were admitted and to which the King attached great importance. But when did the thought arise that Joan had taken the initiative in the question of the King's legitimacy? Seventy years later, in the beginning of the sixteenth century, three chroniclers, who all depended on unreliable sources, and two of whom were anonymous, related that Joan through a revelation had acquired knowledge of a certain prayer that the King in his despair had addressed to God, in which he begged for a sign that would give him certainty regarding his legitimacy. One need not doubt that the King had uttered such a prayer. He must certainly have uttered very many prayers, but, as Cordier has pointed out, if Joan really told him of such a revelation, such an astounding "sign", why then should the King have ordered the subsequent examination covering many weeks, and, above all, why did Joan herself in Chinon and Poitiers clearly and distinctly state that her only sign was that she should raise the siege of Orléans and that her word must be believed? If she had really received this other sign, why should she not have made full use of it when people from all sides clamored for just that?

But it is not the end of the matter. For Joan repeatedly, particularly during the trial, spoke of a secret that she could not reveal and that concerned the King's person and their first meeting. Before pausing for a moment before this riddle, of which I have not the key, I must mention a circumstance that in this connection may be of some importance.

It is a historical fact that visionaries of recognized authenticity, especially youthful ones, often claim to have had secrets given them by the supernatural world that they may not at once reveal. This occurred in the cases of La Salette and of Fatima. In both, secrets were confided to the young visionaries, which they obstinately kept to themselves. Fatima's message is not yet completely known; part of it was confided to the Pope alone, who has not revealed anything about its contents.[3] The phenomenon only shows what is quite natural, that ordinary people whose spiritual perception is blunted cannot be given spiritual truths that they are not yet capable of assimilating.

[3] On June 26, 2000, Pope John Paul II released the Third Secret of Our Lady of Fatima to the public.

Something similar must lie behind the case of Joan of Arc. One must be careful not to see in her only the simple, unsophisticated peasant girl. She was all that, but she was also a visionary, one blessed, to whom secrets were confided and who was used in supernatural connections. Those who see in Joan only France's liberator, who through ignorance, intrigue, and cruelty was brought to her downfall before she could fulfill her mission, see only one side of her life's work. Side by side with this natural line is another, a mystical one. Besides playing her part in the history of France, Joan was permitted to realize the tragic fate of the religious exception, the saint. The culmination of her life was to be placed in the same situation as the dying Savior himself, to recognize and stand firm by the love of God even when it was not manifested, when everything seemed to indicate that she was deserted by God and man. This is the real greatness and majesty in the life of Joan. For this reason, every attempt to present her as a young woman whose highest quality is sound common sense appears pitiful, and Cordier's attempt to reduce her revelations to hysteria and hallucination becomes an unpardonable simplification.

I shall return to this problem, a central one in Joan's life. I have touched upon it here because it is probable that we cannot properly understand her talk of the secret revealed at the castle in Chinon unless we remember what kind of person she really was, not only a purposeful, clear-headed woman, but also a holy woman, one who is what she is less through her own qualities than through the great Spirit who deigns to use her as his instrument.

What has Joan herself to say about her secret during the trial?

The question is not an easy one to answer. The judges never understood her testimony. The reports are obscure. During the most pressing cross-examination, she herself obstinately insisted that nobody should succeed in dragging out of her what she might not reveal. At last they succeeded in breaking her down; she does not know what she is saying, she is even driven into a kind of recantation, but she immediately withdraws it when she has somewhat recovered and collected herself.

During the pressing examination on March 10, in Rouen, when Joan had clearly been driven almost to a breakdown, she gave among others the following answer: Asked what the sign was which she gave her King when she came to him, she replied that it was beautiful, honorable, and easy to believe. It was good and the finest that exists.

It is easy to understand that the judges were puzzled. They understood her to mean that an angel had in the sight of everybody placed a sign in the form of a crown on the head of Charles VII.

One question was: "Was the sign still there?" The answer came: "Naturally. It will still remain in a thousand years and many more."

The judges wondered if the sign was of gold or silver or if it consisted of precious stones or a crown. Joan answered: "I will say nothing more, nor would any man be able to describe anything so wonderful as this sign." After which she wanted to go over to another matter, but was brought back to the subject by the examining judge and then related that on her way to the King she had heard her "voices" say that she must continue on her way.

"When you stand before the King, he shall receive a sign to receive you and believe in you."

The judges asked how she had acted when she came before the King, and she replied that she had curtsied several times and thanked God for making her victorious against all opponents who disbelieved her. She added that it was an angel from God, and no one else, who gave the sign to the King.

Asked if the priests had seen the sign, she replied that when her King and those present had seen the sign and the angel who gave it, she asked the King if he were satisfied, and he replied, "Yes." She then withdrew to a little chapel nearby and was afterward told that when she had left, three hundred people had seen the sign. She also said that it was from love of her and so that she should not be questioned any more that God allowed those present to see the sign.

Later Joan, before a number of priests, withdrew some of her confession and among other things stated that the angel was really herself. To Cordier this settles the matter. Joan withdrew her statement.

It seems to me, however, that this retractation is of small importance since it was the result of a terrifying pressure, and we do not even know if it has been correctly rendered in the report. On the other hand, Joan's own words quoted above have the ring of truth. Here she touches upon a great secret, revealed not in a solitary talk with the King, but before three hundred courtiers and officers. One can never really understand documents of that kind unless one bears in mind that one is listening to a young mystic who in faltering, human language tries in vain to translate a spiritual experience. We know that the majority of saints have lamented that human language never suffices to explain what they have seen and experienced and that they are continually forced to use inadequate symbols. Joan says emphatically that no man could describe the miracle she beheld. The judges understand nothing—they think that she is speaking of gold, silver, precious stones, or a crown when she is speaking of spiritual values, of certainties, of truths. She intimates that at a certain moment the light of the supernatural world broke through so that the doubters and critics, the cowards and sluggards, understood that here was no hysterical young peasant girl but God's own voice speaking through her.

Cordier's rejection of this document, perhaps the most important in Joan's biography, is characteristic of him. He thinks that he can explain Joan's revelations through psychology by references to medical "science", by drawing parallels with mentally afflicted persons. He does not even suspect that he is faced with a person quite unique, an absolutely pure-hearted, healthy young woman who in vain tries to show the theological and juridical experts that God is speaking through her, using her with such strength that a whole sinful court was forced to accept her, at least for a moment. Her testimony corresponds in its nature with all we know of the experiences of the saints and of those chosen by God; and against all human reason she succeeded in really gaining the confidence of the King and his counselors.

Here we are confronted with exactly the same problem as the one connected with the origin of Christianity. What actually happened, the Resurrection of Christ, is and will remain a miracle that human wisdom will always be able to deny; but without this miracle it would have been impossible, from a historical point of view, for Christianity to have arisen.

The Amazon Waits

The time immediately after Joan's first meeting with the King is also wrapped in legend and improbable later additions. If one adopts the principle of refusing to believe in the chronicles and accepting only the testimony of witnesses who can be proved to have been present, a picture emerges that differs in many respects from the traditional one. A great deal of sentimentality, one might almost say vulgar mysticism, falls away, but other matters are unquestionably authentic, and apart

from the fact that they are supported by documents possess such a striking inner truth that they must be accepted. Among these is the subsequent utterance of a man who was soon to become a very close friend of
Joan, the Duke of Alençon.

At the time of Joan's arrival at the court in Chinon, the Duke was
out shooting, but he was interrupted in the middle of his sport by one
of his followers, who gave him the sensational news that a young girl
had appeared at court and declared that she had been sent by God to
throw the English out of the country and to save Orléans. The following day the Duke rode to Chinon and when he came into the King's
presence found him engaged in a friendly chat with the girl. When he
was presented to her as the Duke of Alençon, she said, "You are very
welcome. The more of the Blood of France that are gathered here the
better."

The next day Joan went to the King's Mass and when she saw him
enter curtsied to him and was conducted by the King into a room. The
King asked everyone else to leave except his reader and La Trémoille.
Joan made several earnest requests of the King, among them that he
should present his kingdom to the Lord of Heaven, who after having
received this gift would do as he had done with the King's predecessors,
reinstate him into his former position.

The following anecdote illustrates the strong tradition that Joan
insisted in her meeting with the King that God was the true Lord of
France and the King only his "Lieutenant", his Viceroy. According to
one account, Joan had begged the King to present his kingdom to her,
to which he agreed. Joan then summoned a secretary and had a deed
of gift made out in which the King presented France to the Lord of
Heaven. This deed was read out in public, whereupon, according to the
story, Joan pointed to the King and said with a smile, "There you see
the poorest knight in the land." After that she was said to have ordered
another document to be drafted in which God reinstated the King on
the throne of his fathers.

The person who related this anecdote was in Rome at the time
and probably received it at third or fourth hand, suitably padded and
embroidered.

Let us return to the Duke's account. After referring to the conversation during the King's breakfast, he added, "And after the meal the King
went out to walk for a space to the fields, and there Joan practised with

her lance; and when he (the Duke) saw how skillfully this same Joan carried the lance and ran with it, he gave her a horse as a gift."

As we see, there are not many words, but they are enchanting, they have a freshness, they give a vivid picture of the healthy charm that emanated from Joan's youthful person. The Duke, blasé with many fair women, gazes fascinated as the young amazon gallops across the field handling her spear with strength and skill and can think of only one way of expressing his admiration—by presenting her with a beautiful horse. The scene has the freshness and beauty of a passage from the *Odyssey*, and everything suggests that every detail is true. The profound theological talk during breakfast was a little beyond the Duke's comprehension, and he said that he had forgotten most of it, but the picture of the young horsewoman thundering over the field is one that would remain with him for ever.

Joan appears to have remained a fairly long time at Chinon, where she became acquainted with the principal personages in the King's entourage and went daily to Mass. After a time it was decided that to be on the safe side a formal examination of her case should be instituted. Poitiers was the town where parliament met and where most of the exiled University of Paris was to be found. It may be interesting now to study some important documents relating to the weeks Joan spent in Poitiers. The most important is a letter she dispatched to the English. Unfortunately, an even more important document has been lost—the report of the investigating commission. A third document of great interest is the report of one of its members.

Joan's "Letter to the English" has been the object of many different interpretations, most of them rather sentimental. The Church has held that it was characteristic of her noble nature that, like a good Christian, before fighting she gave her adversary an opportunity of withdrawing from the country, and only had recourse to arms when a friendly settlement was impossible.

Joan was, however, not the originator of the letter, for it was part of the diplomatic and knightly etiquette of the times to issue similar challenges and letters before a struggle began. It was merely a matter of form without practical significance. Joan could not write, and it has even been questioned if she herself dictated the letter, though there is much to suggest that she did. For one thing, she repeatedly mentioned it during the trial in Rouen and only objected to one or two isolated expressions that the secretary may have added or altered. The letter also contained some astonishing passages where one feels one can recognize the eager warm voice of the young peasant girl.

She begins her letter by asking the English commanders to hand over the keys of all the towns they have occupied in France to "la Pucelle", the Maid. They may then withdraw unmolested if they do not continue the war. She then begs all warriors, knights, and others before Orléans to do the same.

She adds: "*Et si vous ne le faites ainsi, attendez des nouvelles de la Pucelle, qu'ira vous voir sous peu, à vos bien grands dommages.*" One might translate this splendid tirade in the following manner: "And if you do not so do, you shall soon hear from la Pucelle, and it will cost you dear."

One can almost see her with clenched hand dictating the letter to a nervous secretary. Further on she says in masterful language: "King of England, if you do not do so, then know that I am now the *chef de guerre* (the military leader), and wherever I come upon your people in France I shall chase them out whether they wish it or not." (During the trial, the expression *chef de guerre* was one among those to which she objected and denied having uttered.)

Here we see a new side of Joan apparently only noticed by Sainte-Beuve. In his unassuming but beautifully logical essay, he points out that there are two Joan of Arcs—the one of legend and the one of reality. The former is full of sentimentality, but everything suggests that the other Joan was of a very different type, a realistic, often even drastic, strong-willed, purposeful being. Sainte-Beuve goes so far that he regards her remark to Robert de Baudricourt about the three children she shall bear as an expression of a kind of rough humor. But he also gives other more convincing examples of her sense of fun.

Continuing, Joan says that she has been sent by God "*corps pour corps pour vous bouter hors de toute la France*" (to throw you out man against man from all of France) and says, as usual, that it is she who has revealed to Charles VII that God is on his side. Afterward there follows a magnificent outburst, the language of which bears signs of having been accurately rendered: "If you refuse to believe this message from God and from the Maid, we shall strike wherever we find you and create such havoc that there has been nothing like it in France for a thousand years...."

There is a further important detail in this remarkable letter that has escaped the otherwise keen-eyed Cordier. The letter ends: "Written this Tuesday, Holy Week".

Holy Week, the week before Easter, is to a devout Catholic the holiest of the year. On Sunday, Tuesday, Wednesday, and Friday the four Gospel accounts of the Passion are read in full. Even though we may assume that Joan might have followed the Easter Passion in a convent, perhaps, in any case she had in those decisive days before her definite appearance lived as close to Christ as any human being can, and hour after hour had been brought closer to the great mystery, the terrible catastrophe that was to lead to the salvation of the world. The previous Sunday she had witnessed the solemn act called *la bénédiction des rameaux* (the blessing of the branches) and seen the monks leave the church in procession, to return preceded by two singers who, when inside the church doors, raised their voices in the beautiful hymn "*Gloria laus.*" There, as she sat with her blessed olive branch in her hand, she must have felt as one of those who greeted our Savior when he entered Jerusalem. When she was taken prisoner in Rouen, she uttered the simple words, "I am only afraid of one thing, treachery"; we suspect that she had in mind the greatest treachery in history—the kiss of Judas, about which she heard day after day during the services of Holy Week.

It is not without significance that Joan enters upon the stage just in this great week, as if she were to receive her last consecration before the beginning of her great act, for she had before only seen small village churches and the convent chapels she had visited on her journey. Now she could every day enter the great temples swelling with the majestic music of organs, where the Church elaborated the whole of her liturgical splendor to commemorate the greatest event in Christendom. When she first stepped forward, it was in the middle of Holy Week, when everything is silent preparation, when the churches are unadorned and the holy pictures veiled, when every day that passes brings the death of Christ closer, and when the Catholic, hour by hour, follows the last footsteps of his Master.

It is in this atmosphere of preparation for sacrifice, in close proximity to the mystery, that Joan publicly appears with her first act, her "Letter to the English".

Thus we must not allow the warlike challenge and gestures to deceive us into believing that Joan had lost sight of what was essential. What is most important for her is that she is sent by God, and as a good Catholic she knows that one whom God has chosen for his instrument must be prepared to sacrifice himself. I do not believe that she as yet had any presentiment of how closely she would be permitted to follow her true King, that within two years she would suffer martyrdom. But even though she does not say so, one must assume that this prospect was always present to her. Once we try to remove Joan from a sphere in which Christ is the center, as soon as we attempt to judge her as a spontaneous outburst of willpower, or of sound common sense—of course with a Christian background, seeing that the times were Christian—we lose contact with the essence of her being. Everything she does, everything she says, has its basis in her adherence to the central secrets of Christianity. She was never able to forget—it had been strongly impressed upon her mind by the example of her two saints—that whom God uses must be ready to die for his sake. It is only against this background that the youthful and violent phraseology in her first public pronouncement can be seen in its right light.

Devoutness has so many gestures, so many masks. Those who dedicate themselves to God often feel that they must act in a solemn and joyless manner. Their soul must die in order to arise again to a new life, but will it ever be really resurrected if it bears those marks of death that are represented by stern and unbending earnestness, mournfulness, and melancholy? One loves Joan because after her first sacrifice, of her family, her home, and her childhood, she does not sigh or moan or adopt the solemn role of a prophetess or a sibyl and does not make a display of her suffering. She is reborn, and her personality has a freshness and power that only the superficial observer would mistake for the mere beauty and freshness of a young woman. Joan is *anima naturaliter christiana* even in her freedom and fun. For hours she kneels on an icy church floor because there are certain things which the human being can only confront on his knees. She listens to mysterious "voices" she sometimes distinguishes among the murmur of the forest, sometimes in the peal of church bells, but which sometimes—even often—speak to her realistically and clearly of coming events, of great deeds, of great suffering. Most certainly she is a mystic, a visionary, and one who hears things. But she is also a young woman who charges over the fields handling her spear with such skill that the experienced Duke is astonished, and who with her fist clenched and her eyes shining with the joy of battle threatens to hurl the King of England and all his men out of the country in the most terrible havoc seen in France for a thousand years. How can one help loving her?

The Examination in Poitiers

Joan's new friend, the Duke of Alençon, with whom we may suppose she had many a pleasant ride at this time and whom she probably induced to go to church with her more often than had been his habit, has related that she became impatient over all the delay, and bluntly told the King that he would have to hurry and use her while there was still time because she had no wish to remain more than a year.

In the *Chronique de la Pucelle*, which is, however, not very reliable, it is said that she did not understand what she was to do in Poitiers, where she was now taken, but "that Messire would help her". She was lodged in the Hôtel de la Rose with the King's friend, the lawyer Rabateau, and his wife, who was known for her piety and goodness. Archbishop Regnault, who was later to play an important though not very honorable part in her life, headed the commission of examination and was assisted by a number of learned, prosy old men: the inquisitor of Toulouse, the Dominican Pierre Turelure, later Bishop of Digne; Jean Lombard, professor of theology in Paris; the Benedictine Pierre de Versailles, later Bishop of Meaux; the Bishops of Poitiers and Montpellier; the Carmelite Pierre Séguin; and several others. The only one on the commission whose findings are preserved is the Dominican Séguin de Séguin, and these are of some interest.

The commission that examined Joan in the Hôtel de la Rose first established what was not difficult, that she was a good Catholic. Séguin relates that the old men "in order to know exactly what kind of personal life she led, placed her in contact with a number of ladies who reported to the Council the details and manner of life she led". So Joan was not only cross-examined but pursued by a pack of old, experienced gossips who observed her in every situation.

During these trying weeks Joan held on to her four cardinal points: (1) The English must be ejected and Orléans relieved. (2) The King must be crowned in Reims. (3) Paris must be conquered. (4) The Duke of Orléans must be returned from his captivity in England.

All this was to happen before long.

Here and there we find small incidents that make the whole situation alive to us. Guillaume Aymeri was an intelligent old man who subtly asked the girl if God could not manage just as well without arms and battle, that is, if he really had promised to liberate the country.

Joan's answer is still preserved and is great in its simplicity and strength, "In the name of God—the soldiers shall fight, and God shall give them victory."

Séguin no doubt felt that he had found a clever question when, in complete harmony with the views then prevalent concerning inspired persons, he said to her that God would not wish that one should believe her unless a sign were given, and that she could not really expect the King to place an army at her disposal merely because she stated that she was sent by him.

Joan replied just as forcefully, "In the name of God, I have not come to Poitiers to produce signs. But take me to Orléans, and you shall have signs showing why I have come."

This answer is of interest because of an important question mentioned before—whether Joan had really given any signs in Chinon. If she had, surely she would now have referred to it, but she did not.

Cordier speaks of the matter in the following way, "It shows that with Joan the emphasis on warlike action came before the mystical construction, which was only the continuation of the former."

As I have shown before, this is completely to misunderstand Joan's deepest inspiration, because she experienced the spiritual world first and only afterward received orders of a political nature. When God through his saints first spoke to her, his orders concerned nothing but her spiritual and moral life. Only when she had gone through this hard school for many years was she ready for her political mission. Mysticism is not, as Cordier thinks, an airy "construction" without particular importance to an otherwise strong-willed and practical character. Rather the latter is born from the former.

The Dominican Séguin de Séguin also asked Joan what language her "voices" spoke, to which Joan replied wittily, "A better one than yours." The monk acknowledged that she had scored, for he himself spoke in the Limousin dialect. Even in this little exchange one seems to come close to Joan. She becomes alive. Here, too, one discerns her sense of fun side by side with her quickness of repartee.

She told her questioners that she had no learning. Pressed by the theologians, she gave an answer that is both amusing and frightening. She said, "*Il y a es livres de Nostre Seigneur plus que es vostres*" (God has more books than you) and added, "God has a book no priest has ever seen." The theologians were silent. But in this answer, we recognize the attitude for which Joan was later to pay with her life. She believed in God more than in men. When the next question came—if she believed in the Church as she believed in God—she could not answer.

Those with discernment can already recognize in these Easter days in Poitiers a menacing cloud upon the horizon. But the sun is still shining brightly.

An important question that had to be decided, and that even the specially recruited female scouts could not decide with any certainty, was the question of Joan's sex and virginity. This was of paramount importance in those days. Were Joan not a virgin she would have lost most of her authority, not only because she always referred to herself as *la Pucelle*, "the Maid", but also because in that period, which was so completely filled with the Christian way of thinking, a fact now forgotten was very familiar—namely, that nobody is summoned to perform an act for God without being first ordered to make a sacrifice. Joan's first great sacrifice was to forswear human love.

This delicate matter was confided to no less a person than the Queen Mother, Yolande, assisted by a number of honorable matrons from the court and from the town. Joan lent herself to the examination with courage, and there could be only one result. It is of some importance to remember that this part of the examination concerned two questions: first, whether Joan was male or female, secondly, whether, if a woman, she was a virgin. For a long time, the suspicion remained that even if she were not a man she was some kind of hermaphrodite. Later, reliable witnesses, in the outspoken language of the times, speak about her typically feminine voice and her well-developed bosom. There was obviously nothing physically abnormal in her, even though one must assume that this boyishly active, strong, and enduring horsewoman, with her tough will and gay fighting spirit, had a more virile endowment than is usual in women.

Among spiritually advanced men, one often encounters such a measure of tenderness and love that the uninitiated are tempted to suspect them of a homosexual tendency that is often in the popular mind connected with celibacy and aestheticism. In the same way—though it is less observed—one often finds in spiritually endowed women, and especially among religious women, a strength of will and qualities of mind that appear almost masculine. If such women become abbesses, the ignorant may easily suspect them of lesbian tendencies. It is, of course, possible that individual homosexual men and lesbian women may be found in monastic institutions though the natural tendency has been sublimated. But people generally miss the real, deeper explanation. The complete man, man as God intended him, must to the so-called natural—that is, the fallen—man appear abnormal because the latter simply does not understand the meaning of complete humanity. Confronted by a strong-minded, clear-thinking female saint or with a monk whose whole nature is tenderness, intuition, love of sacrifice, the natural, the incomplete man's judgment must be at fault. He does not understand that he is dealing with a true human being who possesses strength of will, tenderness, keenness of mind, and goodness, all together, and that the question of sex plays a smaller part.

In Joan of Arc, there are certain features in common with a young hermaphrodite, as has been pointed out before. But this is a superficial view, and it would be more correct to say that in her nature are combined the finest male and female characteristics, strength of will and readiness for sacrifice, leadership and tenderness, qualities found in combination in most of the really great figures of mankind.

We know nothing of the real background that caused the young man in Domrémy to believe that Joan had promised to marry him, but we can venture a cautious guess. My hypothesis, if it can thus be described, is this: I can imagine Joan as a young woman displaying love even toward youths of her own age—love in its true meaning. Richly endowed as she was, she must have been affected by the suffering of others and, like all true Christians, felt the impulse to intervene, to sacrifice herself in order to help others to attain the peace at which she herself had arrived. Such a reaction is love, but it is also love that demands nothing, gives all. It belongs to the experience of Christians that such love can be understood and interpreted as human passion. Is it unreasonable to ask whether this was the background of a curious scene where we see Joan, who had taken a vow of chastity, stand side by side with a love-sick youth who alleges that she had given him a promise of marriage?

The happy result of the examination in Poitiers was to some extent due to the favorable reports gathered by two Franciscans dispatched to Joan's village. But above all it was due to her whole appearance, the power exercised by her pure and honest personality. Nobody had heard such a convinced voice speak of the self-evident victory God had prepared for the French. "The fatherland would soon be liberated", said one witness. Without the intervention of any other factor, the whole situation became clarified in an inexplicable manner when she appeared on the scene. The Treaty of Troyes had no longer any authority. Nor was the faltering personality of Charles VII a good guarantee for his claims, and he had been surrounded by such a number of intrigues, personal animosities, yes, even attacks and murder, that it was not surprising that more than one good Frenchman asked himself earnestly if the necessary strength to rebuild a new united France could ever be born from this weak and purposeless court. No historian has been able to trace the reversal in detail, and the tradition that attributes to Joan omniscience even regarding military affairs is, as we shall show, misleading. And yet the battle has been won in advance through her mere appearance. Here a supernatural factor intervenes, embodied in the will and faith of a pure maiden, the effect of which we cannot analyze but which cannot be denied.

An objective historian like Calmette writes:

> Mysticism becomes an essential spring of history. Between Heaven and Earth, Joan was the expected intermediary. To believe in her was to believe in the right of the Valois. The dissolving agent of doubt which had paralyzed the French energies was dissipated.... From now on there would no longer be two Kings in France.... The dual monarchy is nothing but an empty phantasm, a soap bubble without substance: Should a Prince of Lancaster continue to call himself King of France and England— what difference could it make from now on?

Highly favorable to Joan was the opinion later given by Gerson, the great theologian, leading spirit of the Council of Constance and one of the most esteemed savants of his day. He had taken a strong stand for the King against Burgundy. Jean Petit's defense of the murder of Louis d'Orléans, for which of course John the Fearless was responsible, had been unmasked by Gerson. In the name of the Church, he refuted the cynical theory that murder could be permitted if it resulted in the downfall of tyranny.

In his report he carefully distinguishes between "matters of faith" and "matters of devotion".

When it is a question of faith, the Catholic has no liberty to choose, but must follow the directives of the Church. But when it is a question of the "matters of devotion", everyone is free to believe or not. Those who believed that Joan was acting under divine guidance could do so with a good conscience. But even those who did not believe in her divine guidance could disbelieve so without any sense of disloyalty to the Church.

According to Gerson, three facts support the belief that Joan was an emissary of God.

In the first place, her appearance was impressive. Secondly, a great number of trustworthy witnesses believed in her, as well as the great majority of Christian people. Thirdly, there was nothing in her actions that could be said to be opposed to the truths of the faith.

Gerson brings out several points of his own.

Who but God could have sent Joan to the court and induced the King's counselors to accept her advice? The enthusiasm she inspired in the people clearly had a religious background. Wherever she appears, the enemy flees. Joan and her troops never tempt God.

It is interesting that Gerson's report also contains a warning. He knows the world, he knows how frivolously men deal with religious truths. He foresees that Joan, in whose divine mission he believes, will one day stand powerless, unable to produce any miracles. He knows mankind enough to realize that they will then betray and mock her. He therefore says even at that stage that if such a thing should happen it would be no reason to disbelieve in Joan. It can happen that God will not listen to us because through our continued sins and neglect we have offended him or simply because it forms part of his unfathomable plan to abandon us for a time to despair and misery.

Gerson also goes into the question of Joan's male attire.

He admits that morals forbid a woman to dress as a man, but these morals derive from the Old Testament, while we now live under the new dispensation. Morals are founded on decency, and in the scale of values decency must come a long way behind righteousness, which is the real motive in Joan's struggle for the King against the English. In this situation, it is therefore permitted to Joan to wear male attire. There is also a special lesson in God thus allowing grown men to be led by a young woman—a necessary lesson in humility.

The other examiner of whose opinions we possess a report was the Archbishop of Embrun, the Luxembourger Jacques Gélu. At first he was more cautious and had evidently received instructions and information from the King's chancellor, Regnault, who had never been convinced of Joan's divine mission. It has been assumed that the chancellor was responsible for the strange expression about Joan, "*une puce élevée dans le fumier*—a flea bred on a manure heap"—which made Gélu's first letter of warning famous. But we must not make the mistake of looking upon this expression as altogether too contemptuous. In the document in which he accepts Joan, Gélu maintains that in the same way as God had created creatures such as flies and lice for the humiliation of man, he has also sent to the court a young peasant girl without knowledge, without culture, and who in the eyes of the world appears very insignificant. And this "louse" should be welcomed by the King with great humility. He should listen to her counsel, though with a certain reservation, for it was obvious that when it came to practical matters, the use of engines of war, bridge-building, the supply of stores, forage, ammunition, or the maintenance of economic stability, it was advisable to rely on ordinary human common sense. But if it becomes apparent that celestial wisdom is manifesting itself in special fashion, then human wisdom must humbly give way. In these cases, the Maid's counsel should be sought and preferred to any other. "Who gives life also gives nourishment. He gives tools to his workmen. We must therefore rely on the Lord. He has identified himself with the King's cause. To all those who defend his cause he will give the leadership required for victory. God does not leave his work uncompleted."

Gélu ends by advising the King to perform every day an act agreeable to God and to confer about this with Joan.

It is interesting to observe in this document that it recommends an attitude toward Joan that is almost exactly that observed by the King's commander-in-chief. Joan will not be permitted to intervene in the actual conduct of the war and will not have a command of her own, but when she reveals beyond doubt that she represents a higher command her opinions will be respected.

The King now had Joan equipped with a suit of armor; there is an entry that the paymaster-general of the forces, Hemon Raguier, was ordered to pay out *"cent livres tournois"* for this. The relatively small sum indicates that Joan's appearance must have been a modest one. A kind of staff was also created for her, consisting of her confessor, the Augustinian Jean Pasquerel; a master of the horse, Jean d'Aulon; her two brothers, Pierre and Jean d'Arc, who had joined her in Poitiers (while the eldest brother remained with their father); her two friends, Jean de Metz and Bertrand de Poulengy; two pages, Louis de Coutes and Raymond, who both left accounts of her; and finally the two heralds, Ambleville and Guyenne. The real leader, or shall we say, chief of staff, was her unfailing friend Jean d'Aulon.

Her banner displayed God seated, one hand clasping the globe and the other raised in blessing, while an angel knelt on each side. Over this device were the words *Jesus-Maria*. On her triangular badge one saw the Annunciation with an angel kneeling in front of the Holy Virgin. It has been held that this device was connected with the cult of our Lady at Le Puy, which was the spiritual center of the French kingdom at that time. Le Puy-en-Velay was the Lourdes of those days and also a national stronghold.

Joan's sword became the object of much discussion. It will be remembered that on her way to Chinon she visited the church of Sainte-Catherine-de-Fierbois in which many knights had deposited their arms in gratitude for the assistance they believed they had received from Joan's favorite saint. Charles Martel was supposed to have laid his sword there, but it had disappeared long before the time of Joan's visit. Joan had a messenger dispatched to the church with the information that the sword of Charles Martel would be found in the earth quite near the altar. Her order was carried out, and the sword, adorned with five crosses about which Joan had spoken, was really found there. During the trial, Joan told the court that the sword had been very rusty, but that the rust had been easily removed.

She regarded this sword as a gift from her saint.[4]

At the end of the trial, Joan returned to Chinon, but soon embarked on a trip to Saumur, which is of interest to us because we still possess some characteristic details concerning it.

---

[4] It may have been this sword that Joan happened to break when she one day struck some trollops with the flat of the blade in driving them out of camp. The King is said to have expressed his displeasure and told her to use a stick on such occasions.

Its purpose was to visit the mother and the wife of the Duke of Alençon. Like the Duke himself, they were refugees and resided in the convent of Saint-Florent-lès-Saumur. The Duke's mother was a daughter of the former Duke of Brittany, and therefore a sister of the head of the ducal house of Montfort and of Count Arthur de Richemont, constable of France. The chronicler Perceval de Cagny has told of Joan's visit to these two ladies with whom she appears to have become great friends immediately. "God knows", he writes, "what joy these noble ladies and the young Duke prepared for the Maid during the three or four days she stayed at the place named."

When Joan was about to leave the convent to ride to the front, the Duke's terrified wife came to her with a touching request: Would Joan as *chef de guerre* free the Duke from his post in the expedition that was being dispatched for the relief of Orléans and replace him with somebody else? Joan must have smiled at the anxiety of the young wife, and answered, as the Duke later related it, in these words:

"Madame, do not be alarmed. I will answer for your husband and shall bring him back to you in good health and in the same condition as now, or perhaps even better."

In these words one can recognize her absolute faith, her unshakable religious conviction, and her astonishing authoritativeness. Anatole France, almost against his own will, falls under the spell of her young heroic personality. He concludes one section of his book in the following beautiful and moving words:

Sixty years later a burgher of Poitiers, then nearly a hundred years old, told a young fellow townsman that he had seen the Maid mount her charger in a suit of pure white armor to ride to Orléans. He pointed out a stone at the corner of the Rue Saint-Étienne from which she had mounted. Joan carried no arms in Poitiers. The stone had since that time been called *le Montoir de la Pucelle* (the mounting block of the Maid) by the townspeople.

With what joy must not the saint have leaped into the saddle from this stone to be borne away from flattery and lies to the conquered and afflicted whom she longed to liberate!

CHAPTER 6

Joan and the Military

On April 28, 1429, the Duke of Alençon and Joan of Arc led a small army of two to three thousand men from Blois toward Orléans.

It was now spring.

Joan had ridden from Domrémy for eleven bitterly cold days. During March she had seen spring approaching, and we may guess that now she participated in the splendors of the Pascal liturgy while the trees were in full flower. The nights were cold, and doubtless a light mist covered the fields and meadows when she went to early Mass. But the mists were soon dispersed, and the damp air quivered in the sun. The cherry trees had already finished flowering, but the apple trees scattered over the landscape were in blossom and the anemones shimmered at the borders of the forest.

Spring came earlier here than at Domrémy, and Joan's countrywoman's eye soon observed that the landscape was quite different, that the farmland was more fertile. Above all, she had been privileged to witness the wonder of Easter, and from now on the Alleluia of the liturgy rang out during Mass, and we can imagine the young horsewoman cantering along under majestic trees in full bloom, humming to herself the familiar words of the *Regina Cœli*.

She had also her "voices". She was familiar with them. To the young man who rode by her side, the Duke of Alençon,[1] she had confided that she really knew a good deal more than she had admitted during the examination in Poitiers, but she had considered it useless to expound

---

[1] Joan loved him and called him her handsome duke, but he does not seem to have been a very pleasant man. He had already been taken prisoner at Verneuil and kept incarcerated in the tower of Le Crotoy. He was a weak character, not particularly intelligent, arrogant, violent, and uncontrolled. He dabbled in magic and was extremely gullible. Moreover, his voice was extremely hoarse and caused him much embarrassment.

her knowledge to the pedants who examined her. She was referring to her "voices", which do not seem to have been debated very much in Poitiers. But she heard them all the time. Had not Saint Catherine herself presented her with the sword that hung by her side? Was it not Charles Martel's own weapon, which she had inherited? She enjoyed the company of the strong, rather primitive duke who rode beside her; like him, she loved horses and fine arms, while the learned old men only drew a smile from her. How exceedingly little they knew of the real truth. God and his saints would speak inwardly to man, and man himself had only to obey bravely. It was so simple, but no sooner was this truth put into words and discussed by theologians than extraordinary difficulties appeared, which she would have liked to be able to scatter as easily as she could hack her way through a thorny thicket, as she rode ahead of the slowly advancing troops.

Was Joan really at that time the responsible head of this advance guard and of the main body, numbering perhaps eight thousand, which was to follow after them?

The traditional biographers have only one answer to this. The King had conferred the command of the army upon Joan. In Rouen she seems to have believed this herself, for she says that the King placed ten to twelve thousand men at her disposal and gave her her own staff and the standard of a commander-in-chief.[2] Literature possesses many long dissertations about Joan's military genius, and at least three military writers who have studied her campaigns have found that she acted on sound military principles and possessed an astonishingly good tactical judgment. The faithful Jean d'Aulon stated categorically "*Dux femina belli facta est*"—A woman has taken over the command in war. Assuredly there were at the time many who believed it as firmly as did later the pious biographers. Père Petitot's writings are full of quotations from Marshal Foch intended to prove Joan's military genius.

It is difficult to reconcile this with the reports of Joan's disagreements with the military leaders and with her misfortunes and capture. The traditional biographers are of the opinion that Joan was surrounded by irresolute men who did not understand her military genius and are

[2] In regard to the reports of the trial at Rouen, it must be remembered that the judges were convinced that Joan was a witch, and it was in their interests to make the victories of the "witch" as decisive as possible. Joan herself denied having called herself *chef de guerre* in her letter to the English.

highly critical because her simple advice was not immediately followed and the English swept from the country.

This is a question not easy to decide; it is still in the balance. But if one reads the texts critically and studies modern scholars unaffected by legends and traditions, one finds that in many respects the picture must be considerably altered.

Did Joan of Arc really command the army that carried out the relief of Orléans or did she not? It is self-evident that the campaign against Orléans cannot have been improvised merely because Joan of Arc had foretold that the siege would be easily raised. Careful research has also revealed that all the measures that led to this result had been adopted either before Joan came to court and was recognized, or later without her knowledge. It was clear to the King's military advisers that Orléans must not fall, and the most energetic measures were taken to prevent this. One of these has already been mentioned in the first chapter, the so-called Battle of Herrings, when French attempts to capture Sir John Fastolf and his great supply train came to such a pitiful end. In literature this battle figured as a great catastrophe that more or less paralyzed the wills of the King's men, but this seems to be an exaggeration. The affair constituted nothing more than an annoying setback. Responsibility for it must fall chiefly upon the Count of Clermont, who then for the first time held an independent command. The enterprise really failed because Clermont attacked Fastolf without waiting for the Bastard of Orléans, who, before the attack, had agreed to join in and support it.

Later historians have asserted that this setback caused something like panic in Orléans, and others have tried to prove that Clermont had abandoned the town in a cowardly fashion instead of taking the obvious course of uniting his remaining troops to the garrison. This must be a mistake. Orléans had a large garrison and was in an excellent state for defense. Of course the garrison had to be provisioned from time to time, but this caused no great difficulties as the English were unable to invest the town completely. It will be realized that Orléans did not require reinforcements.

A number of historians, including some of the earlier ones, have believed that as a result of this defeat Orléans decided to negotiate with the enemy; nothing could be more untrue. But it is a fact that the townspeople sent Poton de Xaintrailles and some other burghers to Philip the Good of Burgundy and to Jean de Luxembourg, who supported the

English and had some small detachments of troops serving in the besieging army. The emissaries appealed to the Duke of Burgundy to try to induce the English to end the siege and if possible to bring about the release of the Duke of Orléans.

Superficially this may look like treason against the King of France. Strangely enough, older historians have made the same charge against certain of the King's own counselors, particularly Regnault de Chartres and La Trémoille, who also showed great eagerness to negotiate with Burgundy. There is, however, a much more natural explanation of this, namely, that the King and his counselors had never abandoned the reasonable hope that the Burgundians would at last come to their senses and cease to help the English to conquer France. While the war continued with shifting success, quiet work was going on under cover to induce the Burgundians to change sides.

This was neither treacherous nor unrealistic. We may be certain that Orléans, whose royal troops were commanded by Dunois, was acting in concert with the King's advisers. Investigations have also shown that there was here no question of desperate or childish "last ditch" tactics. Duke Philip the Good had long since had enough of the English and was intelligent enough to realize that in time he would share the fate that the English were preparing for the King. We must also remember that strange rule of the period, which we have already mentioned, that a town could not decently be attacked while its master was held in captivity. The Duke of Orléans was a prisoner of war. How then could his cousin, the Burgundian Duke, assist the English who wanted to seize his town? This was the juridical question of which the leaders in Orléans made good use.

The Duke of Burgundy took the matter seriously. He traveled to Paris, where he had a meeting with the Duke of Bedford and told him of his wishes. The Duke of Bedford answered that he would be most displeased if he found that he had flushed the bird and somebody else came and caught it; in other words, he answered with an impertinence. Angered, the Duke of Burgundy sent a trumpeter to Orléans with orders to recall all Burgundians.

The Orléans message to Burgundy, which has been made to seem an act of treason, was by contrast a clever tactical move that resulted in a success many times more important than the setback in the Battle of Herrings—the first serious rift in Anglo-Burgundian relations and the considerable weakening of the besieging army. Lefèvre-Pontalis, who made a careful study of the campaign, estimated that the English besieging army numbered five thousand, of whom three thousand were in the front line. Against these troops, Orléans had a citizens' guard of three thousand men and two thousand royal troops. In addition, there was the relieving army of three thousand advancing from Blois. Clearly the situation was far from catastrophic.

Since October of the previous year, the King had been working for the relief of Orléans. The difficulties were chiefly financial, and it was impossible to raise the money for a relieving army immediately. When the army assembled at Blois in April, this must have been the result of decisions taken long before the appearance of Joan of Arc. Cordier, whom we can here follow, comes to these conclusions:

1. Dunois insisted that the decision to send Joan to Orléans was made after the preparations for the relief of the city.
2. The Duke of Alençon stated that when he came to Blois the Queen of Sicily was engaged in financing the army.
3. Both these witnesses and also d'Aulon said that Joan held no command whatsoever, but had only a personal *maison* (establishment) under the leadership of d'Aulon. This, however, was attached to the army that was marching to Orléans under the command of the Marshals of France, Rais and Boussac—for Constable de Richemont had quarreled with the court.

But, no doubt, all the leaders considered her presence to be of the highest importance, for moral, psychological, and supernatural reasons. It is not credible that these experienced soldiers should have regarded her merely as a kind of mascot, part of their propaganda. No, they really believed in her mission and were convinced that she was playing an important part, but to interpret this as implying that Joan had obtained the supreme command is to impose the conceptions of our own secularized time on a period that understood the matter very differently. Divine power was respected, as was its inspired representative, but a peasant girl was not given a military command. One turned to God, but without abdicating one's common sense. One prayed to God for victory, but one acted as if all depended on one's own strength.

Joan herself would have approved of the principle: "In God's name soldiers shall fight, and God shall give victory."

Blois lies west of Orléans and, like that town, north of the river. When the army advanced from Blois to besiege Orléans, it was decided to march along the south side of the river with the view of passing by Orléans and provisioning the town from the eastern side by means of boats. West of the town the English held the powerful earthworks Saint-Laurent-des-Orgerils, which it was considered would be difficult to seize.

The Augustinian Pasquerel, whom Joan's mother had sent to her, has related many details about her life and doings and, of course, especially about her piety. He is not always reliable, but if one uses his text with discrimination, much information and many valuable observations can be found in it. Pasquerel relates that Joan had gathered a group of priests around her banner and that these priests always preceded the soldiers. In this order, the army crossed the river on the south side from Blois singing the *Veni Creator* and other hymns.

The hypercritical Cordier believes that one should not credit such a report, and that only Regnault de Chartres could have ordered this. This seems like carrying suspicion too far. After all, Joan was an emissary of God, and in such matters her authority was complete, as we have recently seen from Gélu.

From another source we learn that Joan had a banner mounted in the open air on which was depicted a scene from Golgotha. She told her father confessor to gather the soldiers around her banner in the morning and at night before their departure, where they might pray and sing the *Salve Regina*. She herself went among the men and asked them if they were conscious of any mortal sin and drove their women out of the camp.

However, this source is the usually unreliable *Chronique de la Pucelle*.

The first night they slept in the open. Joan fell asleep in her armor and next morning it was noticeable that her body was stiff and sore from the unaccustomed male clothing. The next day she was met by Dunois, who had reached the south bank of the river east of the town in a small boat. Joan at once asked him if he were the Bastard of Orléans. When he answered in the affirmative, she immediately proceeded to scold him. "Is it you who have planned things so that we should arrive on this side of the Loire and so that I cannot march directly to the place where Talbot and the English are?"

From this it seems apparent that Joan exercised no kind of command. It looks as if she had only gradually realized that they were on the wrong side of the river. She would rather have marched along the north bank of the Loire, straight at the English.

Dunois answered, if he is to be believed, quietly and politely that in his opinion and that of other experienced soldiers it was safest and wisest to take this side of the river.

Joan's answer takes the form of a real scolding:

"In God's name—the advice of our Lord is better and safer than yours. You think that you can deceive me, but you have only deceived yourselves, because I come with a powerful aid which no soldier or city can obtain, namely, the assistance of the King of Heaven, and you shall share in this, not because of any love of mine, but because God himself wishes it. Saint Louis and Saint Charlemagne have appealed to him to have mercy on Orléans, and he does not desire that the enemy should retain the Duke's person [Orléans] and his town."

It is evident from this speech that Joan was furious. She had wished to march directly against the English fortification, Saint-Laurent, on the north side of the river, without any regard to the fact that the force she was leading was not an army equipped for battle, but a convoy with provisions for the garrison. Her words do not show much common sense, and the only surprising thing is that the Bastard did not lose his temper. However, Joan enjoyed extraordinary authority, and even Dunois, the greatest realist of his times, had seen too many remarkable cases of supernatural intervention to dare to reject Joan. But it was now too late to change the plan, and Dunois had his way. He had, probably rightly, decided that the advance should take place south of the river, as the English blocked the way on the north side. After having passed Orléans, soldiers and provisions would be ferried over east of the town, where there were no English. A sound and unimaginative, but probably quite good, plan.

But saints do not always behave in the same way as ordinary people. If the beginning of Joan's campaign is curious, the continuation becomes even more so.

Dunois explained to Joan that the escort had now played its part and could march back by the same road they had come and rejoin the main army. He then proposed to Joan that she should join him and cross to the north side of the river by boat and enter the town where her arrival was eagerly awaited.

Joan's answer was a blunt "No."

According to one source, she mistrusted Dunois so much that she wanted to accompany the troops to Blois as she believed that they would never return.

According to another, more complete report, she replied that she did not wish to leave her banner and her brothers-in-arms who were *"bien confessés, en état de pénitence et de bonne volonté"* (well shriven, in a state of penitence and of good will).

This seems to imply that she thought her men were now in an excellent state of preparedness, not least from the religious point of view, but that one could not tell how long it would last.

But Dunois would not give way. He spoke to the leaders of the convoy and asked them to persuade Joan to go with him to Orléans while they returned to Blois.

In the end, Joan had to agree to do as he wished.

Certainly an inglorious beginning to the raising of a siege. Joan had been made to take a road that she thought was the wrong one. She was not allowed to stay with her own troops as she wished to do. She was separated from the army and had to agree to be sent to the city like a good little girl.

To the older tradition belongs a story of how Joan caused the wind to change at a moment when it seemed impossible to dispatch the boats with provisions for the city. Cordier ignores this story, but it is well vouched for by many witnesses. Perhaps Joan, possessing the intuition of a child of nature, was more familiar with wind conditions than the military leaders.

However that may be, Joan entered Orléans on April 29, accompanied by Dunois, the Bastard of Orléans. We must now say a word about this man, later her faithful friend and brother-in-arms.

He was a son of the murdered Louis of Orléans and a brother of the Duke imprisoned in England. Born in 1403, and therefore of the same age as Charles VII, he may be regarded as the King's most faithful and skillful general. Like his brother in England, who wrote remarkable poetry with an honored place in the history of literature, Dunois was a cultured man and possessed great personal charm. He was a very different type of person from the rather backward Duke of Alençon, whom, strangely enough, Joan considered to be a handsome man. Dunois, however, carried caution to an extreme. His saying that only two hundred Englishmen were needed to put a thousand Frenchmen to flight may have referred to the unquestioned superiority of English military technique.

If we dare to assume that Joan was at first a little disappointed, this must quickly have given way to other feelings, for she was received with an unprecedented enthusiasm. Luillier relates that "she was received with the same joy and applause by people of both sexes, as if she had been an angel from God, because people hoped that through her intervention they would soon be rid of their enemies."

In our principal source for the liberation of Orléans, *Le Journal du Siège d'Orléans*, we find a description of her entry.

Joan rode into the town at eight o'clock in the evening, wearing full armor, her white banner carried before her. The banner displayed two angels, each with a lily in his hand; a picture of the Holy Virgin and of the angel of the Annunciation, who also held out a lily, was painted on it.

On her left rode the Bastard of Orléans in full armor. They were followed by a rich and splendid company composed partly of troops of the relief force—for she had brought with her into the city two hundred "lancers"—and of the garrison. The burghers of the town, men and women, stood closely packed to see her, many with torches in their hands—all had heard of the young girl sent by God for their salvation. In the crush, one of the torches accidentally touched her banner, which caught fire. Joan showed great presence of mind and also her expert horsemanship—spurring her horse, she swung it round and advanced to the fire, which she extinguished "as if she had long engaged in war". Soldiers and burghers watched the incident full of admiration, and her progress through the city to the mansion of the wealthy Jacques Boucher was accompanied with acclamation and applause. Before she reached Boucher's house, where she was received with great joy, she dismounted at the church of Sainte-Croix to give thanks to God.

Perhaps this matter-of-fact and sensible girl may have reflected that nothing was happening as she had expected, that she was being led instead of leading, that she had been acclaimed without having done anything.

But if she felt any anxiety, it surely subsided before the picture of our Savior on the Cross. The series of events that had led her from the meadows of Domrémy to the triumphant entry into Orléans, one of the biggest cities in France, which to her must have seemed gigantic, all this was fantastic enough to give her strength. Behind such occurrences there had to be a power greater than her own.

She had only to advance fearlessly.

Before the Battle

The day after the entry into Orléans the principal officers met in Joan's hotel. There was another discussion of some acrimony, and Joan saw her plans rejected again. Her wish was to attack immediately, but Dunois wanted to wait and to go himself to fetch the relieving army before any other military measures were taken. To us this seems a sensible plan, but Joan protested violently though in vain. She was in a state of great anger when the leaders left her. Again divine guidance was opposed by human wisdom, and it was the latter that became decisive.

Joan's only source of knowledge was the Bible and the legends, which spoke in unmistakable language: human wisdom leads to disaster, unquestioning faith in God's guidance leads to victory. She must have been very tortured by this new trial. Three times in a brief span of time she had been outvoted and forced to obey against her conscience and inner voice in an important matter.

How did she employ her time while Dunois set out to bring back the relieving army? Odd reports show that she continued her task of strengthening and renewing the new moral and religious spirit in the royal camp, a task she had already begun during the march to Orléans. Impatiently she mounted her charger and, along with a troop of horse, accompanied the Bastard of Orléans part of the way, after which she returned to continue the work she had set herself. Jean Luillier, a burgher of the city, has related that Joan encouraged the townsmen to set their hopes on God, saying that if they did so, they would escape with their lives from the enemy. We also know that a great number of the most important citizens of the town, male and female, visited her, some of course out of curiosity, but others to see with their own eyes an emissary of God. One witness relates that the women were especially struck by one fact:

"She spoke only of God."

One is again reminded how firmly this girl was bound to the mystical events of her youth.

Like herself, the burghers wanted to fight. It is said that they gathered outside her house and loudly called to her to show herself, but on the advice of Dunois she desisted. On their own initiative, the burgher militia then made a sortie and attacked the redoubt of Saint-Pouair, but were repulsed after heavy fighting. Joan did not participate in the fight.

But we know of another important act of hers. She wrote, or rather dictated, a new letter to the English, which she dispatched by two heralds. In it she requested the English to surrender the man who had brought her first letter. Dunois on his side bluntly announced that if this request were not granted he would have all English prisoners in the town killed, including a number of messengers who had been sent by certain English leaders to negotiate the exchange of prisoners.

The *Journal*[3] which tells us about the siege of Orléans goes on to say that

> the English answer to this was to return all the Maid's heralds and messengers with the information that they would burn her, that she was nothing but a whore, and that she ought to return home to look after her cows, which disturbed the Maid very much. When evening came she went down the Boulevard de la Bellecroix, out on the bridge, and from there spoke to Glasdale and other Englishmen who were holding Les Tourelles[4] and called on them to surrender in the name of God, and save their lives. But Glasdale and his men answered her insolently, mocking her and calling her a cowherd, and shouting loudly that they would burn her if they got hold of her. This upset her very much and she replied[5] that they lied, and after she said that, she returned to the town.

Joan's young page, who seems to have accompanied her, has given some details. He relates that "she told them in God's name to withdraw, or she would chase them out; and a person called the Bastard of Granville said rude things to Joan if she expected them to surrender to a woman; he also called the Frenchmen with her 'heathen bastards'".

Reports of this Homeric duel of words passed over the country like wildfire. In the *Journal d'un bourgeois de Paris*, it says that Joan and

[3] *Le Journal du Siège d'Orléans.*

[4] Les Tourelles was a bastion at the southern end of the bridge across the Loire; it was held by the English. Joan's first convoy had to avoid this bastion in order to reach the place east of the town where boats took them across.

[5] Can Joan have spoken to the English in French? In that case the English would also have answered in French. Or possibly she was accompanied by an interpreter.

the English were only a few yards away from each other and that she burst into tears when the coarse soldier mocked her virginity. She was also said to have foretold that the English would soon be beaten, but that Glasdale himself would not live to see the defeat. This actually happened.

The eagerness of the population to approach close to Joan assumed such proportions that her host began to worry about her safety and that of his own house. Great crowds assembled in front of the house, and he begged her to show herself at the window, which she did amid wild ovations. She had to ride out in the town one Sunday—everybody wanted to see her! "In the streets that she passed through there were such crowds that she could hardly advance, and the people did not tire of seeing her. Everybody marveled that she could mount a horse as gracefully as she did."

Nearly all descriptions of Joan give one this impression of aesthetic perfection, though it is not probable that her face was actually beautiful; at any rate nobody has said so. As has already been mentioned, her young male friends, and especially the impressionable Duke of Alençon, all spoke of her beautiful figure, but she must also have possessed a natural dignity and ease of manner that impressed her followers strongly. As Frenchwomen often are, she was lively, quick to tears, both before God and when she was mocked. She cried spontaneously and unashamedly the first time she was wounded.

She was easily angered. There are a number of little cameos that show how she acted when her anger was aroused. One witness relates that she would never allow her soldiers to consume stolen meat. When a Scot dared tell her that she had no doubt eaten stolen meat herself, she became so angry that she wanted to assault him. The good Dominican who tells us of it adds that the incident unhappily indicates that Joan was sometimes "inclined to be excitable"—a fine example of understatement.

Another time, Joan heard a knight swearing, or possibly even blaspheming, in one of the streets of Orléans, and she became so indignant that she seized him by the collar and cried out that she would not let him go unless he promised never to use such language again. The alarmed knight promptly assured her that he would never again be guilty of bad language.

During these days when she was waiting in Orléans, another event occurred that deserves notice.

On May 3, the Feast of the Finding of the Holy Cross was celebrated, as it still is in our day, in memory of the discovery of our Savior's Cross by the Empress Helena, mother of Constantine. This Cross was later carried away by the Persians and recaptured by the Emperor Heraclius, who in 628 returned the relic to Jerusalem. In the celebration at Vespers, the words of one of the antiphons are *"Ecce Crucem Domini, fugite, partes adversae; vicit leo de tribu Juda, radix David, alleluia."*

The hymn of the day is Venantius Fortunatus' masterpiece "Vexilla Regis", which with its triumphant first verse seems so suited to Joan's religious attitude.

> The royal banners forward go;
> The cross shines forth in mystic glow;
> Life himself our death endured,
> And by his death our life procured.

Another verse formulates unforgettably the depth of Christian mysticism developed around the Cross:

> O Tree of beauty, Tree of light!
> O Tree with royal purple dight!
> Elect on whose triumphal breast
> These holy limbs should find their rest.

In Orléans, this great Church feast was always celebrated with a solemn procession, which this year was greater than ever. The whole garrison, all the clergy, and the whole population participated, and the spectacle was of a kind that can still be seen in Catholic cities on the Feast of Corpus Christi. Many of the burghers bore candles or torches in their hands as they followed in the procession. Joan herself, in her white armor, rode behind the Blessed Sacrament carrying her banner, and the officers who surrounded her could see tears streaming from her eyes.

Joan in Camp

Dunois returned to Blois without encountering any English troops. It must be borne in mind that the King's Council was still seeking a peaceful solution. There is, therefore, no reason—as was generally done in the earlier Joan of Arc literature—to represent men such as Regnault de

Chartres and La Trémoille as cowardly and compromising. But it is not likely that Dunois presented himself to a bewildered Council inclined to avoid recourse to arms, and that only after a violent argument did he gain his point that Orléans be sent reinforcements. There could, of course, be differences of opinion, but there could be no discussion about the main outlines of the strategic plan that had been adopted, especially now that Joan's arrival had in such a striking manner raised the morale and the fighting spirit in the besieged town.

Dunois therefore, on May 4, approached Orléans at the head of the relieving force. Nominally, the chief commanders were the Marshals Rais and Boussac. As they approached the town, they were met by a troop of a hundred horsemen, under the command of La Hire and Joan of Arc. Chroniclers and biographers have thought that they saw a miracle in the fact that the English allowed these troops to pass without making any attempt to attack them. But it would really have been much more curious if the English had attacked, since their serviceable troops, as has already been mentioned, numbered only about three thousand men. To have allowed the relieving expedition, which in any case numbered three thousand, to be attacked from the redoubts close to the walls of the strong fortress would have been sheer folly. Here, therefore, we need not consider any supernatural intervention. But one can be thankful for the contemporary descriptions since they give an impressive picture of the relieving troops marching close by the English redoubts, their liturgical hymns echoing over the flower-starred meadows.

After the arrival of the troops, Joan was sitting at table when she was visited by Dunois, who informed her that Fastolf, the victor in the inglorious Battle of the Herrings, was sending reinforcements to the English.

Joan sprang up, crying: "Bastard, Bastard, in God's name, I tell you that as soon as you know when this Fastolf is approaching, you must inform me, and if he should pass without my knowledge, I promise you that it shall cost you your head."[6]

After her meal, Joan lay down on her bed to rest after her ride, and her friend Jean d'Aulon did likewise. But after a short sleep she awoke

[6]Appalled by this frankness, a historian, the Abbé Dubois, makes the following comment: "Is it really possible that a young girl of nineteen should have dared to speak so authoritatively to Dunois, the King's commander in Orléans, and threaten to behead him? Could she really have done this?"

and sprang up "in great commotion", as Jean d'Aulon says. Alarmed, he asked what had happened.

"In the name of God," she answered, "my Council[7] tell me that I must set out against the English, but I do not know if I should attack their redoubts or march against Fastolf, who is advancing with provisions."

Jean d'Aulon goes on to say that while he was assisting her with her armor, they heard great commotion and shouts from the town, and it was said that the enemy had dealt a serious blow to the French. He proceeded to put on his own armor, but the Maid left the room unnoticed and went into the street, where she saw a mounted page. She ordered him to dismount and quickly sprang into the saddle and rode rapidly to the Porte de Bourgogne, where the commotion seemed to be greatest.

The *Chronique de la Pucelle* describes the scene thus: "As soon as she was ready she mounted and rode down the street so that the sparks flew; she rode straight on as if she had known the way beforehand."

Perhaps this is romancing, and we will therefore return to Jean d'Aulon's description. "When they reached the city gate, they saw a burgher who had been badly wounded being carried to his home. The Maid asked who he was, and they answered that it was a Frenchman. She then said that she had never seen the blood of a Frenchman without her hair standing up on end."

At last the time for action had arrived.

The French were already retreating, and in Orléans the church bells were pealing out. La Hire and Dunois took up their stations. It is not necessary to believe that Joan assumed the command and gave Dunois orders to cut off the English way of retreat from the redoubt of Saint-Loup, which was the center of the fighting, for he was surely master of the situation. It is, however, certain that Joan attacked with furious energy. Even those who are highly critical of the romanticization Joan's story has often suffered must recognize that she now threw herself into the battle and brought about a decision: "*Laquelle incontinent par lesdits François fut assaillie, et à trés peu de perte d'iceulx prinse d'assault*" (this redoubt being at once attacked by the French and with small loss taken). The redoubt was stormed, and the surviving Englishmen took refuge in the old monastery church, where, to escape massacre, they put on the garments of priests and monks. The French soon realized what

[7] Her name for the "voices".

114

had happened and wanted to cut them down inside the chapel, but Joan intervened and stopped the massacre. "Priests must be spared", she said with a smile, and by her intervention saved the lives of forty Englishmen. Their redoubt was then set on fire.

Joan had won her first victory, which was celebrated in a suitable manner.[8] But the curious fact remains that Joan had not been informed by the military leaders about the attack on the redoubt of Saint-Loup, which can scarcely have been a spontaneous movement of the garrison. The impression of her isolation is strengthened. But this does not mean that her presence may not have helped to bring about a quick decision.

The following day, May 5, was another great Church feast, Ascension Day. The previous night Joan had announced that on that day she would not fight nor even bear arms, but would confess and receive Holy Communion. It appears that on that day she addressed another letter to the English, which was dispatched to them fastened to an arrow, with the cry: "Here comes a message."

The English replied with more coarse jests about the "Armagnac whore", which caused Joan to burst into tears. But she had a public announcement made that within five days all the English redoubts would be captured and not a single Englishman left in the neighborhood of the town.

It can be guessed that the French commanders smiled at, or were irritated by, such amateurish announcements. Joan, however, ordered the population of the town and the garrison to confess and to receive Communion, and we know that such a tough warrior as La Hire did so. Ascension Day was celebrated by enormous numbers.

Orléans Liberated

Joan was now battle-tried and had shown her mettle, but it is plain that she was still kept away from the Council table. Our accounts of what happened that day in Orléans are contradictory, but whichever version we accept, it is plain that in the beginning Joan was not consulted nor

---

[8] "*A icelle heure furent rendues graces à Dieu par toutes les églises, en hymnes et dévotes oraisons, à son de cloches, que Anglais pouvoient bien oyr; lesquels furent fort abaissez de puissance par ceste partye et aussi de courage*", says the chronicler. (At this hour thanks were given to God in all the churches, in hymns and devout prayers, the bells pealing, which the English could well hear; they had been greatly reduced in power in that skirmish, and also in courage.)

included in the Council of War. It is reasonable to see in this no kind of antagonism toward her, or disapproval of her, but simply a consequence of the opinion generally held in those days that a woman should not take part in a Council of War, which was reserved for dukes and princes.

The Council seems to have taken place in the home of Cousinot, the chancellor of the Duke of Orléans, where it was decided that one body of troops were to attack the redoubt of Saint-Laurent where Talbot was in command, while another was to advance out of the eastern gate, cross the Loire, and attempt to recapture Les Tourelles. This was the most important redoubt of the English and was situated opposite the bridge that led to the town from the southern bank.

Joan either participated from the beginning or joined the troops a little later. In any case she soon saw that there was no wish to inform her of the plan of campaign, and with long strides she impatiently paced the room saying that she demanded to know exactly where she stood. Her friend, Dunois, tried to reason with her, begging her not to be angry: "It is impossible to tell everything at once". She listened to him somewhat ironically and said that she accepted the plan if it were only carried out as conceived.

The plan was not realized, and events took quite a different turn.

Evidently some of the burgher militia were anxious to fight as soon as possible, and therefore assembled more or less on their own initiative at the eastern gate, which, however, was barred. Gaucourt, who was the highest civil functionary of the town, guarded the gate in person and refused to open it. The soldiers then sent a message to Joan, who seized her arms, mounted her charger, and cantered to the spot. "Candid and terrible", in the words of Anatole France, she advanced to the aged Gaucourt and, gazing at him sternly, ordered him to open the gate. "You are a bad man not to open for these men! But whether you wish it or not they shall get out and will give as good an account of themselves as they did the other day."

This must have been in contradiction to the decision recently taken, and it is highly probable that the first dignitary of the town refused to obey these arbitrary orders. He was, however, overpowered, while Joan shouted: "Now I shall be your captain."

The militia was ferried over the river and first reached the redoubt Saint-Jean-le-Blanc, which was found to have been evacuated. The French occupied it and set it on fire. Before attacking Les Tourelles, the redoubt of Les Augustins had to be captured, but here there was a body of English troops who engaged the French and drove them back. The French knights had not yet been ferried across, and when they landed with Joan and La Hire at their head they were met by fleeing Frenchmen. A regular siege was now instituted, and no less than four thousand men were deployed while the guns were placed in position. The French commanders, the Bastard and the two Marshals, took over the command.

Joan carried her own banner. A gigantic English knight barred the road, but he was hit by a stone cannon ball; and two of the King's men—one of them a Spaniard, Alfonso de Partada—dashed forward, and the assault began. Soon Les Augustins was in the hands of the French.

This time, too, Joan stopped the massacre.

Again she had made a personal contribution completely unforeseen in the military planning and calculations. The more one studies her military contribution, the more mysterious it becomes. Entirely ignorant of strategy and military knowledge, acting solely on an inner impulse, she places herself at the head of what seem to be the most foolhardy enterprises—and succeeds.

After two engagements, the army of Orléans now stood before Les Tourelles, knowing that if this redoubt could be captured, the town would be free.

"It will take a good month", sighed the faint-hearted, but others remembered what Joan had promised.

Cordier tries to show that Joan played no part of importance in this fighting, but this is quite unreasonable, for, without her, the attack would probably never have begun, as it was due to her that the town gates were opened. And it can be imagined how the Marshals and the Bastard would have dealt with soldiers who disobeyed orders if they had not had to consider the Maid.

The army did not return to the town but dug itself in before Les Tourelles. Barge after barge arrived with provisions. Joan herself seems to have returned to the town for the night, perhaps to begin the next day with a Mass. One report says that she was tired and had injured her foot, and that though it was Friday she had broken her habitual, severe fast and even drunk a small quantity of undiluted wine.

Saturday, May 7, proved decisive. The royalist commander had felt some anxiety during the night lest the English should attack the town from one of the other redoubts while the greater part of the French army was camped before Les Tourelles, but nothing happened. It is possible that Joan intervened here too, insisting on her divine guidance in opposition to the military experts.

When she mounted her charger, a chronicler relates, a burgher, or a fisherman, passed by and humbly offered to her an *alose* (a shad). She said to him, "I shall have it for my dinner. I will bring a *godon* to help me eat it." She added that she would return that evening, not by boat but by the bridge. This bridgehead had been in enemy hands for one hundred and ninety-nine days.

Again she proved right.

There were only five hundred English in the redoubt, and the attackers had a superiority of ten to one. In spite of this, the enterprise was a risky one, and nothing of importance happened during the forenoon. The English had strongly fortified Les Tourelles and surrounded the redoubt with deep trenches. The French did their best to fill these with faggots, stones, and earth, and attacked with assaulting ladders. Time after time they seemed on the point of success and were thrown back. The French could not use their numerical superiority to advantage. Joan, who was in the front line the whole time, herself climbed up one of the ladders, and when she reached the top was struck by an arrow, which entered between the breast-plates above her chest and penetrated her body till the point could be seen on her back.[9] She was hurled down and carried away, and many thought her dead. She was removed to a meadow, where her suit of armor was taken off. She wept like a child, less because of the pain than because she realized that she would not be able to continue the fight and that therefore Les Tourelles would not be stormed. Around her were superstitious soldiers busy with advice. Among other things, they suggested that her wounds could perhaps be healed through magic, but she replied that she would rather die than act against the will of God.

---

[9] The report that Joan had foretold that she would be wounded has been thought to be a later addition, but this disagrees with contemporary documents. Even Anatole France had to admit that we have evidential reports that she had said that she was going to be wounded. Her confessor, who in other connections inclines toward literary embroidering, relates that she had even foretold that she would be wounded above the breast. Joan herself, asked by her judges about the matter, quietly answered that she knew about it before.

After some time she arose and herself drew the arrow out of her body. Those around her staunched the flow of blood, and summoning her confessor she made confession. She sighed and continued to weep, but at length found consolation, after which she returned to the fight.[10]

When she returned, she found the French disheartened by their setback, and it appeared as if Dunois had decided to call off the attack. Here Joan intervened; it is difficult to say in what manner she did so, and it is safest to quote Dunois' own words:

> The assault went on from dawn till eight in the evening, and it looked as if there were no possibility of being victorious that day, for which reason the witness (Dunois) hesitated and wanted to withdraw the army to the town. But la Pucelle approached him and begged him to wait a little longer. Mounting her charger, she rode to a vineyard a short distance from the soldiers and here dismounted and prayed for half of a quarter of an hour. When she returned, she immediately grasped her banner and planted it on the edge of the moat. When the English saw her there, cheering on her men, they trembled and became frightened. The King's men were filled with fresh courage and began to climb the ladders and attack the ramparts, and met with no opposition. The redoubt was captured, and the English, who took to flight, were all killed.

This account appears so fantastic that it would be hard to believe were it not signed by the commander-in-chief, who had no reason to make up an account that makes him appear in rather a poor light.

Jean d'Aulon, who was close to Joan, also gave an account that deserves mention.

> It was decided to give the signal for retreat, and this was done. While this occurred, the man who carried the Maid's banner and still held it upright before the redoubt became exhausted and handed it to another who was called the "Basque"—a certain Seigneur de Villars. And as the witness was aware that this Basque was a brave man and was afraid that

---

[10]Père Pasquerel relates: "*Et apposuerunt eidem vulneri oleum olivarum cum lardo, et post hujusmodi appositionem, ipsa Johanna confessa est eidem loquenti, flendo et lamentando. Et dum sensit se vulneratam, timuit et flevit, et fuit consolata ut dicebat.*" (And they put olive oil with lard on her wound, and after that Joan confessed to me, weeping and lamenting. And because she had been wounded she was afraid and wept, and found consolation, according to her words.)

the retreat would have unfortunate consequences and that the ramparts and the whole redoubt would remain in the enemy's hands, he thought that if the banner, which he knew the soldiers loved so much, were to be advanced, it might be possible to capture the redoubt. The witness then asked the Basque if he would follow him if he descended into the moat and went up to the ramparts, and the Basque said he would. The witness then went down into the moat and advanced toward the ramparts, protecting himself with his shield in case stones should be thrown and leaving behind him his companion who he thought would follow close behind. But when the Maid saw her banner borne by the Basque disappearing in the moat she thought that it was lost, and seizing it cried out: "Oh, my banner, my banner", and shook it in such a way that the witness thought the others would believe that she was giving some kind of signal. He therefore cried out, "Hello there, you Basque, what was it you promised me?" Then the Basque pulled so hard that the banner was dragged out of the Maid's hand and came up to the witness. Seeing this, the men in the Maid's army ranged themselves in battle order and attacked the rampart with such energy that it was soon entirely in their hands.

This description is so strange that it can hardly be an invention. The Maid struggling with an unknown Basque for her own banner in full view of the enemy! And during this struggle her men have the impression that she is raising the banner as a signal for a new attack, which quickly led to victory!

The story is incompatible with Dunois' story about the preceding prayer in the vineyard.

The critical Cordier insinuates that Joan was probably not there at all, but that Dunois thought it a good idea to make use of her banner in order to raise the morale of the soldiers.

One wonders why in that case Dunois should have described the event so differently.

The fighting was renewed despite Dunois' hesitation, and the renewal was in some way connected with fresh activity on the part of the wounded girl. These facts cannot be disputed and are in themselves remarkable.

The captured redoubt was joined to the fortification of Tourelles proper by a wooden bridge. While the fighting had been going on, the townsmen had collected a number of barges, which they filled with combustible material and set on fire. The barges were allowed to drift downstream toward the bridge, which caught fire just when it was needed for the retreat of the English. Armed with an enormous battle-axe, the English commander, Glasdale himself, led the retreat. Around him were the Seigneur de Moulins, the Seigneur de Pommier, the Bailly de Mente,[11] and some of the noblest English knights. Joan came up and recognized her enemy.

"Glasdas, Glasdas," she called out in her curious way of speaking, "surrender to the King of Heaven. You have insulted me, but I am sorry for the souls of you and your men."

Glasdale answered with new insults and oaths. Over his head still fluttered the glorious Chandos banner, which for eight years had been carried in the van of a series of almost uninterrupted victories and which now encountered the banner of the young peasant girl.

At this moment the bridge collapsed, and the English riders in their heavy armor were thrown into the river, where they drowned. The English banner, too, disappeared in the waves. It is related that Joan dismounted and knelt down to pray for her unhappy enemies while tears ran down her cheeks. The emotion felt by her French friends was of a different nature, for they saw the heavy ransom they could have obtained for these English nobles disappear in the waters.

The remaining Englishmen withdrew into Les Tourelles but were pursued by the French. At the same time, the citadel was assaulted from the other side by fresh French troops, and a general massacre followed.

Les Tourelles, the most important stronghold of the English, had been captured, and its capture was very largely due to a wounded girl who had misunderstood the seizing of her banner. Even those who try to extract from the various sources only that which seems credible and to eliminate all later additions must admit that this event, so decisive for the future of France, was the result of causes practically unparalleled in history. Among the strange events is one factor that is crystal clear— the presence of an inspired young woman who, disregarding human wisdom and experience, follows her own inspiration and carries out one by one each of the seemingly incredible promises she has made in advance.

[11] The Lords Moleyns and Poynings and Sir Thomas Giffart.

All this time the main English army, commanded by the experienced strategist Talbot, remained inactive—nobody knows why.

Magnificat anima mea Dominum

Late in the evening the French, or at any rate the officers, returned to the town. We do not know if Joan ate her fish, but we do know that she kept her promise and rode back across the bridge. The victory was celebrated in the cathedral with the Te Deum, and the church bells pealed. Joan had her wounds tended and ate some pieces of bread dipped in wine.

The following day was May 8, the Feast of the Apparition of Saint Michael, and we can guess what were Joan's prayers as she knelt in the cathedral among the officers.

It was the voice of the Archangel that had called to her years before. Orléans was liberated.

The English massed their remaining troops outside the town, and the French advanced slowly from within. The moment for the *coup de grâce* had come. Fastolf was approaching with five thousand relieving troops, but he did not arrive in time, and French superiority was crushing.

Joan was unable to wear her armor because of her wound, and she wore only a light coat of mail. Asked if it would be right to attack on a Sunday, she replied, "We are going to Mass."

Afterward she advised against fighting that day unless the English took the offensive.

"She had a table with a marble top brought to the flower-strewn meadow and called for the priests in their vestments, and with great solemnity they intoned hymns, responses, and pious prayers."

During one of the two Masses somebody appears to have approached Joan anxiously, near the altar, and informed her that the English, who had until then remained quiet and expectant, appeared to be on the move. Without rising or leaving her place, Joan asked in a low voice if the English had their backs or their faces turned toward the French.

She was told that they were retreating.

"God does not wish us to fight them today", she said. "We will catch them another time. Let us thank God."

La Hire and Sire de la Loré placed themselves at the head of one hundred and twenty lancers and followed the English, though without attacking them. It was observed that the English army was retreating toward Meung.

At this moment, a strange figure was seen further away in the field. When it came nearer, the astonished Frenchmen saw that it was a puffing Augustinian who carried on his back a French captain of the name of Le Bourg du Bar. The latter had been taken prisoner in the Battle of the Herrings and kept in captivity close to Talbot's staff until a handsome ransom could be extracted from his relatives. Strangely enough, his prison warder was an Augustinian who appeared more interested in his prisoner's economic worth than in the merits of his soul. When the English commenced their retreat, the captain refused to follow, and the monk was unable to get him onto his feet. With much regret, the monk was about to abandon his valuable prize when the captain hurled himself upon him, heedless of his spiritual dignity, and threatened him with death unless he bore him on his back to the French troops.

The roars of laughter from the French ranks can be imagined when the puffing holy man came nearer with that old fighting man, Captain Le Bourg du Bar, on his back.

Joan did not hear the laughter. She stood in the spring breeze with one hand pressed to her injured shoulder. In the distance was a cloud of dust raised by the retreating enemy, around her swarmed her own people, and for the first time large numbers of children had poured out of the city to roll in the grass and pick flowers. At the slightest gust of wind, the fruit trees shed their white blossoms, and the ground was white as with snow. In Les Tourelles, eager burghers and rapacious soldiers wandered about among the ruins plundering the fallen English and the remaining stores. A dead soldier was thrown over the barricade and fell with a splash into the slow-flowing Loire. The priests, walking softly, were returning to the town, and the soldiers, who had assembled for Mass, had begun to disperse.

Sharp commands were heard in the distance.

Joan remained, her eyes closed in the soft spring sunlight. Over her head the larks were singing, and from the far distance could be heard the bells of small village churches after the great bells of the cathedral had become silent. Nature herself seemed to give a sigh of relief after an intolerably long agony.

In all directions messengers bearing the news of the victory galloped away.

On a warm hillside, the Bastard of Orléans rested, tired and happy.

And proudly the two Marshals of France, who had loyally observed events and conscientiously done their best to prevent or delay victory, entered the town to partake of the banquet that was awaiting them.

The heavy tread of infantry; shy glances of wonder and admiration at the lonely girl.

Her eyes are closed, she leans her head back and takes a deep breath.

Larks trill.

Magnificat anima mea Dominum. . . .

CHAPTER 7

The Legend Is Born

"At the age of eighteen Joan possessed the same military genius as Condé when he was twenty", writes one of her biographers.

Those who were her nearest friends have expressed themselves in a similar way.

The Duke of Alençon says that Joan was very experienced in all things military, whether it was a matter of handling a lance, assembling the army, or of the use of the new weapon of the times—the artillery. Dunois says the same more than once.

It is a fact that many of history's warlike geniuses have been youths, almost boys, and it is only since the art of war has become so highly technical that the average age of military leaders has risen. There is nothing incredible about a girl of eighteen possessing a natural strategic genius. In this connection, we may mention a thing upon which Tolstoy specially insisted. According to him, there have hardly been any generals of genius. When a battle begins, so many imponderable and incalculable factors enter into play that there is no possibility of predicting events. The general "of genius" is, therefore, according to Tolstoy, the general who recognizes these facts, realizes that he can do nothing, keeps calm, and—waits.

But even this explanation does not suffice to preserve the legend of Joan as a great military leader. It has been shown that in any case she never held a command. When she acted, it was always on impulse or by divine guidance, and at such times she placed herself above all human calculations, estimates, and agreements. She wanted to attack the English with a small body of troops intended merely for the protection of a convoy; she placed herself at the head of a rabble of bellicose burghers and assaulted a redoubt; when the commander-in-chief wanted to sound the signal for retreat, she misunderstood a strange episode connected with her own banner, her men followed her, and a decision was reached.

All this is so astounding, so irrational, that it is only because we possess definite documentary evidence that we can believe it at all. True, Dunois always chivalrously recognizes her genius and especially her own importance, but when at the age of fifty-one he was questioned about her contribution at Orléans, where he himself held the supreme command, these were his words:

"Asked if he thought it probable that Joan was sent by God to intervene in military matters rather than that she was impelled by human motives, he replied that he thought she was sent by God and that her military contribution depended on divine rather than on human inspiration."

It could not have been put better.

When victory had been won, and won with the speed and almost precisely in the manner that Joan had foretold, rumor became rife all over the country. Modern research has shown how rapidly and how effectively the King's chancellery worked. An intense propaganda was set in motion, couriers were dispatched, often with letters drafted by the King himself, to various towns to tell the story of the great victory, and of the miracle by which Orléans had been liberated. Other documents too were rapidly circulated, and in French archives we can still find traces of them. Thus Joan's "Letter to the English" was copied and distributed, as were the findings of the Court of Examination in Poitiers, and an anonymous Latin poem in sixteen verses, in which the "white virgin" was described as having been sent by God. The exposition of the theologian Gerson was also widely read.

In the Vatican library is preserved the manuscript of a work printed in 1479 in Poitiers, the *Breviarium historiale*, which purports to describe nothing less than the history of the world from creation until 1428. At the end of the manuscript, a note has been added that reads as follows:

"Since I have been in Rome after finishing this work, among the events which have occurred in the world there is one which is so great, so remarkable and incredible, that I do not believe anything similar has happened since Creation. I must therefore write an addition to my book and say a few words about this event. A maid called Joan has appeared in the Kingdom of France, and this girl has performed deeds which appear more divine than human...."

The countries neighboring France too possess documents that bear witness to the general amazement caused by Joan's appearance, and it is natural that legends grew up rapidly. As a matter of fact, after the liberation of Orléans it is almost impossible to find reports that are not exaggerated, highly colored, or romanticized. The most childish tales were told and believed. In the *Journal d'un bourgeois de Paris*, we read that the author, who after all was a Burgundian himself, had heard how Joan as a small girl was able to summon the birds from the sky and the forest, and they would come to her and be completely tame in her presence. On June 21, 1429, Perceval de Boulainvilliers, counselor and chamberlain of Charles VII, and Sénéchal de Berry, wrote to the Duke Visconti in Milan telling him of sensational happenings connected with Joan's birth. When Joan was born all the people in the neighborhood, for some reason not to be comprehended, were filled with joy, and everyone sought for an explanation. Nobody understood that the reason was that this girl had come into the world. But it was not only men who felt this supernatural joy. Even the roosters, who at this time of the year are generally quiet, began to crow with tremendous inspiration and strength and, flapping their wings, continued thus for two hours.

The jungle growth of legends went on. A contemporary author, whose name we do not know, relates that strange visions and revelations appeared all over the country—fully armed knights were seen in the air, mounted on huge white chargers, and over their heads fluttered a great white streamer that reached from Spain and stretched on toward Brittany where the whole duchy was in revolt. At the castle of Dien, near Talamont, the people saw a horseman with a drawn sword coming out of the sky and charging at the castle with the rapidity of lightning. Everybody believed the castle would be set on fire by lightning, and the people fell on their knees, crying to heaven in their terror, but the horseman repeated three times, "Fear not", and then disappeared.

Then there were, of course, white doves over Joan's head, strange divine phenomena at her birth, etc.

As with nearly all saints, Joan had scarcely appeared before human folly almost submerged her acts in sentimentality and superstition.

When the devil cannot prevent the appearance of a noble and pure soul, he revenges himself by distorting the picture of this soul in the minds of others. That which was simple obedience becomes sentimentality and unctuousness. That which was bitter sacrifice and pain becomes magic and mystery. Around that which was health and strength, simple-hearted willingness to listen and obey, is spread a miasma of lies and false mysticism. In the end, the real picture vanishes so completely that it cannot be rediscovered except by an experienced historian.

The truth about Joan of Arc is sufficiently brilliant and astounding. Apart from the external events which I have touched upon, Joan's personality has a purity, a light, an absence of pride and self-sufficiency, which is very rare, and is usually found only in people who have had a whole lifetime of chastening through suffering and sacrifice. But this is not enough. The mendacious propaganda and the sentimentalizing attain such dimensions that they finally become a danger not only to her mission, since they give a false picture of what she is and what she stands for, but even to her life. Joan is condemned to death and shortly after executed as a witch. Why? Because her judges honestly believed that she was a witch sent by the devil. And the evidence on which this belief was based was found, almost entirely, not in the true facts but in the sentimental myths that had been created round her person.

This fact, to which I shall return later in greater detail, should be brought home to all the sentimental, pious Christians who cannot come into contact with a saint without dragging her down to their own spiritual level. This kind of meddling officiousness is always distasteful and morally depressing, but in this case a saint had to pay the price herself— with her death.

When one reads foreign observers and chroniclers such as Morosini and Windecke, one finds a whole flora of sentimental fabrications.

A priest during Communion is said to have presented two hosts, one consecrated and one unconsecrated, and Joan had immediately recognized the former.

Joan's daily food was said to consist of less than one ounce of bread.

She had liberated city after city without an armed force.

The Bishop of Clermont had refused to deliver the crown of Saint Louis to the King, whereupon Joan had written to the burghers of Clermont threatening disaster, but in spite of this the crown was not surrendered. So a terrible hailstorm began, which so alarmed the bishop that he burst into tears and repented deeply.

When the royal army had devastated the vineyards near Reims, the vines had, after the King's coronation, burst into fresh buds.

On one occasion, Joan had ridden up to a soldier and revealed that the soldier was a disguised woman who was pregnant, and that she had earlier murdered another child of hers.

On one occasion during a meal with the King, Joan had broken into loud laughter. In reply to a surprised question, she said that she could not help laughing because at that moment five hundred English soldiers on the way to France had drowned. This was, of course, verified three days later.

A white dove bearing a gold crown had descended on Joan's banner.

All these stories were harmless enough when told in those parts of France that were loyal to the King's cause. The English listened just as eagerly, but gave the rumors quite a different interpretation. The Duke of Bedford himself gave his opinion on the matter. In a report about the death of Salisbury, "caused by the curses of a diabolical woman", he refers to a "disciple and bloodhound of the devil, called la Pucelle", who occupied herself with magic and curses and in this way caused the death of English Christian knights. In a letter to Charles VII, he speaks of Joan as a satanic and shameless heretic. There exists also a document indicating that special measures had to be taken to check the English soldiers' fear of this witch, for quite a number of English soldiers had deserted and fled back to England and did not dare to take the field again.

There is a celebrated episode when a citizen of Toulouse suggested to the town council that Joan should be consulted as to which currency the town should adopt.

The Count of Armagnac wrote to Joan and begged her kindly to inform him by return which of the Popes who now warred against each other was the true one.

Hundreds of such examples could be quoted. They show that in a very short time Joan's real personality had disappeared in a cloud of misunderstandings and falsifications.

Modern research has not by a long way yet cleared up this jungle.

"If Messire Did Not Protect Me"

According to the traditional picture of the period following these events, Joan received sole credit for the liberation of Orléans. The delighted King gave her the command of his army. At Joan's orders, a campaign was undertaken that mopped up the remaining English garrisons in the Loire, whereupon, faithful to her revelations, she advanced on Reims to crown the King.

In all the literature about her, we find statements like "Joan took the command", "Joan realized that the Loire district must first be cleared of the enemy", "Nobody could now challenge Joan's right to the supreme command."

The truth is probably quite different.

We know that Joan had received clear orders that after the freeing of Orléans she should lead the King to Reims to be crowned. This and nothing else was her aim, and she adhered to it. It was the King's advisers who took the decision—obviously the right one from a military point of view—that the Loire district must first be cleaned up. For it was known that the English under Fastolf were advancing from Paris to join the remnants of the army that had besieged Orléans. Quick action was therefore needed. There seems to be little foundation for the traditional belief in the slackness, cowardice, and passive attitude of the King's commanders. Just as the liberation of Orléans was prepared and carried out with skill, so also was this new task.

An important document for this period of Joan's life is a letter written to their mother by Gui and André de Laval. They are burning with eagerness to take part in the continuation of the war and beg their mother to pawn their possessions to help the King finance it. The letter includes a vivid picture of Joan herself.

Selles-en-Berry was to be the starting-point of the new campaign. When the two young de Laval brothers appeared there, one of them visited Joan in her quarters, where she offered him wine and said jokingly that she hoped next time to offer him a glass in Paris. The young man also saw her setting off in the company of Marshal de Boussac and some others, and he described the scene to his mother with all the enthusiasm of a modern newspaper-man.

> I saw her mount her charger wearing a complete suit of white armor but with her head bare and carrying a little battle-axe in her hand. The horse, a big black charger, was very fresh and made it difficult for her to mount. She said, "Lead him to the cross", which was close to the church, beside the road. Then, when she mounted, the horse stood still as if he had been tethered. She then turned to the church door, which was quite close, and said in her clear, girlish voice, "You priests and you people, go in procession and pray to God." Turning in the saddle, she called out, "Forward! Forward!" A page bore her furled banner.

The King showed her great gratitude and kindness. We possess an account of how she gracefully bowed her head from the saddle to greet him at their first meeting. However, she did not greatly appreciate his long conferences. Once when the King sat in council, Joan knocked on the door and entered. With the King were Gérard Machet, the King's confessor, Christophe d'Harcourt, the Bastard of Orléans, Sire de Trèves, and perhaps someone else. Embracing the King's knees, in accordance with the custom, Joan said, "*Gentil Dauphin*, do not gather together so many people, and do not hold such long councils! Instead set out at once for Reims and let yourself be crowned!"

Christophe d'Harcourt gazed attentively at the girl. Was it true that she had revelations? He used the opportunity to ask her if it was her "voices" that made her say such things to the King.

She said "Yes", and added, "they have urged me much lately."

Christophe d'Harcourt asked her if, in the presence of the King, she would not tell them about her "voices".

The King saw that she hesitated and asked gently if she perhaps did not like to speak about such things before strangers.

Joan gave an explanation that one can only read with great reverence. She had never before to such a degree revealed her secret. "When in some way I feel sad because I am not easily believed regarding what Messire has said to me, I go away and lay the matter before Messire and express regret to him that those to whom I talk do not immediately believe me. And when I have ended my prayer I hear a voice which says: '*Fille de Dieu, va*', and when I hear the voice I feel great happiness. And I wish I could hear it always."

These words speak for themselves. No young mystic could describe her meeting with the supernatural more simply. God's formula, "*Fille de Dieu, va*", is sublimely simple, and it is touching that she feels it hard to leave the state of ecstasy and joy she attains at such moments.

Those who are familiar with the lives of the saints will recognize the situation.

The writer adds that when she uttered those words she had a luminous look and there were tears in her eyes. Anatole France, who reports the episode, comments drily, "It was no ecstasy but an imitation of one." This is not so certain. What he regards as "a scene combining artifice and naïvete" is more probably something spontaneous. Joan did not display the phenomena which in many cases, though certainly not in all, accompany mystical experiences. The word "ecstasy" is also disputable, but there can be no real doubt that we have here a case of genuine contact with the supernatural.

She was not immune to temptation. We remember how she once spoke of the possibility that she might feel temptation among the handsome young knights who surrounded her; another incident shows that she realized the danger of temptation of a different kind. Simple people paid her homage, even worshipped her, and kissed her hands and feet. A member of the committee that examined her in Poitiers, Pierre de Versailles, observed this and said to her: "You are wrong to permit that kind of behavior. Be careful, for you lead people into idolatry."

A person less honest than Joan would have protested, but Joan was as humble and clear-sighted concerning the temptations of pride as she was concerning those of the flesh. "Yes," she replied, "I should never be able to save myself but for Messire."

It is small traits such as these that display Joan's real secret. Few have had such a sharp light focused upon their whole life as Joan had, few have been examined by such pitiless judges, and yet nothing in her life shows a trace of impurity or arrogance. With sublime simplicity, she moves in a proud, intriguing, and mendacious world impersonally, one might almost say anonymously. She is the "instrument". She obeys and listens, and God speaks through her. The history of the Church can show a venerable gallery of devout men and women, and the Church has acquired a profound knowledge regarding temptations of all kinds to which even these chosen ones are exposed. Joan was one of the very few who are not required to take the long road toward perfection. Her inner struggle took place mainly between the age of thirteen and seventeen, after which she was purified. Because of this, everything she does appears in the eyes of men to possess a strength beyond human understanding. It is for this reason that God cut short her triumph and reserved her for the greatest of all tasks—to be united with Christ in his own suffering, to become a martyr.

On another occasion Jean d'Aulon put a similar question to her. Could she not show him this secret council of which she speaks? She replied, "You are not worthy or pure enough to have such a vision."

She was not so naïve that she did not recognize the price she had to pay. In Rouen, faced with death, she complained touchingly because her pure body, which had never been defiled, had now to be burned.

132

She also, without any arrogance, recognized her spiritual power. "I know that I can help people a little", she said to her confessor on one occasion—we may well believe softly, almost shyly.

The confessor answered with astonishment, "But one has never seen the like of what happens in your life! There exists no book containing its like."

In her inimitable way, Joan said to him, "Messire has a book no priest has ever seen, however *parfait en cléricature* he may be."

A proud reply that expresses beautifully the certain faith in her young soul.

Patay

The military situation in the Loire district is easily described.

The English held the town of Jargeau, twelve miles to the east of Orléans, where the commandant was Lord Suffolk. They also held the town of Meung twelve miles to the west, and the town of Beaugency a further six miles to the west.

Immediately after the raising of the siege of Orléans, the Bastard of Orléans made an attack on Jargeau, which, owing to bad preparation, was repulsed. The French army consisted of eight to ten thousand men. Fastolf's force of five thousand was forty miles to the north and advancing southward.

On June 11, when the French again stood before Jargeau, news came that Fastolf was approaching. The French commanders were almost in a panic, unable to decide whether they should continue the siege or turn against Fastolf. The Duke of Alençon relates that Joan intervened with her customary resolution. She saw the anxiety of the generals and assured them that they had nothing to fear as God was on the side of the French. There is a story, which may perhaps be true, that one of the generals objected and begged her to stick to practical facts, to which she answered that she would much rather look after sheep than give such advice without being certain of God's help. The battle was resumed with Joan's white banner as usual in the van, though she did not herself take an active part in the fighting. At Rouen she insisted that she had never killed an enemy.

During the battle, we hear the voice of Joan: "*Avant, gentil duc, à l'assaut!*" (Forward, gentle duke, to the assault!)

Somebody thought that it was too soon to launch the attack, but Joan replied, "Fear not. It is always the right time when God decides", and added a simple maxim: "Act, and God will act!"

Then she said with a smile to the Duke of Alençon, "Didn't you know that I promised your wife to bring you back safe and sound?"

In the same account occurs an anecdote that indicates Joan's contempt for her own safety and concern for that of her friends. Noticing that the spot where she stood was under fire, she begged the Duke to move away from her. Almost immediately afterward a soldier dropped dead at the very spot where the Duke had been standing.

During the attack, Lord Suffolk called out that he wished to confer with the Duke of Alençon, but no attention was paid to this. During the fighting, Joan was thrown to the ground when a cannon ball struck her helmet. She rose immediately, crying, "*Amis, amis: sus, sus!* God has doomed the English. We have them beaten! Courage!"

The town was captured, and Lord Suffolk surrendered, according to later reports, to Joan in person. Nearly all prisoners were killed, and it was only with difficulty that the richer and more important captives were rescued and placed on barges.

Joan was unable to prevent the massacre.

Jargeau was taken after twenty-four hours' fighting, and the victorious army marched back to Orléans. Homage was paid to Joan, a Te Deum was sung in the cathedral, and there were great festivities in the town.

Two days later, the French army began the siege of Beaugency, during which a curious episode occurred. A new army appeared in the distance and was at first believed to be the advance guard of Fastolf. However, it proved to be a Breton force of six hundred lancers and four hundred infantry, under the command of no less a person than the High Constable of France, Arthur de Bretagne, Sire de Richemont.

As has been mentioned earlier, this eminent noble had been driven from court by the King's new favorite, La Trémoille. The whole winter he had carried on a personal campaign against the troops of La Trémoille, but he now came to join the French army against the King's express orders. The reason for this was, of course, the reports concerning Joan of Arc and her victories. He was accompanied by a number of the leading nobles of Brittany.

The High Constable was a small, ugly, limping man with a weather-beaten face and protruding underlip and was called by Charles d'Orléans, "*Ma vieille lippe*".

The Duke of Alençon had received orders from the King under no circumstances to accept help from the High Constable. To prevent a meeting between the King and the High Constable, La Trémoille had at that very time invited the King to be his guest at his castle of Sully on the Loire, but he had not reckoned with Joan of Arc. Faced with this new problem, the Duke of Alençon evidently lost his head and threatened to raise the siege—a strange decision indeed when before him he had a commander offering help and in his rear a large English army advancing under Fastolf. When two Breton nobles, the Seigneur de Rostrenen and Le Bourgeois, rode up to the Duke to request night quarters for the Breton army, the Duke replied that if the army came any nearer he would fight. Even Joan seems at first to have believed that it would be necessary to fight the Bretons, and among her own troops there were protests showing that there were those in the French army who would rather fight for the High Constable than for "all the virgins in France".

Everything suggests that an armed clash would have been unavoidable had not Fastolf's army at that moment arrived on the scene. Before this new threat, Joan was able to reconcile the Duke and the High Constable. "We must stand together" were the words she used according to one witness.[1]

One account states that the High Constable met Joan and the French commanders, the Duke of Alençon, the Bastard, Monsieur de Laval, and Monseigneur de Lohéac, at a place called La Maladrerie. Here, Joan dismounted, as did the High Constable. She greeted him with deep respect, and he said to her, "Joan, I have been informed that you will fight with me. If you are of God, I have no fear, because God knows my good intention, and if you are of the devil, I fear you even less."

Joan then seems to have obtained the solemn promise of the High Constable to be faithful to the King, and a document was drawn up confirming this.

Now that the two armies had been united they could face together the army advancing under Fastolf and Talbot.

---

[1] *Quod opus erat se juvare.*

The English had held a council of war in Janville, at which the two commanders disagreed violently. Fastolf was cautious and favored the establishment of a new line of defense by occupying fortresses and towns where possible, instead of trying to relieve the English garrison in Beaugency. Talbot disagreed and said his intention was to take the offensive, whereupon Fastolf, realizing that he could not influence his fellow commander, left the room in anger. The next morning the English army began to advance in battle order.

On the French side, Joan counseled immediate attack, but as usual was met by faint-hearted objections, to which she replied, "But I suppose you have good spurs!"

The Duke of Alençon apparently understood this to imply a retreat, and asked her if that was really her intention. "*Nenni*", she replied with a smile, adding that the spurs would be needed for pursuing the fleeing English.

Three English knights rode up to the French lines and challenged three French knights to single combat, but were answered by Joan or her men, "You go back and sleep, since it is late. Tomorrow we will have a closer look at you."

The next morning the two armies deployed for battle and watched each other threateningly, but there was no fighting. When the garrison of the town saw that Fastolf and Talbot were retreating, they lost courage and surrendered the town on condition that they were allowed to retreat unmolested. This impressed Fastolf so strongly that he ordered the army to retreat immediately to Paris—an order that was eagerly obeyed. The French followed in the wake of the English army, and Joan was angered when she was refused permission to command the advance guard—a privilege given to La Hire. Instead, she followed behind La Hire's horsemen with the rest of the army.

Another remark of Joan's has been preserved for posterity. It seems to have deeply impressed the Duke of Alençon, who stated in his testimony during the Trial of Rehabilitation: "Many of the King's men were afraid ... but Joan said, 'In the name of God, we must fight them; and if they hung on to the clouds, we will still get them!'" (*En nom Dieu, il les fault combatre; s'ils estoient pendus aux nues, nous les aurons!*) She added that she was sure of victory.

La Hire's force advanced rapidly toward the English, whose shouts when they drew a deer from cover in the forest told the French that they were in touch with the retreating enemy. When Fastolf was informed of the nearness of the French advance guard, he ordered his rearguard to make a stand. The dreaded English archers immediately set about driving their lances into the ground and joining them together by means of chains, but before they had completed these preparations, La Hire made one of the many famous cavalry charges of French history, overcoming all resistance before a single arrow could be shot.

Fastolf's main army was now approaching, but the commander of the English rearguard seems to have believed that Fastolf was retreating before the French army under the Duke of Alençon, and he thought that all was lost.

Fastolf fled, and his troops hardly offered any resistance. Two thousand Englishmen were cut down with scarcely any loss to the French. Sir John Talbot galloped off, but La Hire and Poton soon caught up with him and took him prisoner, he bitterly cursing "the fortune of war".

Fastolf continued his flight. At nightfall, he galloped into Étampes and the following day reached Corbeil. The Duke of Bedford, infuriated by his cowardice, tore off his Order of the Garter. Talbot never forgave him.

The whole English army had been crushed by the French at very small loss.

A Maid and a Wounded Enemy

Cordier claims that the real victor in the Battle of Patay was the commander of the French cavalry, La Hire, and that Joan is hardly mentioned in trustworthy records. This may be true, but on the other hand, this astonishing success is inconceivable without the previous contributions made by the presence of Joan.

We possess one recorded incident about her, however, which is worth serious attention. Cordier says casually that she saved an English prisoner of war who was being ill-treated by a French soldier, but the incident does not seem to us so insignificant.

When Joan appeared, the usual butchering of unremunerative English prisoners was going on. She saw a Frenchman who was guarding a column of prisoners strike an Englishman with such violence that he fell to the ground as if dead. Joan swung herself out of her saddle and ran up to the dying man. She was able to find a priest, and the Englishman confessed. During his confession, she held his head on her knee and tried to ease his pain.

The great cynic, Anatole France, who, however, was able to recognize intuitively that which is human and of genuine worth, says of this episode, "That was her part in the Battle of Patay. It is that of a Holy Maid.'"

The incident is not only beautiful, like a medieval illumination on an old blood-stained manuscript, but it carries our thoughts back to another scene—to Joan's great predecessor, Catherine of Siena, who refused to leave an Italian youth condemned to death until he had been reconciled with God.

Through the bloody chaos of history runs an unbroken line of sacrifices and acts of love, often unrecognized. It begins with Christ weeping like an ordinary man over the suffering of his friends and awakening the dead, though he himself is later to give his own life for mankind. It continues through the martyrs, century after century, even up to today, in, for example, the martyred Russian and Polish churches. In this noble company, there is a striking proportion of young women.

Already as a young girl, Joan had been fascinated by the attitude with which Saint Catherine and Saint Margaret confronted the brutality of the world. At Patay she does not share in the intoxication of joy over the victory, but from her charger looks with compassion on her enemies. This is the same woman who a little while before cried out that even if the English were to flee as far as the clouds she would catch up with them. The thief on the cross in a flash of insight discovered who the man was who was being tortured at his side, and a single generous emotion in his darkened soul sufficed for the Savior to promise him Paradise. The unknown English soldier who had seen around him only brutal and irreconcilable enemies did not know that he rested in the pure arms of a young saint.

The picture is one of eternal beauty. The modern historian regards it with indifference and records that Joan played no great part in the Battle of Patay. When one day there is an end to killing and the hour of the Final Judgment approaches, the true direction of the main highway of Western history will be made clear. It can usually not be perceived by human eyes. Its acts of heroism are unrecognized, hidden in quiet convents and monasteries, in lonely cells, in the silent performance of duty, in lifelong unnoticed acts of sacrifice. But occasionally the laws of history permit us to see this highway in its sublime beauty.

A maid kneeling at the roadside while around her echo the whinny of horses and the shrieks of the murdered.

She presses the head of an unknown, dying enemy to her breast and prays for his soul.

CHAPTER 8

Waiting at the Loire

The military situation in France was radically changed by the Battle of Patay.

For decades the English had been invincible, and there were few who believed that Charles VII would be able to hold out indefinitely, still less to drive the enemy out of the country.

The attitude of the High Constable is significant. It is true that he did not obtain quite the reception he hoped for and was turned away, but he showed plainly that he knew which side would be victorious.

In Burgundy, the Battle of Patay made an even greater impression. Philip the Good had performed his tight-rope act with great skill, but he now began to suspect that he had been too cunning.

It would have been reasonable for the French army to march on Paris now, which overwhelmingly supported Burgundy. The Duke of Bedford, who had his headquarters there, expected an immediate attack and moved out to Vincennes. Rumors spread over the whole country that Paris had fallen, but the Parisians began eagerly to fortify their city, to dig trenches, strengthen the ramparts, and place artillery in position.

But a strange thing happened. The French army showed no inclination to take advantage of its tremendous success, and the historical problem this presents is still hotly disputed. The old view—that Joan alone represented initiative and courage in the King's headquarters and that otherwise he was surrounded by cowardly and irresolute men—has now been abandoned. There is nothing to support this belief. On the contrary, as we have shown, the King's commanders acted with great resolution and never missed an opportunity, in spite of the great difficulties, particularly of an economic nature, under which they had to act. After this victory at Patay, there followed a period of inactivity, and we may be sure that there were good reasons for this.

The Duke of Alençon pursued the fleeing English to Janville, whose English garrison capitulated; whereupon he returned to Orléans, from whence the troops for the Loire campaign had set out a week earlier. The King himself was visiting his favorite, La Trémoille, at his castle at Sully, which rests like a clenched fist on the slowly flowing Loire. The inhabitants of Orléans were not pleased at the King's absence and grumbled loudly.

After a few days of feasting in Orléans, the commanders made their way south to consult with the King. The records do not make clear what happened. One of the problems was what attitude should be adopted toward the High Constable, that great soldier who with his Breton army had played no unimportant part in the recent fighting. "The King ordered the Lord High Constable to return home...."

But the High Constable humbled himself enough to beg his enemy, La Trémoille, to intercede for him with the King. Joan, who had earlier assisted in the reconciliation between the High Constable and the Duke of Alençon at Beaugency, now made a fresh attempt to soften the King. The King granted her request and declared that he forgave the High Constable, but out of regard for La Trémoille he could not permit him to accompany the new expedition that was being prepared.

Charles VII could have reached Paris in two days without meeting with any resistance, and the city would certainly have quickly surrendered, but he did not do so and only appeared before Paris eleven weeks later. All records agree that instead the King wished to march to Reims to be crowned.

It is self-evident that this was connected with Joan's insistence that she had been sent by God above all to free Orléans and to crown the King in Reims. There are historians who have eagerly and indignantly blamed her for this and insisted that it would have been wiser first to conquer Paris. It is, however, clear that Joan needed no other motive than her revelations. She can certainly never have weighed the arguments for and against in a realistic manner. The voice of God had told her what to do, and she acted accordingly. It would have been completely foreign to her to consider whether or not the occupation of Paris would have been, from a moral and psychological point of view, of greater value to the King than his coronation in Reims. Such calculations, however, must have occupied the minds of her advisers. It was they who had the final say, and when without great hesitation they decided to agree to Joan's proposals they must have had good reason. One can certainly not reject completely Anatole France's view that Archbishop Regnault of

Reims, the King's counselor, was anxious to return to his see with its rich emoluments.

Politically, the most important person in the King's entourage was certainly La Trémoille. It seems that at an earlier stage he had not been greatly in favor of Joan, though he refrained from openly opposing her. Now, however, he sides with her and decides, clearly against the advice of the highest military authorities, for a march on Reims and the crowning of the King instead of exploiting the recent military successes.

One asks why.

La Trémoille, whom Anatole France describes as a "barrel, a wine sack, a kind of Gargantua who would devour the whole country", is worthy of a chapter to himself. He was about forty[1] and enormously fat. He owed his life to his corpulence, for once, when an attempt was made to assassinate him, the dagger, though thrust with great strength, could not penetrate through the layers of fat to any vital organ. He had originally served the Duke of Burgundy and never relinquished his great aim of bringing about a peaceful understanding with Burgundy. After becoming *grand-maître des eaux et forêts*, he was guilty of such scandalous transactions that the matter was raised in parliament. He was continually occupied with financial schemes and loans; he lent the King and the Crown his own money, at a very profitable rate one may be certain. While in Paris, he barely escaped being killed by the populace, who were infuriated because of his immoral life and gluttony. He had been the lover of Queen Isabeau and thoroughly approved of her way of life. He fell in love with Catherine de Clermont-Tonnerre, then married to Sire de Giac, a favorite of the Dauphin. De Giac was arrested in bed, tried, and sentenced to death by drowning. He then requested a strange favor—that before being thrown into the water his right hand should be cut off, as he said that he had sold it to the devil. La Trémoille witnessed the drowning of his rival with much pleasure. As for his own wife, Jeanne de Bretagne, he placed her on such short commons that she wasted away and died.

La Trémoille had for long been a friend of the High Constable; it was the latter who originally advised the King to place the direction of his affairs in the hands of La Trémoille. The High Constable was

---

[1] In 1429 Joan was seventeen, the Bastard of Orléans twenty-six, and the Duke of Alençon twenty.

also involved in the murder of Sire de Giac. The friendship, however, turned into enmity. Immediately before the appearance of Joan, the High Constable had been waging a private war against the King and had devastated, among other places, the personal domains of La Trémoille in Poitou. This was the reason why La Trémoille advised the King to reject the High Constable's advances.

What lay behind La Trémoille's decision to march on Reims instead of on Paris?

The older historians arrived at a definite opinion, which is concisely expressed in, for instance, the book of Père Petitot. La Trémoille was a ruthless climber and egotist and cared nothing for the welfare of the State so long as he could gain wealth, and now, purposely, he endeavored to cross all Joan's plans. He sent away the High Constable with his thousand men and treated in a similar way a number of other Frenchmen who desired to be reconciled to the King. Petitot goes so far as to accuse him of having used all his powers to break up the army the generals had assembled. He depicts him as an intriguer and scoundrel, as the King's "evil spirit".

One is very puzzled after reading a number of works containing similar judgments on him and comparing them with the policy he actually pursued. Many authors consider his connection with the Duke of Burgundy to be the most weighty evidence of his treachery, but it is difficult to understand why his attempt to bring about more normal relations between the King and the Duke of Burgundy should be regarded as a treacherous policy. It is, further, quite unreasonable to suggest that in this matter La Trémoille was opposed to Joan, for she had never shown herself disinclined to a peaceful solution; on the contrary, and this applies to both the English and the Burgundians, she always tried to settle every conflict without recourse to arms.

It is impossible for us to know how La Trémoille regarded the propaganda value of the King's coronation, but he had other reasons for supporting the idea strongly. The most important was that he could make use of the coronation in support of the policy to which he so strongly adhered—to further the cause of peace with the Duke of Burgundy. He preferred to exploit by diplomatic means the military successes that had been gained. If, instead of fighting the English and Burgundians, the King had himself crowned in Reims, and at the same time appealed to the Burgundians for collaboration and support, the French cause would at once be enormously strengthened. To keep Paris occupied would be a heavy burden unless the hostility of the Parisians could be overcome by a reconciliation with Burgundy. This political line of thought seems a very sound one, and there is no reason to doubt that it had the full approval of Joan too.

But Joan was tortured by inactivity. A little vignette is preserved from those days that gives a clear and touching picture of her.

Not far west from Sully on the Loire is a famous monastery, Saint-Benoît-sur-Loire (earlier called Fleury), with a great white Romanesque church. It was to this church that the relics of Saint Benedict, the great pioneer of monasticism in Europe, were brought from Monte Cassino when it was plundered by the Lombards. These relics are still preserved in the crypt of the church. About the year 1000, the famous Abbo, leader of the school of Fleury, which played such an important part in the development of French culture, worked here. One writer says that there were at least five thousand students in his school. During the time of Joan, here as well as elsewhere in the country, monastic discipline had relaxed, and the spiritual life had lost something of its honesty and depth, but Mass was said under the beautiful white arches as it had been in earlier centuries and as it still is in our day.

Joan came riding through the silent landscape where the Loire moves forward so quietly that the eye can hardly discern a ripple of movement in the water. High above the group of gray buildings rises the tower of the basilica. Endless cornfields, cultivated ground, and orchards extend as far as the eye can reach, and tiny, insignificant dwellings cluster tight around the great basilica, God's house. The sun shines in broad beams over the wide scene. The wind sighs in the treetops.

The King saw that Joan was crying and said awkwardly that now she deserved a little rest. That is all we know about this episode. But we can guess at the sorrow of the Maid over these endless delays, her sadness because her faith—so self-evident to her—was not shared by the King and his counselors, and because there were discussions and compromises instead of the action God had commanded. Possibly, too, she felt homesick. Perhaps she was merely overwhelmed for a moment by a longing to escape from a task that was proving so difficult to carry through.

In any case this picture of the weeping girl on horseback outside the white monastery church remains engraved on one's memory, appealing and accusing.

On June 24, the army, under the Duke of Alençon, Joan's most faithful friend, left Orléans and marched to Gien, another small town on the Loire not far from Sully, where they were to be joined by other parts of the army. From here, proclamations concerning the impending coronation in Reims were dispatched to different parts of the country. In the proclamation to the burghers of Tournai, it said:

Jesus and Mary.

Noble and loyal Frenchmen of Tournai, the Maid salutes you through this proclamation and lets it be known that she has in eight days, by means of attacks and in other ways, thrown the English out of all the places they held on the banks of the Loire. Continue as good and loyal Frenchmen, I beg of you; I beg and exhort you to be prepared to present yourselves at the coronation of the noble King Charles in Reims, where we shall soon be found. . . .

Whatever credit we may give to those scholars who hold that Joan did not participate in purely technical questions of a military and political nature, we cannot deny the fact that it was she and no one else who wrote this proclamation in her own name, though, of course, it must have been written with the full approval of La Trémoille.

The same must be the case with a letter she addressed to the Duke of Burgundy, which has not been preserved. From this we see that from the very beginning Duke Philip the Good was invited to take part in the coronation. But he did not do so.

Even the few days at Gien have given us a little indication of Joan's impatience. Perceval de Cagny, citing the Duke of Alençon, relates that Joan became so tired of waiting that she departed suddenly with a small body of men two days before the King and the main army set out. The few words he uses give us very much the same picture that we have seen before: "In her irritation, she rode off and camped in a field two days before the King set out."

On June 30, the army stood before Auxerre, which Joan had visited during her first ride. The town of Saint-Germain, with its two mighty churches, had been under the Crown since 1371, but had recently been conveyed by the Duke of Bedford to his ally Philip the Good. Like a number of other smaller towns, Auxerre did not feel very warmly toward Charles VII, as soon became apparent. "The town of Auxerre did not entirely surrender for they came before the King and begged him to march past; they implored him to be spared war."

According to a rather unreliable report, Auxerre had bribed La Trémoille with two thousand *écus d'or* so as to be spared from siege and bloodshed.

In fact the King and La Trémoille acted realistically. They knew that a siege would take time, and that not only Auxerre, but also other towns that sympathized with Burgundy, such as Troyes and Châlons, would espouse the King's cause automatically as soon as an understanding was reached with the Duke of Burgundy. They therefore decided to advance quietly on Troyes.

This town cannot have had pleasant associations for the King, for it was here that his mother, the vicious Queen Isabeau, had fled from Paris. Here too he had signed the treaty by which he formally gave up his right to the French throne, and here the marriage between Henry V and Catherine of France had been arranged.

The burghers of Troyes hastily sent a message to Reims to say that the enemy, that is the King's troops, were approaching and that they would be loyal until death to the King of England and the Duke of Burgundy. They stated that they had confirmed their resolution by swearing an oath on Christ's holy Body. Very naturally they were counting on English military aid.

Already from Brienon-l'Archevêque, the King had addressed a letter to Troyes ordering the town to open its gates and declare their loyalty to him. At the same time, Joan, no doubt with the approval of La Trémoille, wrote a passionate letter in her personal style ordering the town in God's name to surrender to "the noble King of France, who will soon be in Reims and Paris no matter who attempts to prevent him".

If they refused, the Maid assured them that the King's army would find its way into the town in spite of all defiance. "I recommend you to God, God protect you, if he will. Reply briefly...."

The burghers of the town were in a dilemma and replied to the King that they had sworn fealty to the King of England and the Duke of Burgundy and that they were in any case powerless as there was a strong garrison in the town. Joan's letter, however, had greatly disturbed them. Like everyone else they had heard rumors of her magic and incantations. They therefore refused to acknowledge her letter and cast it into the fire, referring to her as "a madwoman" and "full of the devil". At the same time, a messenger was dispatched to Reims with a request for immediate reinforcements.

In Troyes at this time was a man who in the future was to have a certain importance for Joan and her faith. This was the preaching monk, Richard, a pupil of the great Saint Vincent Ferrer. Nothing gives one a clearer picture of how God's chosen were regarded at that time than the accounts of the works of this Spanish saint, with which Joan must have been familiar. He has been called "the greatest miracle-worker in Christendom", and the stories concerning him are so fantastic and yet so well authenticated that scarcely any historian has dared to undertake the task of reducing the material to reasonable proportions.

When before his death he was asked how many miracles he had performed, he replied calmly, "Nearly three thousand." He was said to have resurrected more than thirty people from the dead. One writer said that he performed miracles as easily as we raise a hand. Not even in the time of the apostles has any discharge of supernatural forces been seen comparable with the works of Saint Vincent Ferrer. In no place where this giant set his foot could the Reformation make any headway. When only a student in Barcelona—he was of English extraction—he was already looked upon as a saint. Once, when a mason had slipped from the scaffolding of a building and called out for help, he answered: "Just wait a moment while I ask permission." He then went to the Prior, received permission to intervene, and returned to the mason, who was still floating in the air and only sank slowly to the ground when ordered to do so by Vincent. In 1367 he became a Dominican. His fame grew and spread throughout Christendom. He could make himself invisible. The Queen of Spain always knelt when speaking to him. He could read men's souls as if they were an open book. At international congresses he spoke his own language, but everybody easily understood what he said whether they were Bretons, Flemings, Lombards, Englishmen, or Frenchmen. There is such a wealth of evidence concerning him that one enthusiastic biographer has maintained that the phenomena are as well authenticated as the conquest of Constantinople or the Peace Treaty of Versailles.

It is in this morbid atmosphere, in which truth and falsehood can no longer be distinguished, that Joan appeared. Magic was the highest sign of spirituality that those times could imagine, a fact that explains why Vincent Ferrer had so many followers. He made church bells peal for three hours without being touched by human hand. He caused figs to burst into ripeness on a bare tree. He read the future without any difficulty. One day he encountered a man being led to execution. Was he guilty or not? At that moment the body of a dead man was being carried past, whereupon he turned to the corpse and said, "Is this man innocent?" The corpse sat up and replied, "Yes. He is innocent", and then lay down quietly again. When Vincent preached, demons were heard shrieking around him. He declared openly that he was the angel of the Apocalypse. When people refused to believe this, he turned to a dead man who was being carried past. The dead man raised himself in his coffin and said in a loud and distinct voice, "Yes, this holy man is what he says he is, the angel who shall announce the final judgment for all." In a letter to the Pope, Benedict XIII, Vincent compared himself to Moses and John the Baptist. When he died and was buried in Vannes in 1419, two dead men who lay by his side came to life and stood up. It was believed that it was only because of the intervention of Vincent Ferrer that the final judgment was postponed.

This fantastic personality, with his unbelievable hypnotic power, had a number of pupils who imitated to the best of their ability his apocalyptic visions and miracles. One of these was Brother Richard, who had made a pilgrimage to Jerusalem, and who preached during Advent in Troyes in 1428. He predicted that the Last Hour would soon come and exhorted people to penance and better living. He appeared in Paris in April of the same year, and for a fortnight preached out of doors every day from five to eleven o'clock. People would gather in thousands to hear him speak of the impending arrival of the Antichrist. He related that he had seen the Jews in Syria streaming toward Babylon because they knew that the true Messiah had been born who would restore their country to them. This Messiah must be the Antichrist of whom it had been said that he should be born in Babylon, grow up at Bethsaida, and afterward appear in Chorazin. It was with him in mind that Jesus had said, "Woe unto thee, Chorazin, Woe unto thee, Bethsaida."

According to this monk, the year 1430 would be decisive. Huge crowds were terrified by his preaching and burned or threw away their dice and balls, musical instruments, and precious clothes. Everywhere in Paris great bonfires burned in the streets. Brother Richard also thundered against the magical use of mandrakes and distributed instead small medallions bearing the name of Christ.

He gave out an announcement on May 1 that he would preach on Montmartre at the very spot where Saint Denis had suffered martyrdom. Early in the morning thousands were gathered on the hill, but no preacher appeared. It may be that he was prevented by the authorities—according to some reports the Duke of Burgundy in person had driven him away.

He then fled to Auxerre, where he continued his activities. When the Maid approached the town, he advanced toward her to ward off the danger and was about to sprinkle holy water on her when she said with a smile, "Come nearer. I shall not fly away."

She understood that he thought she was a witch and calmly awaited what she knew was coming to her.

The strange thing is that the fanatic immediately became convinced, and from that moment never doubted that Joan had been sent by God. According to one report, he undertook to deliver Joan's letter to the authorities, who, as we know, still adhered to Brother Richard's earlier opinion that Joan was a witch sent by the devil.

The King's counselors now conferred as to what should be done. Was it safe to leave this relatively strong place unconquered in the rear, or would it be better to risk an assault? According to one report, Joan intervened as usual.

Entering the chamber where the Council of War was being held, she uttered the following words, "*Noble Dauphin*, give orders to your army to besiege Troyes immediately, and do not linger longer over this council table. In God's name, I promise that in three days I shall lead you into Troyes—*through love or through battle and violence so that false Burgundy shall be astounded.*"

From the same source, we learn that Joan immediately commenced preparations and that during the night she worked as hard as two or three experienced soldiers. This so alarmed the burghers of the city that at dawn they rushed to the churches and prayed to God.

Another account indicates a difficult problem facing Joan and the King's leaders, the scarcity of provisions and consequent dissatisfaction of the troops.[2]

---

[2] "And there was among the host great scarcity of bread and other victuals, for among this host there were six to seven thousand men who had not eaten bread for more than eight days, and these people had lived on beans and crushed wheat grains."

It is said that Joan then pretended to begin the attack on the town and that before long it surrendered. We must suppose that here, too, Joan acted in complete harmony with the King and his counselors. The same applies to the reports that she sent out her followers with orders to shout to the defenders of the different redoubts, "Surrender to the King of Heaven and to the noble King Charles."

The *Chronique de la Pucelle*, which, however, is more like a romance than a history, gives many details of this siege and describes dramatically Joan's entry into the Council of War. Only one of the episodes described in this chronicle sounds probable; this at least can hardly have been a complete invention.

In the terms of capitulation was agreed a right of free passage. Joan rode up to observe the departing army, but noticed that the Burgundians were dragging with them some French prisoners of war captured earlier. Spurring her horse she galloped up to the Burgundians and made them free the prisoners. This was probably not quite in accordance with the custom of the times, for the King had to solve the problem created by paying ransom himself for his captured soldiers.

Joan was at the King's side when the army entered Troyes and during the great church ceremonies, but soon after she seems to have left the great nobles and withdrawn to the army. It was here, a chronicler relates, that she was visited by a townsman who begged her to carry a newborn child to the font, to which she agreed.

Brother Richard had completely changed his attitude toward her and made glowing speeches in the town in her honor and defense. He described Joan as better able to penetrate the secrets of God than any saint in Paradise, with the exception of John the Baptist. He also told his audiences that Joan, if she wished, could lead the King's armies over the ramparts, and many other wonders. This hysterical babbler contributed largely to the distortion of the picture of the real Joan, and it is no exaggeration to say that he and others like him were collecting fuel for the pyre upon which Joan was burned. Every exaggeration, every false report, every superstitious falsification that he and his like in pious eagerness spread over the land, was turned in Rouen into an accusation.

The view of an enemy is shown in an account by a Burgundian soldier who saw her at the time of her intervention in favor of the French prisoners of war. He was not impressed by her. "By God, I have never seen anything more ordinary", he muttered contemptuously. "There is not the least sense in anything she does—just a silly girl."

One prefers this rough but frank opinion to the pious lies spread by her admirers.

The Duke of Bedford followed with anxiety the reports of the King's advance and wrote to England for reinforcements. Something strange then occurred. The Cardinal of Winchester had just succeeded in raising an army for dispatch to Bohemia to put down the Hussite heretics, but on July 1, it was decided that this army of crusaders should be sent to France instead. Thus by July 25 a new English army of 3,500 men had already arrived in Paris. Philip de Moulant, commandant in Nogent-sur-Seine, wrote to Reims, saying that there was no need for discouragement as English reinforcements were on the way.

The Duke of Burgundy, after taking certain measures, proceeded to Paris to consult with the Regent, the Duke of Bedford, about the new situation. Discussions continued for five days, accompanied by solemn Masses and great military parades. The Parisians were made to swear fealty to the Regent and the Duke of Burgundy, which they seemed to do willingly, and in their turn the dukes promised to defend Paris. Philip of Burgundy agreed to send an army to reinforce Bedford, and the latter was very pleased with the zeal of his ally. He wrote that the Duke of Burgundy "in several respects had proved himself a true friend and loyal vassal to the King (of England)".

But in Reims there was anxiety. Guillaume de Châtillon, who commanded the garrison, informed the burghers that the army that was to take the field against the King of France would not be in a position to do so for about two months. The burghers were infuriated and appear to have driven the Burgundian representatives out of the town.

The King advanced steadily with his army. In Châlons, which offered no resistance, Joan met some old friends from Domrémy. She saw there Jean Morel and her godfather Gérardin d'Épinal, and dismounted to embrace them. When her godfather admired her red cloak, she presented it to him.

From these talks with her old friends, an important reply of Joan's has been preserved. Somebody asked her if she was never afraid, to which she replied, "I am only afraid of one thing—treachery."

At last they stood before Reims. The city offered no resistance, and the King was met by a deputation offering surrender.

On the morning of July 17, 1429, four horsemen rode up to the monastery of Saint Rémi in Reims where *la sainte ampoule*—the holy vessel—was preserved. They were in full armor and each carried his own banner. They were recognized as great lords, the Marshal de Boussac, Sire de Graville, Sire de Rais, and the Admiral of France, Louis de Culan.

The abbot, Jean Canart, received the eminent guests and conducted them to the church of the monastery. Slowly the small procession advanced between the Romanesque columns—the church is filled with a Benedictine peace and its architecture gives a feeling of wholeness and holiness—the light only sparingly penetrates through the small windows. The visitors knelt before the high altar and then followed the abbot to the tomb of Saint Rémi where the holy vessel is preserved. The abbot raised it up while the four nobles bent their knees. Solemnly they made their way to the church entrance, from where they proceeded, accompanied by a great procession of horsemen and monks, to another of the city's churches—that of Saint Denis, where Archbishop Regnault awaited them. Reverently he received the holy vessel from the abbot.

Again the procession moved on and advanced through the streets up to the cathedral. The populace was kept back by serried ranks of soldiers. The Archbishop and the King, the peers and generals, the clergy and the most important court functionaries, as well as the delegates of the different towns, marched up to the cathedral doors.

It may have been the first truly great cathedral that Joan had seen. Far out on the plain the great towers had become visible, but as she got nearer, the massive building seemed as if it were raised up high by the widespread wings of angels.

In amazement she had stood, small and insignificant, before the majestic façade.

Above her, a throng of figures over the portals. In Chartres the Jewish kings, the prophets, and the popes stand listening as if they are all waiting for the return of the Savior coming from somewhere beyond the great plain. But on the portals of the cathedral at Reims life is presented in vivid, dramatic scenes. At the right-hand portal stands John the Baptist, solemn, stern, his forehead lined with suffering, prepared to descend silently and make way for one greater than himself. On the central portal, an angel inclines his head with a smile very moving in its gentleness and delicacy; calm, as if in a dream, submissive and waiting, the Virgin Mother stands at his side. She is faced by Saint Joseph, mustachioed, a handsome figure of a man, more like a knight than a humble carpenter, but his countenance illuminated by intelligence and sensibility. At the same portal stands a pope, a boyish figure with raised hands and a gentle face expressive of poetic and tender feelings. But there is also a row of stiff, rough-hewn men: Simeon with the child Jesus, another John the Baptist, Isaiah, Moses—heavy, bearded figures, strangers to the demands and enjoyments of cultured life, devoted entirely to their supernatural tasks.

The whole of human life is mirrored in these portals; the cathedral is not only the center of the daily life, it is a symbol of the cosmos of man with all its facets—the daily labors, the changes of the seasons, cattle and trees, commerce and manufacture. Against this background stand the solemn, devout figures who take part in the greatest scenes of history—the Crucifixion, the Annunciation, the Crowning of Mary, the Eternal Judgment ... Joan knows that in this world she has her place, just like one of the small figures in a weather-worn frieze—small, almost invisible, but still *belonging*, an intrinsic part of the structure of holiness.

The procession enters the church and advances to the choir, where the Archbishop places the holy vessel on the high altar. According to custom, the great lords enter the cathedral mounted and only dismount in front of the choir.

Joan goes slowly forward carrying her banner in her hand. On both sides the windows glow in splendid colors. She follows these sights with her eyes and gives a faint cry when she sees the inside of the west façade—two gigantic rose windows, glowing like oriental carpets brought from the Crusades, and around the lower and smaller rose window a gallery of figures in serried ranks—God's servants, the heroes of the legends, warriors, saints and prophets, separated by exquisitely sculptured foliage.

Joan stood entranced. This was the world where she belonged. She did not know that another age had begun. Had she been born a few centuries earlier, when the Gothic cathedrals grew up in France and its King Louis was himself a saint, she would have been understood in a different manner. In her time, ecclesiastical art was declining, holy men were expected to produce magic and signs, and the devil had wormed his way deep into the life of the Church, dividing her servants into two irreconcilable camps whose enmity contributed toward the terrible crisis that was threatening to devastate Christian France. Joan had no inkling of all this. She had never been able to understand the evil in men and believed that the souls of others were as pure as her own.

And this was not the moment for pessimistic reflections. She was dazzled and blinded by the enormous height of the Gothic vaulting overhead, by the forest of columns, by the blue windows sparkling with beauty and by the gigantic rose windows that seemed to float mysteriously. As if from a great distance, she heard the King's herald call in a ringing voice upon the twelve peers of France. Of the six secular peers, none is present. They have all betrayed the King and his cause.

In their place the Duke of Alençon, the Counts of Clermont and Vendôme, the Lords de Laval, La Trémoille, and de Maillé step forward.

Of the six ecclesiastical peers, only two answer the call, Archbishop Regnault and the Bishop of Châlons-sur-Marne, Jean de Sarrebourg.

Absent too is the High Constable of France, Arthur de Richemont, who is carrying on his own war in Brittany against both the English and the King's followers. The sword of the King is therefore carried by Charles d'Albret in his place.

Contrary to traditional procedure, Joan herself stood at the King's side, carrying her own banner. Her judges later cross-examined her as to why she was present. In reply to the question why her banner should appear so near the King, she answered simply and a trifle bitterly, "It had been present in so many difficult situations that there was good reason why it should now be honored."

This reply shows that she had begun to feel disturbed by what the future might bring.

The Archbishop now stepped before the King, asking him whether he would always protect the cause of the Church. Without rising, the King answered affirmatively with a solemn oath.

After this the two bishops assisted the King to rise and presented him to the peers and the representatives of the people, who hailed him with ringing shouts. As silence again descended on the cathedral, Charles laid his hand on the Bible and took his royal oath, promising mercy and justice to his people.

Now the Duke of Alençon buckled on the King's spurs and gave him the accolade; the Archbishop blessed the sword and handed it to the King, who received it kneeling and then placed it on the altar. From there the Archbishop took it and handed it back to the King. He now passed it on to the representative of the High Constable, who during the remainder of the ceremony held the naked blade raised before him.

The Archbishop then proceeded to the ceremony of the anointing.

The abbot of Saint Rémi opened the casket in which the holy vessel was kept and handed the vessel to the Archbishop, who passed a fraction of the coagulated oil onto the paten.

The cathedral choir sang, "The glorious Frankish people together with its noble King have been sanctified by Saint Rémi with oil from heaven and with holy water, and have been given the riches of the gifts of the Holy Spirit."

The Archbishop now anointed the King's head, "I anoint you King with the holy oil, in the name of the Father...."

He then anointed the King on his neck between the shoulders, on his right and his left shoulder, and on his arms.

After more prayers, the King knelt and the palms of his hands were anointed, whereupon the sceptre was placed in his right hand.

The peers of France were then summoned to the altar, and the Archbishop raised the crown above the King's head; supported by the peers the crown was slowly placed on the King's head: "Accept the crown of the Kingdom...."

At this moment, the trumpets rang out, the crowds outside shouted joyfully and pushed into the cathedral as the doors were thrown open: "Noël, Noël!"

After the coronation, the King created several knights and raised others to new honors. La Trémoille was made Count.

During the long ceremony, Joan had stood immovable at the side of the King. How many times had she not said, using her favorite expression: "*Par mon martin*, I shall lead the noble King Charles and his army and he shall be crowned in Reims."

Now the army had marched through a countryside that only recently had been regarded as hostile to the King and without striking a blow had reached Reims.

Now the King was crowned ...

She had fulfilled the second of her four promises.

When the solemnities were over, she advanced to the King and knelt before him. She must have remained in this position quite a long time weeping. The Chronicle relates: "When the Maid saw that the King was crowned, she knelt before him in the presence of all the great lords, embraced his knees and said, shedding hot tears, 'Now the will of God is done. The will of him wished that I should raise the siege of Orléans and lead you to the city of Reims, so that you should have a holy crowning and thus show that you are a true king and he to whom the country should belong.' "

This was the first time that she had addressed the King, not as *Dauphin* (crown prince), but as *Roi* (king).

A New Line

Joan of Arc had met with great difficulties, but in nine months she had accomplished a task that has no parallel in the world's history. She had fulfilled all her promises; she had freed Orléans, vanquished the English, and led the King to Reims and crowned him.

Her father, Jacques d'Arc, now appeared in Reims. We know nothing of his reactions, but we can guess them. Even at a time when the presence and power of the supernatural was recognized in a way beyond our understanding, Joan's deeds were striking and unusual. The father who had been angered because she had left Domrémy without his permission, and who had said that he would rather drown her than see her set out into the world, saw her now standing with her own banner at the King's side before all the nobles of the kingdom. He saw her in a beautiful suit of armor, surrounded by many attendants, and on familiar terms with dukes and courtiers. Jacques d'Arc made use of his opportunity and obtained an audience with the King, in which he described the conditions in burned-down Domrémy. He obtained from the King a promise of freedom from taxation for himself and his neighbors. He was the guest of the city and before leaving was presented with a horse.

In Reims Joan also met her first faithful helper, Durand Laxart, and this meeting may have helped to arouse in her a feeling of longing for home. At any rate it is clear that at this time she began to show signs of fatigue.

As a matter of fact, her successes ended with the coronation at Reims. From man's point of view, it is possible to find explanations for this, and the next chapter will give an idea of the men who prevented the expulsion of the English and the capture of Paris. But all such explanations are insufficient. We must seek elsewhere for the profound reason why Joan's fate now changed, why after the most glorious victories she is now caught in hopeless intrigues, why military operations turn unsuccessful, and in the end she is taken prisoner, to die at the stake. But, as always when one deals with the deepest significance of a great human tragedy, the greatest caution and the most careful reservations are called for. The only fixed point for such reasoning is the logic we recognize in the fate of other saints. Almost all end in suffering, if not in destruction. A Joan of Arc who after a successful war of liberation would spend the remainder of her life in peace and happiness is an impossible conception.

Why that should be so is more difficult to say.

Without question, Joan was called to a unique historical act, the salvation of France. This act was performed in a manner without parallel in history, and if any historical event calls for a supernatural explanation, this surely is the one. But with persons who have attained such spiritual maturity, we cannot apply the same logic as with ordinary mortals. The tasks that confront them, tasks which they seem almost to grow into and become part of, are of a wholly different kind, tasks of such terrible nature and enigmatic meaning that the ordinary man instinctively shrinks from them. If Joan's lifeline appears to decline after the coronation in Reims, this is only because we look at it from a limited point of view; in truth it is now that she begins to rise to the real heights. Can one conceive of a Christ victorious in the human sense of the word, receiving the homage of a united Jewish people, and proceeding as a universally beloved High Priest to spread his teaching to all mankind, without being met by fierce resistance? Why should this thought be inconceivable? Because the highest that a man can give is his life. Because man's need and fear are such that nothing but the punishment of the innocent can counterbalance them.

One cannot grasp the supreme logic in Joan's life if one does not see it as an imitation of Christ. She is not merely a morally purified person, a prophet, a visionary, a genius of action, a unique instrument of God. She is also a mystic, that is, a soul that moves ever closer to Christ in order to become not only like him but united with him.

Joan's spiritual development during the few years of her active and suffering life is astounding. The young amazon is changed into the saint who humbly accepts what from man's point of view seems maddening and revolting—death by torture, martyrdom.

This means that a new line cuts through her life—in part crossing the first one. Both are of God. First God ordered her, after years of purification, to carry out a definite historical task that, from man's point of view, seemed quite unreasonable, for which there have been no precedents, and the like of which may never be seen again. By her complete obedience, humility, and faith, Joan carries out this unreasonable task and liberates her country. But through her very obedience and faith, she grows into a different person and therefore knows that greater tasks are demanded of her. She no longer loves merely her country and dreams of its salvation before anything else—now she loves Christ more than anything else upon earth. And the one who loves Christ above all—which means that he destroys his own ego with all its desires and allows himself to become nothing but the receptacle of divine love—this person is ripe then for another task than to lead armies and gain victories by means of miracles: he is ready to be killed, to die. Such is man's terrifying condition, so appalling the misery of mankind, that nothing can help but the sacrifice of the best and noblest for the most degraded, the highest for those that have fallen lowest, the pure for the unclean, the noble for the common herd. The true history of mankind is the account of such successive ransoming by voluntary sacrifices. In this royal line, that of the martyrs and the saints, Joan has her place.

I have said that this second line crosses the first one in her life. When from our human point of view we follow the course of her destiny, we stop short at this point, shocked and horrified. Why was this necessary? Why could not Joan be allowed to continue her task?

Perhaps she herself could not have found the answer to that question, for she was never a great theologian. To the very end, it seems as if she was never able to find a satisfactory formula for her faith. On the other hand, some things seemed more self-evident and elementary to her than they are to modern people. Among these was the idea that the man who gives himself to God must accept being broken by him. Joan had learned this with great clarity in her childhood, when she pondered alone over the destinies of Saint Catherine and Saint Margaret: pure women who had to give their lives, not in order to realize earthly tasks, but for the glory of God.

Joan had anxious presentiments that she was to be faced with something new, something frightening. She had, as I have mentioned, spoken of being taken prisoner. She sensed that a far greater task lay before her than to make the will of God obeyed among men who had never heard her "voices". Her new opponent was more dangerous than any of the others—it was herself, the remnants of selfishness in her own nature. Was she ready to make the supreme sacrifice? She had sacrificed a great deal, but there were still some things that were her own. One of them was her undefiled, virgin body. Would she, if God demanded it, be prepared to sacrifice this too?

Perhaps she could not entertain the thought. Her soul was in agony. She could not look into the future, but she sensed that it would bring her terrible suffering. Again she sought refuge in the only thing that was firm and secure—in God himself as he led her toward the company of his saints.

Again she heard the "voice": "Daughter of God—onward, onward, onward!"

CHAPTER 9

Failure before Paris

It is an arguable question whether or not it was right to crown the King in Reims instead of immediately following up on the recent military successes. After the coronation, the proper strategy was obvious—to conquer Paris immediately and to drive the English out of the country before they could again consolidate their position.

This was not done.

Instead the King spent months in meaningless operations and then retired to the line of the Loire without having achieved anything.

The reason for this has been much discussed.

The older literature felt no doubts; the King was vacillating, his entourage cowardly and actuated by selfish motives, and Joan slowly outmaneuvered. Anatole France alone has insisted that this view is too one-sided. Though he feels no sympathy for the King's closest counselors, particularly La Trémoille, he maintains that the latter pursued a consistent policy and showed great energy and initiative. Curiously enough, Joseph Calmette leans toward the older opinion. To him, La Trémoille is the King's "evil genius" who betrays the true interests of the country: "La Trémoille was '*l'homme néfaste*'. He was responsible for all Joan's misfortunes, he lay behind this retreat into doubt and indifference...."

Even those who have the greatest dislike of La Trémoille find it difficult to share this opinion. He pursued another aim, reconciliation with Burgundy. One may criticize this policy, and one can see—in retrospect—that the cunning Duke of Burgundy hoodwinked La Trémoille by carrying on intrigues with both sides. But this does not mean that the policy of reconciliation was not a reasonable one.

In Paris, the Duke had effected a reconciliation with Bedford. On the way from Paris to Artois, he dispatched a delegation to Reims to resume negotiations with the King. Their arrival was received with joy—and nothing suggests that Joan of Arc, any more than anybody else, saw through the Burgundians' game. Everybody believed that there would soon be a reconciliation and that the war against the English could then be pursued with redoubled strength. Those who insist that the army should have advanced on Paris without delay forget an important fact: Paris was in the highest degree hostile to the King, and to attack the capital before reaching an understanding with Burgundy would have been very hazardous. It would still be possible to reach Paris before the arrival of the English reinforcements (these did not enter Paris until July 25).

When the Burgundian delegates arrived, Joan sent a letter to the Duke of Burgundy in which she insisted that the King of France and the Duke "conclude an honest and enduring peace". She added that as good Christians they should forgive one another and that if the Duke felt he must fight, he should march against the Saracens.

The fact that Joan speaks of the King and the Duke forgiving one another shows that the letter cannot have been written in the King's chancellery and merely signed by her. La Trémoille would hardly agree that the King and he had anything for which to ask forgiveness.

The next part of the letter seems very typical of Joan's own point of view: "Duke of Burgundy: I beg, appeal, and urge you as strongly as I can that you do not continue to fight against the Holy Kingdom of France and that you at once withdraw your soldiers who are still in occupation of certain towns and castles belonging to this Holy Kingdom."

She emphasizes that everyone who wages war against France thereby also fights against "the King Jesus, King of Heaven and Earth".

The style of the letter is most informal, the language is colloquial and shows signs of improvisation, and everything points to its coming direct from Joan.

From July 18 to 20, the King negotiated with the Burgundian delegation. At the time, the English reinforcements were approaching nearer and nearer to Paris. The only result of the negotiations was an agreement that peace should be maintained for a fortnight and that new negotiations should be conducted in Arras.

Nothing can be said with certainty regarding the Duke's intentions, but it is probable that he deliberately tried to deceive the King: he did not wish to begin serious negotiations until he held in his hand a trump card—the arrival of the English reinforcements in Paris. He was very successful, and the decisive days passed without any action on the part of the French. The King confined himself to receiving the homage of a number of lesser cities: Château-Thierry, Coulommiers, Crécy-en-Brie, and Provins.

On July 27, a startling event occurred: the royal army left Soissons and marched—south. On August 1, the army was in Montmirail, on the 2nd, in Provins. In a few days it had marched seventy miles southward. Everything indicates that for some reason the King preferred to retire after the coronation to the line of the Loire.

Most writers profess their inability to understand this action, but it is far from inexplicable, for there were towns, such as Auxerre, south of the royal army, which were, to put it mildly, unreliable. Reims was situated in a part of the country that still to a great extent favored Burgundy. The Duke of Burgundy was assembling an army, and on July 28 his troops stood in Châtillon-sur-Seine. If, as is not unreasonable, an attack on Paris was regarded as too great a risk, there were military reasons for a withdrawal to a safer line.

In itself therefore the retreat southward cannot be criticized, but it is more difficult to understand why it was immediately halted. From August 2 to 5, the army lay in Provins; then suddenly it wheeled and marched north in the direction of Compiègne. Why?

The reason may have been the fact that Bedford, on receiving news of the retreat of the royal army, had immediately marched off to overtake it and offer battle. When the English army advanced along the left bank of the Seine, the King evidently thought the situation precarious and preferred to take up a new position near the castle of La Motte de Nangis in Brie. Here the army formed in battle order and came into contact with Bedford's troops, though no actual fighting took place. According to one source, Joan and the Duke of Alençon hailed the halting of the retreat with joy, and this seems probable.

Another reason for not continuing the retreat was of a psychological nature. The retreat of the royal army had produced panic in several of the towns that had recently espoused the King's cause and could now expect frightful reprisals; this was especially the case of the coronation city, Reims. We know the letters in which the city's administrators spoke of their distress and their regrets over the King's retreat. Faced by these appeals and under pressure from the English army, which tried to cut off their retreat toward the south, the King's counselors chose to march north. This is quite understandable, but one is left with an impression of hesitancy and irresolution.

At this moment, Joan again intervenes with a letter to the city of Reims that was a reply to earlier appeals from the city council. This letter is very informal and clearly written on the personal initiative of Joan.

She explains that the King had wished to observe the two weeks' truce, but adds that she herself is not enamored of such agreements.... She cannot even promise that she will observe the truce. If she does so, it will only be out of consideration for the King's honor. She also indicates that the object of this delay had been to enable the Duke to surrender Paris peacefully to the King....

Bedford discovers that the royal army is withdrawing and addresses a letter to the King, whom he calls "Charles de Valois". He insults the King, asserting that he has no right to the royal title, grossly insults Joan, and finally proposes a meeting somewhere in Brie or in Île-de-France, where terms for an eventual peace could be discussed.

Strangely enough, the English army does not follow the King's army but returns to Paris.

On August 10, the royal army had reached Crépy-en-Valois. According to one source, Joan here uttered one of her best-known remarks. She was riding between Dunois and Archbishop Regnault and observed how touchingly the people greeted their King and paid homage to him. "Look, what splendid people", she said. "I have never before seen people so truly joyful at the sight of their noble king. May heaven grant that when I end my days I may be buried in this earth."

Astonished, the Archbishop asked her, "Where do you think that you will die?"

Joan answered, "Where it pleases God. I know not the time nor the place any more than you do; perhaps it might be agreeable to God, my Creator, if I now withdrew, laid down my arms and served under my father and mother, and looked after the sheep with my sister and my brothers, who would be so glad to see me again."

Her anxiety is noticeable. There is a new note in her speech; never before has she spoken thus about herself; it is evident that she has been asking herself whether her task were not now completed.

The Duke of Bedford was now ready for fresh action. On August 13, he marched toward the King and took up his quarters in the town of Senlis, twenty-five miles north of Paris. The following day the royal army advanced against him and took up a position near Senlis at the village of Montepilloy. But here too there was no serious fighting. The English had fortified their position, and the King was advised not to attack. There were small skirmishes so that the neighborhood was covered with a cloud of dust, but no decisive battle.

From August 18 to 28, the King lay in Compiègne, and the Duke of Burgundy brought forward his terms. In spite of his victories, the King could not obtain any real recognition. It is the Duke who wins all points. The King deplores and condemns the assassination of the Duke's father, John the Fearless, and promises to punish the assassins and to erect a chapel on the bridge of Montereau where a Mass shall be said every day and to establish a monastery for twenty-four Carthusians in the town. Further, the Duke was to keep his independence in relation to the Crown and gained a number of other advantages. One cannot see that the King gained anything, and it is scarcely possible to conceive a greater diplomatic defeat.

On August 21, the Duke's representatives arrived at Compiègne to conclude a peace treaty. However, the only result reached was an armistice until December 25. The Duke agreed not to attack the French north of the Seine during the following four months. The King was to give up a large number of towns though they were loyal to him, such as Compiègne, Pont-Sainte-Maxence, Creil, Senlis.

La Trémoille's efforts had resulted in a complete fiasco.

Clearly this was recognized by the King and his entourage, and a new effort was made to improve the situation by an attack on Paris. The Duke of Bedford's action now was as puzzling as the King's had been before. He who had recently been so bold and had twice left Paris to offer battle now hastily retreated and led his troops back to Normandy.

Despite the diplomatic defeat, a new chance thus offered itself. Joan made an intensive effort to save the situation. The Duke of Alençon tried to persuade the King to attack Paris with the entire army. At last, on September 5, the King did leave Senlis and rode to Saint-Denis.

In Paris preparations were made to meet an assault. There were rumors that Joan had threatened to massacre the population. The French erected a temporary bridge over the Seine not far from Saint-Denis and captured a couple of important redoubts. The King and La Trémoille were somewhere between Montmartre and the city.

The army was divided into two groups. One of these, commanded by Joan, Count de Laval, and the Marshal de Rais, advanced against the

Porte Saint-Honoré. The other, commanded by the Dukes of Alençon and Bourbon, advanced toward the Porte Saint-Denis.

The assault began on September 8. The first outworks outside the Porte Saint-Honoré were captured. Joan took a personal part in the battle and was seen to snatch a sword from a Burgundian soldier. Artillery was brought up. A first trench was forced when another was unexpectedly encountered, which was no less than sixty feet in width and filled with water. It would take time to bring up enough material to fill this enormous trench, and the work began immediately.

Joan followed these maneuvers and herself tested the depth of the ditch with her lance. She was wounded in the calf by an arrow. She was led away and at the same moment the energy of the French was diminished.

Joan's "voices" told her to hold out. She sat on the ground and told those standing around her that they must not give up—Paris must be captured. Then came an order from La Trémoille that the battle must cease. Desperate, Joan refused. The Duke of Alençon tried to calm her, assuring her that the battle would be resumed on the following day. She still refused. Sire de Gaucourt then seized the wounded girl and forcibly dragged her away. She was taken to the Saint-Denis chapel.

The next day the situation seemed more hopeful. Baron de Montmorency with sixty men had succeeded in escaping from Paris and reported for service with the King. A new assault was prepared. Just as it was about to begin, the Duke of Bar and the Count of Clermont rode up and ordered the Duke of Alençon and Joan to withdraw immediately to Saint-Denis.

A new development lay behind this order. Sire de Charny had appeared in the King's headquarters as representative of the Duke of Burgundy. He gave the information that the Duke was prepared to induce Paris to surrender if a promise were given that the city would be spared. This offer was taken seriously. The following day La Trémoille demolished the bridge that Joan and the Duke of Alençon had thrown across the Seine.

But the Duke of Burgundy had never meant what he said. While these maneuvers were going on, he was negotiating not only with the English but also with La Trémoille's enemy, the High Constable de Richemont, and had suggested to the latter that he seize all La Trémoille's landed possessions in Poitou.

On this occasion, Joan is said to have exclaimed, "There can never be peace with Burgundy except at the point of the spear." Archbishop Regnault began new negotiations with the Burgundian representatives Jean de Luxembourg and Sire de Lannoy, but of course no results were reached.

It was now too late to renew the attack on Paris. Joan solemnly deposited her sword at the altar in Saint-Denis, and on September 13 the retreat southward began.

The morale of the army gave way, and it looked as if the troops were fleeing southward after a defeat. The town of Sens refused to open its gates. On September 20, they reached Gien on the Loire, and the army was disbanded.

Dunois and La Hire disappeared.

The Duke of Alençon returned to his family.

Joan found herself alone at court, abandoned by nearly all her closest friends. Everything that had happened since the coronation in Reims had failed. We know nothing about her own reactions, but we may assume that she felt the greatest grief. Why had God suddenly forsaken her? This question has been asked by many a saint in similar situations. Joan was to learn that to chosen souls God sometimes manifests himself by his apparent absence. It is only a question of accepting his will in order to hear him, despite his silence.

In eighty-five days, the royal army had marched more than six hundred miles and gained practically nothing by it.

Joan, who at the time of the departure had been surrounded by friends and enjoyed the confidence of everybody, was now made responsible for the defeat before Paris. Earlier she had seen clouds on the horizon. Now they were massing over her head. She knew that the storm was close at hand.

Full of anguish, she must have asked herself what God now wished to do with her life.

She herself could only wait. Nothing is more difficult for a genius of action.

Joan in Bourges

From this period of waiting, we possess a description that is one of the most valuable documents concerning Joan of Arc. It is the work of a wise and experienced woman who knew Joan very well, who had spent many days in close intimacy with her, and had pondered deeply over her mission and her character.

Joan had come to Bourges and found quarters there in the home of Régnier de Bouligny, a rich and honored financier in the service of the King. For three weeks, Joan lived in his house and became a close friend of his wife, Marguerite La Touroulde. According to the custom of the time, the two ladies shared the same bed. They went together to the public baths, where Joan's hostess believed that she could establish that Joan was a virgin. They went for walks, performed household duties, and made excursions together. This is one of the few completely relaxed periods of Joan's life.

Marguerite La Touroulde, who described her impressions in detail during the Trial of Rehabilitation, soon found to her astonishment that Joan was ignorant to an extreme degree and had practically no knowledge of the world and world affairs. On the other hand, she was extremely disciplined in her religious life and frequently went to confession. She often asked her hostess to accompany her to Matins in the cathedral.

Marguerite's description contains a number of other details that give a clear picture of Joan's religious life. She was realistic and sober-minded. There was nothing overwrought or superstitious in her spiritual life. When her hostess once spoke about the remarkable fact that Joan never felt fear in battle, she added that she thought that this might have been because Joan could not be killed.

The worthy lady was therefore not immune to superstition, but Joan immediately denied the suggestion. "I am no more immune to danger than any other soldier", she replied calmly. As a matter of fact, she had, as we know, been wounded several times and had been very close to death.

Another incident may be related, as it is very characteristic of Joan's religious life. Burghers' wives often came to Marguerite's house and wished Joan to touch and thereby bless and give power to their rosaries. But Joan only smiled and said to her hostess, "Touch them yourself, do! It will be just as effective if you touch them as if I did."

She could not have demonstrated in a more categorical way that she regarded herself as a quite ordinary woman without any kind of spiritual eminence. There is nothing in her whole life indicating that she regarded herself as equipped with any special powers. She heard her "voices", but that was all. Other Christians, too, could hear God if they only listened.

Joan was extremely generous. She had considerable funds—among other things she had a personal salary from the King—and she gave generous alms. Her hostess remarked that she once said, "I have been sent to console the poor and the suffering."

There is a new note in this utterance of Joan, though it is related to her love for wounded soldiers and her care for the dying, even for those who were enemies and had only just before sought her life.

It may be said that all this is very ordinary and occurs in the lives of most pious women. True enough, but this natural simplicity and humility of the miracle-performing heroine to whom the whole country was paying homage is worth noting. Despite her triumphs and honors, her personality still displays the same touching sincerity as in her youth. The genuinely Catholic in her type of piety is what I have earlier referred to as the *instrumental* side; she herself is absolutely nothing; she is the instrument, the means by which a gentle and high power deigns to work.

The same witness relates that Joan objected to luxury and to a certain kind of empty pleasure; for instance, she had a horror of games of dice. Perhaps she remembered that the soldiers threw dice for Christ's clothing.

Her astonished hostess relates, however, that there was one activity in which she was a complete master—that of handling horses and arms: "She mounted her charger and handled her lance as skillfully as any knight; the whole army admired her."

One may regret that Joan was forced into inactivity during these weeks, but one must be thankful that they have provided this intimate picture of her. She is magnificent in her sublime moments in the great hours of peril and inspiration. She is disarmingly pure-hearted and simple when she moves about privately in the peaceful home of a burgher.

The Duke of Alençon, her closest male friend, wished to make use of the pause in the war to make an expedition into Maine in order, if possible, to reconquer his own territorial possessions. Quite naturally he was anxious that his comrade-in-arms, Joan, should accompany him, but there is documentary evidence that La Trémoille did not permit this. He and his friends "did in no manner wish to consent, to participate, to suffer that the Maid and the Duke of Alençon should be together", it says in strikingly energetic language. This need not be interpreted as evidence of ill will. On the contrary, it may mean the very opposite: that Joan should be preserved for greater tasks. For Joan this separation from the Duke must have been a sore trial; they were never to see each other again.

To tell the truth, the Duke's later life was much to be deplored. At the side of Joan, he performed many admirable deeds, but on his own he soon became the victim of temptations he could not overcome. The end of his life was pitiful.

Meanwhile the King's enemies were displaying great activity. The King still imagined that the Duke of Burgundy had been serious in his promise to surrender Paris, but Philip the Good appears never to have had the remotest intention of doing so. On September 21, at the head of an army of four thousand, he arrived at Senlis, where the King's men, the chancellor, and Archbishop Regnault de Chartres resided. The latter, who still dreamed of a peaceful solution to the conflict between the Crown and Burgundy, received the Duke with reverence. The Duke continued his advance to Paris, where he met the English leaders, the Duke of Bedford, and the Cardinal of Winchester. It was still regarded as advisable to negotiate with the King. On October 10, Archbishop Regnault as the delegate of the French king, the Cardinal of Winchester as that of the English king, and Jean de Luxembourg as that of the Duke of Burgundy conferred in Saint-Denis. The principal subject of their discussions was a proposed peace conference in Auxerre on April 1, 1430.

All this was make-believe. At the very same time, the Duke of Bedford and Philip the Good were conferring about the continuation of the war. The Burgundian played his cards very cleverly: having already received the title of Governor of Paris, he was now nominated Regent of the whole of France by the English king. In other words, he now occupied the position hitherto held by the Duke of Bedford.

It was agreed that the new English army should be dispatched to France, that the district around Paris should be cleaned up, and that, if possible, Guyenne, which had shown itself to be loyal to the Valois, should be conquered. The High Constable, de Richemont, who had waged his private war against the English in Brittany, was, if possible, to be bribed to change sides and join the English with his considerable army.

Everything was designed so that a great blow should be struck the following spring, which would finally crush Charles VII.

The latter, however, was not entirely inactive. In particular he thought it important to safeguard his position in the Loire district, where the English and the Burgundians still had powerful sympathizers here and there. In October therefore the King's counselors decided that the two rebellious towns, Saint-Pierre-le-Moustier and La Charité-sur-Loire, were to be occupied. For this purpose, a new army, which Joan joined, was assembled in Bourges.

Of the siege of Saint-Pierre-le-Moustier, we possess a remarkable description by Joan's own master of the horse, Jean d'Aulon, the true meaning of which is not easy to interpret. The first attacks failed, and as usual it was decided to retreat. Then occurred one of the strangest episodes in the history of Joan. The account of the witness is very clear and so can hardly be the result of imagination, so we must regard it as reliable.

The French had begun to remove their artillery, and everything was prepared for breaking up. Jean d'Aulon, who himself had been lightly wounded in the foot, was seated not far from the ramparts watching the raising of the siege. He noticed that Joan had disappeared and felt anxious. He therefore had himself lifted onto a horse and rode toward the ramparts. He found her surrounded by a handful of soldiers just in front of the moat. He asked her what in the world she was doing there, and why she did not withdraw like the others.

Joan raised her visor and replied, "I am not alone. I have about me fifty thousand of my own men. . . ."

It is clear that Joan was here referring to supernatural powers that were at her disposal. She feels herself abandoned by men; in the most paradoxical form she indicates that God is more powerful than all enemies. Jean d'Aulon shrugged his shoulders and called to her to leave immediately. She did not listen to him, but cried loudly to the soldiers to bring up material and fill the moat so that it could be crossed. And what is remarkable is that this happened and that the town which just before had so successfully defended itself was easily captured.

In connection with this, Cordier speaks of a "passing hallucinatory disturbance". The contact of a saint with the supernatural world will in all times appear thus to those who recognize no other world than that of time and space. It is unusual, however, for hallucinations to conquer a strongly fortified town.

After the storming of the town, the usual plundering and murdering commenced, but Joan intervened with great energy and, among other things, succeeded in saving the church from plunder. It was always the same: she herself had to intervene to get anything done. No sooner had a town been conquered by the help of God than the victory was abused by those she had helped and led. She had to wage a new fight to prevent violence, murder, and fire.

In a letter written immediately afterward to the burghers of the town of Riom, Joan requests assistance for the continuation of the campaign. She writes calmly and confidently, "Dear and good friends! You are aware that the town of Saint-Pierre-le-Moustier has been stormed...."

She knows that God has not abandoned her.

The town of La Charité-sur-Loire remained. At the end of November, Joan stood before the town, which was defended by a well-known adventurer, Perrinet Gressart, who had entered the service of the Duke of Burgundy. There is little to tell about this siege except that it was a total failure, probably because the troops had not received their pay from the King.

This was the second time that Joan had been checked; the first time was before Paris. It caused a great sensation, and it is clear that even during the trial in Rouen the matter was still very much alive. The judges asked her if her "voices" had really told her to attack this town. Joan replied that she had done so neither with nor against the orders of her "voices". The King had asked her to, and she had obeyed. One can feel that here she had acted without certain inspiration.

A Witch: Joan Is Taken Prisoner

At this time a woman named Catherine de la Rochelle appears on the scene who to a certain extent can be said to have been Joan's rival. She came with the rather suspect Brother Richard, who often associated with strange soothsayers and female magicians and clearly did not distinguish Joan from the others.

Catherine believed she could persuade the Duke of Burgundy to conclude peace, and it is possible that it was to her that Joan angrily uttered the words about the impossibility of obtaining peace with the Duke except at the point of the spear.

Catherine appeared at court and made some impression on La Trémoille and the King. She had extraordinary visions and revelations. She saw a female figure dressed in white and gold, and this apparition told her that she should pass through the towns of France accompanied by heralds and trumpeters crying out that all must give her their gold and treasures in order to finance Joan's troops.

Joan was grateful for the suggestion, but with her sober-minded way of looking at things felt skeptical about Catherine. To the King, she said that it was all nonsense and inventions and that the best thing Catherine could do would be to return to her husband and children.

Catherine, however, insisted on her revelations and told Joan that she was quite willing for her to control them. As the revelations occurred at night-time, she invited Joan to share her bed. Joan accepted. She spent a sleepless night by the side of the snoring soothsayer, but there was no sign of any revelation. She asked her companion if the visions would soon occur and was told that they would begin very soon. Joan herself relates that she then consulted her own saint, who informed her that it was all pure invention.

When her judges in Rouen took up this matter and asked her why Catherine's visions should have been so inferior to her own, she answered that if Catherine's revelations, like her own, had been seen and admitted by recognized ecclesiastical authorities, archbishops, bishops, and others, she would never have been requested to control them.

Catherine was neither a virgin, a visionary, nor a warrior; when it was suggested that she should take part in the assault on La Charité she excused herself by saying that the weather was rather chilly.

This witch later took a mean revenge. When Joan fell into the hands of her enemies, Catherine said that she ought to be carefully guarded so that the devil could not come and free her.

Despite the reverse, Joan's position was still a strong one, and there is no reason to believe reports that a malicious party at court under the leadership of La Trémoille was working against her. At the end of 1429, Joan was raised to the nobility together with her parents and brothers and all their descendants. The document conferring the patent of nobility states that the King wished to give expression to his gratitude for the "innumerable and shining signs of God's grace of which we have become the recipients thanks to the intervention of our dear and well-beloved Maid, Jeanne d'Arc from Domrémy...."

The document also expresses the King's hope that Joan would in the future continue to confer benefits on the kingdom.

La Trémoille had supported her elevation to the nobility. He was morally suspect, but there are no indications that he deliberately tried to push Joan into the background or even to oppose her. Even if he did not believe in her divine mission and was incapable of appreciating the purity of her personality, he was enough of a realist to recognize her importance.

Another sign that Joan still retained her popularity was the homage of the city of Orléans. Great festivities were held in Joan's honor, and she was presented with a large residence for her free use for fifty years. That Joan continued to be in close touch with the King's policies appears from a letter to the Hussites in Bohemia. She may not have written this letter herself but it is probable that she approved of it.[1]

But though Joan may have had nothing to do with this letter, one cannot fail to recognize her voice in two letters she sent at that time to the burghers of Reims, whom the Duke of Burgundy's concentration of troops had naturally made very anxious.

Around the turn of the year, Philip the Good had displayed ceaseless activity. He raised troops and money and cleverly manipulated popular feeling in towns that had not yet dared to choose between him and the King; and he assembled his Burgundian and Flemish troops at the end of March and the beginning of April. His friend, Jean de Luxembourg, approached Reims threateningly. At the same time, the Duke continued the negotiations for peace. But the arrangements for a conference in Auxerre on April 1 were altered, and the meeting postponed until June 1. The Duke hoped that long before this date he would have conquered much of the loyalist territory, especially as Henry VI of England landed in Calais at the end of April with two thousand soldiers.

Strangely enough, these plans miscarried. In Paris, there were riots and conspiracies fomented by La Trémoille; the hesitant towns did not surrender so easily as had been expected, and one of the Duke's allies was thoroughly beaten at Anthon by the King's general, de Gaucourt.

---

[1] According to Calmette this letter was a fake. The letter "is probably really a school essay and there is reason to believe that Joan never knew anything about it". But if the letter is not a fake, it may, according to Cordier, have had some reference to the fact that the troops which the Cardinal of Winchester had had brought over to France were originally recruited for a campaign against the Hussites. By taking its stand against the Hussites, the Royal Chancellery could emphasize the absurdity of troops intended for combating heretics opposing France.

It was in this disturbed situation that Joan sent her first letter to the burghers of Reims. There is a striking difference between this letter and the formal, lifeless epistles she sometimes signed with her name. She promises to return soon to Reims, and if, against expectation, the English or the Burgundians should get there first, she would know how to deal with them.

One cannot doubt that the letter mirrors her happy optimism and certainty of victory.

Not until May do the King and his counselors appear to have realized that the Duke of Burgundy could not be trusted. Their whole policy, which had occasioned the retreat from Paris, had ended in complete fiasco. War was now the only possibility.

It is a mistake to believe that this was a victory for a war policy backed by Joan in opposition to, for instance, La Trémoille; earlier, probably, she had shared his views, but it is clear that she was delighted to see the Duke of Burgundy unmasked.

The first military task for the King was to prevent the Duke's two armies from joining hands; he had therefore to prevent the Burgundians from becoming masters of Champagne and the valley of the Oise. The large towns of Champagne, such as Troyes, Châlons, and Reims, remained loyal. To keep the Burgundian army assembled in Flanders from marching on Paris, Compiègne must be held. For this purpose, an army, which Joan accompanied, was dispatched to the north.

It was to be her last campaign. Some sources suggest that she was in an uncertain mood at the time of her departure from the Loire district. One of them says that she left for the town of Lagny-sur-Marne without informing the King. In any case, it is certain that during Easter Week Joan was before Melun. She must have followed the Passion, as the story was told day after day in Mass during Holy Week, with the deepest emotion. For she knew now that she herself was close to a sacrifice, close to suffering. It was in the moat outside Melun that her intuition first became a certainty. Or in her language: the "voices" told her what was going to happen. She told her judges in Reims that her "voices" had told her that she would be taken prisoner before the Feast of Saint John the Baptist (June 24), that this had to be, that she should fear nothing, and that God would help her. Questioned by the judges, she further stated that this message had recurred repeatedly and that she would die soon without suffering long imprisonment. But she had never been able to learn the hour of her end, though she had often tried. The judges asked her if she would have marched on, even if she had known the exact time. Joan replied—with Christ before her eyes—that if she had known the time, she would have marched less eagerly, but that she would have obeyed her "voices" come what might.

According to her own statement, Joan after this revelation handed the initiative to the military leaders.

Melun surrendered.

The King's troops won another minor victory over a Burgundian force commanded by a celebrated and feared adventurer and condottiere, Franquet d'Arras. Later Joan was blamed by her judges for having contributed to the execution of this officer. In actual fact, she at first wished to have him exchanged for a French officer, but when she learned that the latter was already dead she permitted the authorities in the town of Lagny, who had suffered from his misdeeds, to judge and execute him.

In Lagny, an incident occurred that was later to be misinterpreted. A child had been born almost lifeless. On the third day, it was taken to a church where prayers were said that the child be permitted at least to live long enough to be baptized. Joan participated in these prayers; the child showed signs of life, and it was possible to baptize it before it died. Later Joan was accused of having boasted that her prayers had resurrected the child. She denied this emphatically.[2]

The Duke of Burgundy now made every effort to capture Compiègne, a town that should have been his according to the treaty with the King, but whose citizens refused to obey orders. When Joan heard that Compiègne was about to be attacked, she hastened there. It was May 13. She was received with joy by the townsfolk, went to church, and remounted.

At Pont-l'Evêque, however, the French were thrown back by the English and Burgundians.

Archbishop Regnault was in favor of marching up to Soissons, crossing the Aisne, and attacking the Duke of Burgundy in the rear. Joan accepted the plan. But before Soissons her soldiers seemed to have lost courage. The town refused them quarters within the walls, and they had to bivouac in the fields. In conditions that are not very clear, on

---

[2] "*Je ne m'en enquis point*" (I do not know a thing about it).

the morning of May 23, Joan returned to Compiègne with only four hundred men. She heard Mass in Saint-Jacques, went to Communion, and spoke to some small children who recognized her. In this church, according to one source who is not entirely without value, she said, "My good friends, my dear little children, they have sold me and betrayed me. I shall soon be given over to death. Pray to God for me. I can no longer serve either the King or France...."

Even if this is apocryphal, it may well express her feelings at the time. She must every day have told herself that the war was being conducted in a noticeably slack manner; she must also every day have seen the great personal risk to which she was exposed.

The end could not be far off.

The English and the Burgundians lay scattered over the neighborhood in small detachments. Jean de Luxembourg stood with his Picards on the banks of the Aronde at Clairoux. Five hundred Englishmen under Montgomery stood at Venette. The Duke himself was with his detachment at Coudon. Baudot de Noyelles, with a small detachment, was in the village of Margny overlooking the Seine.

It was this village that the French now decided to capture. Joan mounted a particularly fine horse, and we have a splendid picture of her on her departure.[3]

Joan was at the head of a detachment of a few hundred men under the command of Captain Baretta. She carried a Burgundian sword she had taken at Lagny. She was equipped for a parade rather than for battle.

There were certain risks about a sortie of this nature, and the commandant in Compiègne, Guillaume de Flavey, consequently took precautions. He placed a small troop at the bridgehead and saw to it that there were boats ready to bring the advancing troops back to the town in case of need. Joan is supposed to have said that she wanted to capture the enemy commander-in-chief herself. The idea behind the sortie, however, was undoubtedly a different one: to effect reconnaissance and, if possible, to capture the strategically important village of Margny.

It was five o'clock in the afternoon when the detachment rode over the bridge and disappeared from the sight of the garrison.

[3] "She mounted her horse, armed like a man, wearing over her armor a coat of scarlet and gold. She was riding a very fine and proud charger, and in her armor and bearing was like a captain leading a large host. And so, around four o'clock in the afternoon, with her standard raised high and fluttering in the wind, accompanied by many noblemen ..."

The fighting began well; the Burgundians defended themselves but without great energy. Joan must have had high hopes of capturing the village.

However, at precisely that time the Burgundian commander-in-chief, Jean de Luxembourg, accompanied by some ten men, was out on reconnaissance not even armed for battle. He discovered the attack and joined the troops at Margny, dispatching a message to Clairoux demanding reinforcements. At the same time, messages were sent to the English at Venette and the Burgundians at Coudon.

The village was captured, and Baudot and his men driven back. But instead of merely setting fire to the buildings and retreating with their booty, the French detachment fatally delayed their departure. The Burgundians, who knew they were about to receive reinforcements, counterattacked. As a matter of fact, the Duke himself was on his way to the village. It is also possible that Joan had been recognized. After some fighting, the French were forced to draw back. Now, however, they noticed the approach of the English reinforcements who were trying to cut off their line of retreat to Compiègne. The French were seized by something like panic, and they all tried to get down to the river as quickly as possible. The commandant, however, had the drawbridge raised, fearing that the enemy might attempt to use it. Some men threw themselves into the boats; others dived into the water to swim across.

A small force was pressed up against the bridgehead. Among them was Joan of Arc. She appeared as calm as ever and anxious to attack. Her well-known battle cry was heard, "Forward! They are ours!"[4]

Her own soldiers seized her bridle to force her to retreat with them, but she resisted. She wanted to fight, indifferent to the fact that in this situation even the greatest bravery would be quite futile. The English pressed forward between her and the bridgehead—she had now only a handful of men around her who continued to fight. One of the enemy dragged her from her horse. She rose to her feet, and from all sides heard cries urging her to surrender. It was clear that nobody dared—or wished—to kill her. Perhaps she was feared as a witch. Or perhaps it was the thought of the handsome ransom the King could be made to pay for her.

---

[4] *"Allez en avant! Ils sont à nous!"*

One of her last remarks appears to have been, "I have sworn fealty to one other than you, and I mean to keep my oath."

She surrendered at last to one of the enemy who assured her that he was a knight, which implied that her life would be in no danger. His name was Lionel de Wandomme. It was said that he was as happy as if he had captured a king.

At the same time her brother, Pierre, was taken prisoner, as well as her faithful master of the horse, Jean d'Aulon, and Poton, nicknamed "the Burgundian".

The garrison of the town remained completely inactive. No attempt was made to save her who had saved France. Later investigations have, however, acquitted the commandant of blame: it has been shown that he could not have acted otherwise.

Joan of Arc was a prisoner.

This occurred about six o'clock in the afternoon of May 23, 1430.

CHAPTER 10

In Beaulieu and Beaurevoir

Joan had surrendered to a knight who served under Jean de Luxembourg, an experienced soldier thirty-nine years old, who had always been faithful to the cause of Burgundy. He immediately informed the Duke of Burgundy in his headquarters at Coudon. Philip the Good at once jumped into the saddle, anxious to make Joan's acquaintance as soon as possible. His chronicler was present at the meeting but makes no reference to it. Calmette wondered if the reason for this silence might possibly be that the Duke of Burgundy had not behaved very chivalrously on this occasion: "One would have to be bold to assert this, but it is permissible to suspect it."

On the following day the ducal chancellery sent out letters with the great news.

Joan was held prisoner for three or four days in the camp of Jean de Luxembourg. On June 6, she was taken to Noyon. The Duchess of Burgundy had expressed eagerness to meet the much-discussed girl from Domrémy, but we have no information about this meeting either. From Noyon, Joan was taken to the castle of Beaulieu in Vermandois about twenty-two miles from Compiègne. There she remained during June and July. At this period, she was still treated with respect, and Jean d'Aulon had charge of her quarters and meals.

Joan's friends were helpless; their troops were too weak to intervene on her behalf. The King himself lay inactive on the Loire. Nobody can blame Dunois or La Hire for not trying to rescue Joan. It is also wrong to blame the commandant in Compiègne for hoisting up the drawbridge before Joan could cross. From a human point of view, she was herself to blame for her capture.

She retained her gay courage.

Jean d'Aulon said one day with a sigh that the town of Compiègne too, which Joan had relieved, would now fall into the hands of the enemy. He added that he had heard that the Burgundians would massacre the whole population. Joan replied, "Oh, no. That won't happen."

She went on to say that all the towns God had allowed her to conquer or liberate would doubtless keep the enemy at bay.

She very soon made an attempt to escape. Later she spoke to her judges about the incident, pointing out that there had never been a prisoner who had not wanted to escape. She had meant to hide, and then to have locked her guards in the tower. However, the gatekeeper discovered her: "God did not wish me to escape that time. . . ."

In the early part of August, Joan was taken to Beaurevoir near Cambrai. This was the residence of Jeanne de Luxembourg and Jeanne de Béthune, the former an aunt of Jean de Luxembourg and very devoted to him, and the latter his wife. Jeanne de Luxembourg was sixty-seven, very delicate in health and very pious, and for a long time she had been trying to bring about the canonization of her brother, the Cardinal of Luxembourg. Both ladies treated Joan with exquisite kindness. They offered her decent clothes, that is, feminine garments, but she declined the offer, saying that her "voices" did not yet permit her to discard her male attire.

We know of another episode from this time. A Burgundian knight, Aimond de Macy, got to know Joan and was attracted by her. One day he tried to caress her breast, but was vigorously repulsed by the angry girl.

Joan made a second attempt to escape. She told her judges that her reason for this was that she had heard she was to be handed over to the English, and also that she was in despair about the terrible events that were said to have occurred in Compiègne, where all the inhabitants over seven had been murdered. She was asked if her "voices" had really approved of this attempt—which was almost in the nature of attempted suicide—to which she answered in the negative. Saint Catherine had almost every day impressed upon her that she must not throw herself from the tower; God would help both her and Compiègne. Joan had then answered Saint Catherine that if God would help Compiègne, she would want to be there herself. But her "voice" had told her that she must accept her fate. In any case, she would not be free till she had met the English king, to which Joan replied that she had no wish to meet him and that she would rather die than fall into the hands of the English.

She crept out of the window and hanging by her stretched arms allowed herself to drop, commending herself to God. She dropped sixty feet, and by a miracle escaped without serious injury, though she lost consciousness.

It appears that in spite of all she succeeded in hiding in a watchtower of the castle and remained there without food for three days but with no possibility of making her escape. She was then discovered.

She willingly admitted that she had done wrong and would have been wiser if she had listened to her "voices". Nevertheless, the saints had saved her from destruction when she fell.

A Shepherd Boy

On June 25, the news of Joan's capture reached Paris. The very next day the University of Paris in a solemn address to the Duke of Burgundy requested that the prisoner be handed over to the Inquisitor General of France, the Dominican Martin Billoray, for questioning.

It is probable that this letter was the result of direct pressure on the part of the Duke of Bedford, who was convinced that Joan was a witch and who also realized how important it was that she should be sentenced by the ecclesiastical authorities, in order that her influence might thereby be finally broken.

We must assume that the men of the University of Paris acted in good faith. All they knew about Joan was through rumors, often insanely exaggerated. They knew that she did all kinds of supernatural things; all the myths set in motion by Joan's foolish admirers appeared in Paris to be just so many proofs of her guilt. These men were, of course, supporters of the Duke of Burgundy, and the terror created by the Duke of Armagnac in Paris was fresh in their minds. They were surely loyal and sincere in their faith in the English cause and cannot be blamed for what they did, especially as rumor was rife concerning the horrible massacres Joan had intended for Paris once she got within its walls.

Anatole France says quietly: "They were men; one believes that which it is in one's interest to believe; they were priests, and everywhere saw the devil, especially in a woman...."

What did the foremost ecclesiastical authority on the other side, Archbishop Regnault of Reims, do at that time?

As has already been mentioned, several visionaries appeared around Joan, among them Catherine de la Rochelle, whom Joan had time to expose personally. But it is a strange fact that some time before Joan was taken prisoner a young shepherd, Guillaume from Gévaudan, had strange revelations while he was watching over his sheep. These revelations also concerned France and her future. He went to Mende and told of his revelations and asked to be taken to the King. Pious people believed him and arranged for him in due course to be taken to the King. He related that God had told him to accompany the army and conquer the English and the Burgundians.

When the King and his priestly advisers asked him for proof or a sign, the youth—who had never touched a woman—showed that he had the stigmata. He had so deeply entered into the sufferings of Christ that his body bore the same wounds as that of Christ. This was, of course, in itself no evidence of his holiness, but nevertheless it made a strong impression.

The King sent the youth to Archbishop Regnault, who received him in a kindly manner. There the youth learned that Joan had been taken prisoner. "This will only bring them more misfortunes", he said. Guillaume immediately adopted a hostile attitude toward Joan and explained that her downfall was due to her pride, that she had worn too costly clothing and instead of obeying the will of God had followed her own. The opinion of a shepherd boy may seem unimportant, but it deserves a moment's thought.

It is evident that from the time of the coronation in Reims Joan had lost her earlier unfailing confidence. She herself admits that on some occasions she had acted, if not in opposition to her "voices", at least without their approval. One is sometimes tempted to wonder if in her later, often inexplicable, actions she was led by the will of God, or by her own will. The question cannot be answered with any certainty. But it is reasonable to believe that the words of the mystical youth made a certain impression on Joan's old friends, who had probably themselves noticed the beginnings of her uncertainty and had puzzled over the question why she should seem to be forsaken by the strong powers who had before protected her.

Archbishop Regnault himself at that time addressed a letter to the burghers of Reims, where Joan was greatly beloved, endeavoring to explain the matter. It is possible that when writing this letter he had been influenced by the youth's opinions. In any case he wrote that Joan had only herself to blame. "She would not listen to advice but did exactly what she herself wished."

However, we may suspect that the Archbishop's chief regret was that Joan had not listened to *his* advice.

But now God had intervened and sent to him a remarkable youth: "To the King has come a young shepherd who guarded his animals in the mountains of Gévaudan in the parish of Mende, and this shepherd said neither more nor less than Joan and asserted that God had allowed Joan to be taken prisoner because she had fallen victim to pride and because of the costly garments in which she clad herself."

This letter has for centuries roused the greatest indignation among Joan's admirers. And yet it is not so unreasonable. In what other way could an old theologian who had never been really convinced of Joan's divine mission judge her appearance and her downfall?

Calmette claims that "La Trémoille was overcome with delight" over what had occurred, but nothing points to this. What we do know with certainty is the extraordinary emotion and sorrow in the towns that had come to know and love Joan. In Tours there were public prayers for her liberation, and a great procession of the whole of the clergy marched barefoot through the streets. In the towns of the Dauphiné, special Masses were said for Joan. In the Postcommunion, God was implored to free "the Maid who, while carrying on the work which God had inspired her to do, had been and still is incarcerated in the prisons of our enemies".

The theologian, Jacques Gélu, who at the beginning had adopted a very hesitant attitude, addressed a courageous letter to the King in which he asked him to consider carefully whether it could not possibly be his own sins and omissions that had led to the punishment by God that was implied in the capture of Joan; he ends it by imploring the King to spare neither money nor other means to liberate the Maid and save her life. If this were not done, the King would incur the risk of "bearing the ineffaceable shame of a most condemnable ingratitude". Gélu proposed that prayers for Joan's liberation should be said in all churches in order that God pardon the sins of the King or the people that had perhaps led to this national catastrophe.

We do not know if the letter made any impression on the King.

183

Cauchon was Bishop of Beauvais, so it was within his diocese that Joan was captured.

Very early this prelate had thrown himself into the political arena and had even fraternized with "the scourge of Paris", Caboche. For decades he had served the Dukes of Burgundy and the English, and he was one of the closest confidants of the English court. As the town of Beauvais sided with the French king, Cauchon had a permanent residence in Rouen, but he never forgot that he was a Bishop of Beauvais. He became one of the strongest forces in the trial of Joan and in the end succeeded in bringing it to the desired conclusion.

His later life was also remarkable. The Pope appointed him Bishop of Lisieux, and in this connection he became liable to pay four thousand gold florins to Rome. The money never arrived, which annoyed the authorities so much that Cauchon was excommunicated. This did not put him out in the least, for he continued to say Mass and administer his high office. He then received advice from Rome that if he did not immediately submit, the order of his excommunication would be displayed on the church doors and all faithful forbidden to have anything to do with him. Cauchon yielded and was pardoned.

He died in 1442 of a stroke while his servant was shaving him.

Cauchon hated Joan of Arc and was clearly of the honest opinion that she was in the service of demons. He appeared before the Duke of Burgundy on July 14, 1430, with a long and eloquent letter from the University of Paris.

The learned men of the University were seriously concerned. They feared that the lord of the nether regions might, with the help of men of ill will, enemies, and opponents of the Duke, free his pupil, Joan. Such a shame must never under any circumstances fall on the most "Christian name of the House of France". Wherefore the University once more respectfully requested that the Duke surrender the said witch either to the Inquisitor General or to the Bishop of Beauvais, under whose spiritual jurisdiction she had been taken prisoner.

In a similar letter to Jean de Luxembourg we read: "The first duty of a knight is to safeguard and defend the honor of God, the Catholic faith, and Holy Church. You had this holy oath in mind when you exercised your high power and person to take prisoner a woman who calls herself the Maid and through whom God's glory has been terribly violated, for by means of her intervention idolatry, confusion, evil doctrines, and other evils have descended on the kingdom to an immeasurable degree."

Jean de Luxembourg was asked to prevent Joan from escaping and to hand her over to the Bishop of Beauvais, the pillar of faith and the Church.

At the same time as Cauchon presented these two letters, he laid on the table, if not a purse, at least the promise of one. He offered to pay the—for those days enormous—sum of ten thousand francs if Joan were handed over to the English.

This sum indicates the tremendous importance of Joan to her opponents.

In London, it had been suggested that the witch should be put in a sack and thrown into the Seine. But others pointed out how great would be the political effect if the people of France became convinced that Charles VII owed his victories to a woman guaranteed by the Church to be a genuine witch. Until the appearance of Joan, the English had had scarcely any serious reverses in France; therefore she must be in the service of the devil. If this could be confirmed by the Church herself, and if the King of France could be thus implicated, the war would in all probability be won. Nothing can be said against the logic of this argument.

Obviously the offer made a great impression on both the Duke of Burgundy, who had incurred heavy expenses during the campaign, and his lieutenant, Jean de Luxembourg. Both well knew what happened to witches; they were burned without mercy.

An important precedent had recently been established. The unfortunate monk, Brother Richard, had taken not only Joan and Catherine de la Rochelle but a number of other women under his protection. One of these women, Pieronne from Brittany, was captured by the English and very thoroughly questioned in Paris. Despite threats and exhortations she gently insisted that God had more than once revealed himself to her and spoken to her, and that she was convinced that Joan had been sent by God.

She was burned alive. Both knights understood that the same fate could await Joan without any benefit to them. During the course of the night, they probably eagerly discussed what was the right solution:

Would the King of France pay as much, or perhaps more? In spite of Cauchon's pressure, a decision was postponed, and to prevent the risk of any contretemps Joan was moved from one castle to another. Thus in September she was brought to Arras; there, strangely enough, she was visited by a Scotsman, who painted a kind of portrait of her, showing her kneeling in full armor before the King and handing him a letter. We also know that one or two visitors offered her feminine clothing, which she always declined.

Another reason for Joan's removal may have been that the fortune of war was not wholly favorable to the Duke of Burgundy. Despite tremendous efforts, he never succeeded in capturing Compiègne. The besieging force was crushed between the garrison and reinforcements under Marshal de Boussac. Simultaneously other detachments of the King's army made raids in the neighborhood of Paris. La Hire was fighting in Normandy, and Marshal de Boussac made thrusts between the rivers Seine, Marne, and Somme.

In the circumstances, Jean de Luxembourg finally agreed to the proposal of the English and surrendered Joan. To avoid any risks she was to be taken to Rouen, where she could be regarded as out of reach of the King's forces.

From Arras, she was taken to the castle in Drugy, then to Le Crotoy, where her friend the Duke of Alençon had been incarcerated after the battle of Verneuil. She was still allowed to receive visitors. Many inquisitive people came to see her, and she was allowed to talk with priests and to confess.

From Le Crotoy, Joan was taken by boat to Saint-Valéry, from there to Dieppe, and then to Rouen, which she was never to leave.

In Rouen: The Iron Cage

In Rouen, she was conducted to the old castle that had been built in the reign of Philippe Auguste. There, since August, had resided the young English king, Henry VI, under the supervision of the stern Lord Warwick. Joan was incarcerated in one of the seven towers. The tower had three floors; Joan was imprisoned on the middle floor, which consisted of one single large room the diameter of which was forty-three paces.

How she was imprisoned there is not easy to decide. An iron cage has been spoken of in which she could not hold herself straight, but this story has not been confirmed.[1] What is certain is that she was chained by the neck, hands, and feet from the first moment until the beginning of the trial. Night and day, she was fettered in chains. Her guard consisted of five English soldiers, of whom Anatole France says that they "did not belong to the flower of chivalry". Three of them spent the night in the same room as Joan. That they did not at once sexually assault her must have been due to their fear that she was a witch.

At the beginning many visitors were allowed to come in and gaze at the imprisoned girl, among them a lawyer of Rouen, named Pierre Daron, who has given an account of his visit. He asked her if she knew that she was going to be captured, and, as usual, she answered in the affirmative. Why then had she not been more on her guard? Joan replied that she had no knowledge of the time and the place.

Another visitor tells that Joan was tied by means of a long chain attached to a post with manacles on her ankles.

She was, of course, also visited by her powerful opponents, Jean de Luxembourg and his brother the Bishop of Thérouanne, Lord Warwick, and Stafford. Jean de Luxembourg appears to have intimated that he might ransom her if she would promise never again to fight against Burgundy. One can suspect that this was due to secret pressure on the part of the King of France. Joan rejected the suggestion with contempt. She knew that she was in the hands of the English and that nothing could save her: "I know very well that the English intend to kill me and think that after my death they can take the whole kingdom of France. But even if another hundred thousand *godons* come, they will never be able to take France."

When she uttered these words, one of the Englishmen lost his temper and would have run her through if he had not been stopped by Warwick.

Jeanne de Luxembourg had until the last fought against the handing over of Joan to the English. Generally speaking, Joan gained the sympathy of women, even of those upon the side of the enemy. When the wife of the irreconcilable Duke of Bedford visited Joan in her prison, she

[1] However, it is quite certain that such a cage was constructed. "He also said that he had heard of Stephen Castille, a locksmith, that he himself had constructed for her an iron cage, in which she was kept standing, chained by her neck, her hands and her feet; and that she was kept in this condition from the day she was brought to Rouen until the beginning of the trial."

was seized with pity and at once offered her female clothing. She even gave orders on her own initiative that a long and warm cloak should be made for her by her tailor, Jeannotin Simon, and came to Joan accompanied by him. When the tailor wanted to try on the cloak, he happened to touch Joan's breast. He had an immediate box on the ear.

The French writers who have described Joan's imprisonment have not been squeamish in their expressions.[2] Even recognizing their exaggerations, we have to admit that her trial must have been a terrible one. Joan was alone in a prison tower, surrounded by brutal soldiers who insulted and wounded her. She was still suffering from the effects of her fall in Beaurevoir. It was a cold winter—Christmas was approaching, and she was not allowed to confess regularly or to go to Mass. The holy anticipation of Advent was lost to her. She never heard from her friends. She knew nothing of her family, and she was only twenty years old.

Above all, she must have pondered over God's intention in these happenings. Was it conceivable that he had abandoned her to this? Yes, if she had sinned through pride and self-will. But had she done so? For what could she blame herself? For she had had her faithful confessor by her side from whom she hid nothing. Would he not have warned her if she had been guilty of sin?

Joan had now entered into a state with which suffering saints are familiar and that must be borne as a special trial; great difficulties are encountered, and one cannot with any certainty determine if they are the result of one's own sin or if they are the direct will of God. Whichever is the case, the trials must be loyally and humbly accepted. About this there can be no question. But from a purely practical point of view, it is of importance to know if one is within or outside the circle of grace, if God acts as he does because he wishes to chastise, or if he is preparing a mysterious destiny, a great suffering for one who is innocent. We may assume that such thoughts occupied Joan's mind, too. In her agony, she appeals to her warders and begs them to allow her to go to Mass, confession, and Communion. Warwick has her informed that women of her kind cannot be allowed to approach the sacraments.

During the peace of Christmas, Cauchon worked energetically preparing for the impending trial. At the moment there was no bishop in

[2] The Jesuit Father Paul Doncoeur, in his work *Le mystère de la Passion de Jeanne d'Arc,* gives the following description of Joan's warders: "The warders lie full of whisky and pudding, stretched on their benches, and snore like pigs."

Rouen, and he had therefore to ask the Chapter for permission to conduct the trial at a place not within his own diocese. This permission was granted without any difficulty.

Cauchon now appointed judges and officers of the court. He shunned no difficulties. The accumulated experience and authority of the Church was to be mobilized against the young witch and against Charles VII.

He first turned to the University of Paris, with whose position he was very familiar: all who might conceivably have defended Joan had long since left the city. Six learned men came from Paris: Jean Beaupère, Thomas de Courcelles, Gérard Feuillet, Nicolas Midi, Pierre Maurice, and Jacques de Touraine. They were all famous theologians.

Then Cauchon turned to the powerful monastic orders. He sent letters to the abbots of the great Breton and Norman monasteries. Mont-Saint-Michel, Fécamp, Jumièges, Préaux, Mortemer, Saint-Georges de Boscherville, Trinité-du-Mont, Sainte-Catherine, Saint-Ouen, le Bec, Cormeilles. He also wrote to the priors of Saint-Lô, Rouen, Sigy, and Longueville.

The most important of these monks was perhaps the abbot of Mont-Saint-Michel, Robert Jolivet, who was completely pro-English and had earlier wanted to surrender his monastery to the enemy. The powerful abbot of Fécamp, Gilles Duremort, was during the trial to appear as an irreconcilable enemy of Joan. In addition to these great personages, there were the canons of the College of Rouen and a number of private advocates and theologians from different parts of the country.

The majority of the judges—there were about a hundred—were recruited from three groups that had all proved themselves reliable enemies of Charles VII: the University of Paris, the great Norman monasteries, and the canons of Rouen.[3] There is nothing to suggest that these men were thoroughly dishonorable. They were probably average men, strongly influenced by their political leanings and in certain cases, as we shall find, afraid to express their real opinion. But they were on the whole, both before, during, and after the trial, honestly convinced that

[3] Of Normandy's four bishops, one, the Bishop of Bayeux, was in Spain; the second, the Bishop of Évreux, was in Paris; the third, the Bishop of Séez, was close to Charles VII, and was visiting him; the fourth, the Bishop of Avranches, Jean de Saint-Avit, advised Cauchon to turn to the Pope and Church Council. Cauchon never entered this advice in the proceedings of the trial, but the following year had his colleague thrown into prison because of his French sympathies.

in Joan they were dealing with an authentic witch, an emissary of the devil, whom they must as Christians and priests try to save or, if she did not submit, sentence to death.

Perhaps one can assume that, by and large, they had as good a conscience as the Jewish clergy who pressed for Christ's crucifixion. To assume that the noblest representatives of mankind have been the victims of conscienceless and shameless men is to lessen the real tragedy of history. On the contrary, there is reason to believe that both Christ and Joan were in part sentenced by men who acted in good faith, who represented a good average of judgment and legal knowledge, and who honestly believed that they were intervening in favor of a holy thing that must not be defiled without punishment.

That is not to say, of course, that one or two of the judges were not lacking in conscience and objectivity. We will return to these cases.

Preparations for the Trial

What form did such a trial take?

Before the beginning of the actual trial, a preparatory trial was held, a *procès préparatoire* or *procès d'office*. The object of this preparatory trial was to examine the person under suspicion. On the basis of the evidence collected, it was then decided if the actual trial should take place. The evidence of the prosecutor would be that produced during the *procès d'office*.

During the Middle Ages at a trial of this nature, there should have been only two judges and an unlimited number of jurymen. All these had the right to put questions and intervene in other ways.

Further, the accused was not represented by counsel. It was only if the accused was found unable to understand the proceedings that the judge could choose a counsel for the defense.

After this preparatory trial had succeeded in its task, the proper trial, the *procès ordinaire*, commenced. From the records of the earlier examination, the prosecutor established a number of articles more or less based on extracts from the evidence produced. The accused was given the opportunity of replying to the accusations article by article, and the new record was then placed before the jury.

It was now Cauchon's task to prepare what he himself called "a good trial". This was not altogether easy. Among other difficulties was the following:

Joan's case had already been thoroughly gone into by the commission in Poitiers. The president of this commission was Regnault de Chartres, Archbishop of Reims, who was in fact the superior of the Bishop of Beauvais, Cauchon himself. In other words, the implication was that a subordinate prelate did not accept a result at which his superior had arrived: a bishop disavowing an archbishop.

It was therefore of the greatest importance for Cauchon to give his trial at least the outward semblance of complete legality.

What he first required was evidence that could make it possible to take up the case in a legal manner. At an early stage, he sent out emissaries to scour the country for compromising facts. The facts were brought in but were unfortunately found to be favorable to the accused. However diligent the search, it was impossible to produce any witnesses willing to testify to any shameful or compromising occurrences in which Joan had been involved, and in order to condemn her it was necessary to have recourse to the pious gossip we have already mentioned. When one of these scouts, Nicolas Bailly, reported the results of his investigations to Cauchon, he was roundly abused by his master, treated as if he were a traitor, and not paid for his trouble. During the whole of the trial, not a word seems to have been said about these investigations, nor were they mentioned in the promemoria or in the summing up.[4] It was also of importance to try to establish that Joan was not a virgin. Again she was forced to undergo an intimate examination, though it is probable that this would not appear as repellent to people of those days as it does to us. And it was the Duchess of Bedford, with her noble mind and sympathetic attitude toward Joan, who undertook this task. One source, perhaps not very reliable, suggests that the Duke himself was secretly present at this examination. It is not impossible.

Here again Cauchon was unable to show that the examination in Poitiers had in any way been at fault.

His first attempt at collecting damning material had therefore failed miserably.

He then assembled a number of persons upon whom he looked as reliable and asked them what they considered the best course to take.

---

[4] Nicolas Bailly declared that in Joan he had found nothing that he would not have wished to find in his own sister, though he had made his investigations in five or six neighboring villages and in Domrémy itself.

They, of course, answered that it was necessary to begin with "instruction", that is, to collect evidence as the basis for an accusation. Cauchon replied that this had already been done, but did not mention that the findings were worthless. He promised soon to produce the reports. The officers of the court, prosecutor, clerk, etc., were then chosen.

On January 13, Cauchon stated in a minute that he had already furnished the promised evidence, and on January 23, that on the basis of the evidence he had established a number of points that could be used as the basis for the trial. On February 19, the first report seems to have been produced, and because of its nature it was decided to charge Joan with heresy.

Though this seems very straightforward, it appears that it was in fact very much the reverse. Cauchon had failed in his first attempt to produce compromising evidence and now secretly replaced these reports by others. He established a system of espionage in Joan's prison. He got more or less disguised henchmen to enter Joan's prison, pretend to be her friends, and lead her into a confession of guilt. Even the prosecutor, Jean d'Estivet, took part in these sordid maneuvers, but one of the most prominent in them was a canon of Rouen by the name of Nicolas Loiseleur, who pretended to come from Lorraine and thereby soon became intimate with Joan. He brought her greetings from the King and asked if he could not be her confessor. Two notaries were placed in the adjoining room, from where by means of a hole in the wall they could listen to Joan's answers and put them down.

Joan immediately fell into the trap and spoke freely from her heart. Probably it gave her much joy to confess to this priest. In order to gain her full confidence, he warned her to be careful of the priests who were going to try her; she must not do as they advised her; that would be disastrous....

A rumor was spread in the town that Loiseleur had dressed up as Joan's favorite saint, Saint Catherine, and had succeeded in deceiving her. The report cannot be verified, but it is not quite incredible.

On such evidence Joan was accused of heresy....

Who were the men who principally opposed Joan? We already know Cauchon.

The *promoteur*, that is, the prosecutor, was Jean d'Estivet, nicknamed "Benedicite" because of the appalling insults, blasphemies, and curses continually pouring out of him. He seems to have been a thoroughly conscienceless person, though he was still a canon in Bayeux and Beauvais. He used the coarsest words about Joan, even to her face, calling her a whore and worse, and on one occasion behaved so brutally to her that even Warwick, who was fairly tough, was moved to have him thrown out.

The *conseiller-instructeur* was Jean de la Fontaine. He seems to have been an ordinary, honorable lawyer, but he lacked the courage to object to all the illegalities he must have witnessed. It was he who, during the trial, whispered to Joan that she must appeal to the Pope. When he learned of Cauchon's fury about this, he fled from Rouen.

The senior clerk of the court was Manchon, who proved to be an honorable and courageous man and refused to distort Joan's replies. When his colleagues produced the record of Joan's words overheard and taken down secretly in the prison, he demanded that she be allowed to see the notes before they were accepted as correct; and when the unscrupulous priest, Loiseleur, dictated statements of Joan, he demanded that these be approved by Joan herself before they were produced in court. He also refused to put down her words to the same priest in prison. Later he courageously refused to admit the recantation Cauchon asserted that he had heard as Joan was dying. He was obliged to be present at her death, but he says of it: "I shall never again weep so over anything I may experience, and for a whole month I enjoyed no peace. With part of the money I obtained for my services I purchased a little missal so that I could pray for her."

Manchon's pronouncements during the Trial of Rehabilitation are without doubt the most important material we possess concerning the trial at Rouen.

The other clerk, Boisguillaume, was also a decent fellow whom Joan seems to have liked. On one occasion, when he made a slip, she said teasingly to him, "Take care or I'll tweak your ear."

Another friendly-disposed person was Massieu, the sheriff's officer. He did not believe in Joan's guilt and did not hesitate to say what he thought, which earned him a torrent of abuse from Cauchon. He was perhaps regarded as too insignificant to deserve serious punishment. Once the public prosecutor saw Massieu allowing Joan to pray before the door of a chapel that was on her way between her prison and the courtroom. "Benedicite" asked how Massieu dared to permit the "excommunicated harlot" to be in the vicinity of a church and threatened the good man with prison. When Massieu did not take these coarse outbursts literally but continued to allow Joan to pray, "Benedicite" sent guards to put an end to the mischief.

Joan took a great liking to this kindly man and told him about the coarseness to which the English warders exposed her. He showed her great kindness during her last days and did everything in his limited power to make her suffering more bearable.

Cauchon also required the support of the Inquisitor General, but this potentate had disappeared—to Coutances, it is believed. There may be a significant reason for this disappearance. The Inquisition hesitated.... It is suggested by modern Dominicans that the Inquisitor General understood the purely political import of the trial and preferred not to be involved in it.

Cauchon turned to the deputy of the Inquisitor General, the prior of the convention of Rouen, Jean Lemaître, who replied that he could not act on his own initiative and wished to have nothing to do with the matter without orders from the Inquisitor General. But on the other hand, he felt that he could not object to Cauchon's holding the trial without his collaboration. He seems not to have believed in Joan's guilt, but dared not express an opinion. If he cast his vote for the burning of Joan, it is because he knew that he would otherwise be jeopardizing his own life.

CHAPTER 11

February 21

On February 21 at eight o'clock in the morning the trial opened in the
castle chapel, which had been turned into a courtroom. There were
forty-two assessors present. At first Pierre Cauchon was the sole judge.
Later he was joined by the uncertain and hesitant prior, Jean Lemaître.

Cauchon opened the proceedings by reading a letter from the English
king, dated January 3, in which he solemnly delivers Joan to the Bishop
of Beauvais for trial and sentence.[1]

Thereupon the prosecutor, "Benedicite", announced that Joan had
agreed to be present but had demanded that judges from the King's side
should also be present and that she be allowed to go to Mass.

Cauchon ignored the question of other judges but announced that a
decision regarding her being allowed to go to Mass must be postponed.

Joan was brought in; she was not fettered, but came direct from her
prison. A murmur went through the chapel.

Many of the learned men present saw her now for the first time; a tall
young woman, her hair now perhaps rather long, cut in the style of a
page, attired in male clothing. The minutes of the trial make clear how
great was the scandal of a woman in male attire in those days; to parallel
the effect of Joan's appearance in male attire we can only think of the
way in which a naked woman would have been regarded by nineteenth-
century English nonconformists. The Franciscans, Jean de Nibat and

---

[1] "... and because she has been declared, known, and reputed by several as given to superstition, false teachings and other sacrilegious crimes against the Divine Majesty, we have been
very urgently asked by the most reverend Bishop of Beauvais, our dearly beloved and loyal
adviser, under whose ecclesiastical and ordinary jurisdiction this same Joan belongs as she has
been taken prisoner in his diocese; also urged by our dearly beloved daughter, the University
of Paris, we herewith give, assign, and deliver this same Joan to the aforesaid very reverend
Sir, for him to interrogate and examine her and to proceed against her according to the rules
and regulations of divine and canonical laws; call therefore those who have to be called...."

Jacques Guesdon, stared; the Augustinian hermit, Jean le Fèvre, covered his eyes with his hands; the Carmelites, Pierre de Houdenc, prior in Rouen, and Guillaume Le Bocher, smiled mockingly; and the Benedictine abbot, Guillaume de Conti, of Sainte-Catherine in Rouen, forgot the saint whose name his monastery bore.

Joan, on the other hand, must have recollected the legend of Saint Catherine and her discourse with the fifty learned men. She had convinced them, and in the end they had wanted to embrace her own faith.

She herself had triumphantly emerged from a similar trial in Poitiers.

Cauchon then told Joan to take the oath to tell nothing but the truth with her hand on the Bible.

Joan answered: "I do not know what you are going to ask me. Perhaps you may ask me questions to which I will not reply...."

"Swear to tell the truth regarding that about which you will be questioned, concerning the faith and all that you know."

Before these stern words Joan raised her head. She sensed that Cauchon hated her. Why? For she was herself nothing. She only obeyed God....

"I will willingly give the oath regarding that which concerns my father and mother and everything that I have done since I rode to France, but as to the revelations that have come to me from God, I have never spoken of them to anyone but to King Charles, and I will not do so here, even if my head be cut off; I receive them from my 'voices' and have no right to reveal them to any man. But in eight days I shall know if I may speak."

As we have mentioned before, Joan had many times spoken of her "voices" to her friends; we have related how she was directly questioned about them on two occasions. But here she had something else in mind. It is difficult to decide what this is. It must be revelations of a very special nature of which she had only spoken to the King.

She took the oath kneeling, with both hands on the Bible: "I swear to tell the truth regarding that about which I shall be questioned concerning the faith."

The preliminary questions concerned her name—she was called Jeannette at home, Jeanne in France—her village, her parents, her baptism, her godparents, her age....

In answer to the last question she replied: "I am nineteen years old, I think...."

She relates, what we already know, that it was her mother who taught her the Paternoster, the Ave Maria, and the Credo. Cauchon orders her to say the Paternoster, at which she raises her head in defiance, wearied by his questions: "I will not say that prayer if you do not let me confess."

She wishes to confess to the implacable man before her who is determined to kill her at any cost!

Cauchon replies that he will place two French-speaking priests at her disposal if she will say the Paternoster before them.

She replies that she will not do so if she is not allowed to confess. This altercation was heated, and there were excited murmurings in the courtroom. Perhaps one should remember the comparison made with a naked young woman before a nineteenth-century English evangelical convention: that such a person dare defy the bishop is something unbelievable. Her request to be allowed to confess must be a trick of the devil. Some of the English king's secretaries have entered the courtroom; loud commotion breaks out, the assessors argue with each other, and the clerks can no longer distinguish questions and answers.

When relative calm has settled over the courtroom, a curious incident occurs. In order that Joan shall not understand them, Cauchon and the English lawyers turn to the clerk, Manchon, and dictate in Latin what he is to write. But Manchon refuses! He says that he has heard at least enough to know that the accused said something quite different.

Joan becomes aware that she has friends in the courtroom.

Cauchon wants to adjourn the hearing, but he first asks the assessors if Joan is to be held in an English prison or in the guard of the Church. Jean Fabri says quietly that she must, of course, not be held by the English as the King of England has surrendered her to the Church. For a while this point is discussed. Cauchon announces that out of consideration for the English he cannot demand this; clearly he is under very severe political pressure.

He then turns to Joan and asks her to promise not to leave her prison in the castle.

She answers forcefully: "I certainly do not promise this. If I flee, nobody will be able to charge me with having broken my promise, for I have not promised anything to anyone. Ever since I was brought here my hands and feet have been fettered with iron manacles that hurt terribly. . . ."

Cauchon replies that there is proof that she has several times tried to flee and that it was for this reason that he gave orders that she must be fettered.

"That is true", Joan replied, and continues, "I should like to flee now too; it is the right of every prisoner...."

She looks at him calmly and says, "I know that you are my enemy."

He replied that he had the King's orders to conduct the trial and that he meant to obey.

Now three Englishmen, John Gris, William Talbot, and John Berwoit, are delegated to be Joan's warders and are required to take a solemn oath.

Joan is taken back to prison. It is probable that she is not placed in her cage but sits chained. Perhaps it was that very evening that one of her warders tried to assault her. She complains to Cauchon, who speaks to Warwick about it. The latter upbraids the warders and gives orders that henceforth three of them must always remain in Joan's room.

The deputy inquisitor general, the prior Jean Lemaître, must on that day decide if he will be assistant judge or not. He is uneasy and says to a friend that it will cost him his life to refuse.

So he accepts.

February 22

On the following day, February 22, a vast banqueting hall adjacent to the King's room in the castle is the scene of the trial. Joan notices that she is not taken by the same way as before; she is not to be permitted to gaze on the Sacrament during the hearing.

Again Cauchon orders her to take the oath. She replies calmly that she had done so the day before and "that will suffice". Cauchon cannot make her budge. He delegates the lead in the examination of the day to Jean Beaupère, a strongly pro-English priest. The latter asks Joan in a kindly way to answer truthfully all the questions that will be put to her. Again she answers with an energetic "No." She is ready to answer certain questions but by no means all, and adds: "If you knew for certain who I am, you would not want me to be in your hands. Everything that I have done I have done through revelations."

A majestic reply that one would have thought should have reminded the judges of another scene that took place fourteen hundred years earlier. But not one of them senses that they are witnessing and taking part in a trial that history will one day liken to those of Christ and Socrates. They all have an easy conscience.

A number of unimportant questions follow.

How old was she when she left her parents' home? She answered that she did not know.

Had she as a child been taught any profession? She answered smiling that she could sew and spin and could challenge any woman in Rouen at these crafts.

From the reply, one discerns that she is not depressed but keeps her good humor. She does not understand that these are purposely haphazard and illogical questions to lull her into self-confidence so that she may suddenly reveal her diabolical nature.

Was she in the habit of confessing once a year? She replied that she was. She relates that she used to confess to her parish priest and sometimes with his permission to another priest. She had also two or three times confessed to mendicant friars. She always communicated at Eastertime. Asked by the judge if she had also communicated at the time of other Church festivals, she replies impatiently, "Leave that alone."[2]

During the trial that was to be her invariable answer when unnecessary questions were put. It is not clear why this particular one should have irritated her.

Then came the first question about her revelations. We have already given an account of her answer: she presents a clear picture of her whole life story, the "voice", her first alarm, her new "voices", how she came to Vaucouleurs, how she rode to Chinon, how she arrived at Auxerre and there heard Mass. She added that just then she had heard her "voices" unusually distinctly.

Beaupère asks her on whose advice she adopted male attire.

She refuses to answer.

Her silence must mean that this particular detail was of special importance to her and belonged to the revelations of which she is unwilling to speak. But finally she says that she cannot place the responsibility for her adopting male attire on any human person—an evasive but clear answer.

---

[2] "... *dixit interroganti quod ipse transiret ultra....*" In the French translation: "*Passez outre!*"

The question is again put to her after a while, and then she answers that she had to change her attire and dress as a man. "I think that the advice I then received was good."[3]

Suddenly the judge asks her about her first letter to the English. He has a copy read out. Joan listens and admits that the letter is genuine, but adds that there have been alterations in it. She had never called herself *chef de guerre*; she had not spoken in her own name but in that of the King.

The judge asks her about her meeting with the King. She tells that she had a revelation as to who was the King. Was it true that she then, as when she had her first revelation, saw a light?

Joan refuses to answer.

But did she not see an angel above the King?

She does not answer. On the other hand, she relates that the King himself had had several revelations before the beginning of the campaign. The judge asks her what they were. She refuses to answer. Why not send a message to the King to inquire...?

Her irony is apparent. At the same time the meaning of her information deserves reflection. She is a theologically ignorant, spontaneous religious type. She is unaware of the obstacles that intellectual education and personal sin place in the way of a man listening to God. With her veneration for the King, she thinks him as she is, i.e., that he too in his actions is guided by revelations. And it is not inconceivable that she can in some way have been right—that Charles VII, despite his sickly, nervous, sensitive disposition, had some kind of a religious sensitivity. We know nothing of this for certain, but it is clear that on a high spiritual plane a kind of contact had been established between Joan and the King, a contact that she was afterward not to hold with anyone else.

She answers naïvely that both the King and his entourage heard the "voices" that spoke to her. She must have meant simply that they became convinced of the genuineness of her heavenly mission. She adds, glowing with confidence: "Not a day passes without my hearing the 'voice', and I need it."

Now the judge prepares a cunning trap: What is it she questions her "voices" about? One can feel those present holding their breath in

[3] *"Item, etiam credit quod consilium suum bene sibi dixit."*

suspense: now the diabolical inspirations can be revealed; the girl is so naïve, so confident, that she will surely betray herself. . . .

She answers calmly and with dignity: "I have never asked for any reward other than the salvation of my soul."[4]

Has she always obeyed her "voices"?

No, not always. The "voices" had, for instance, told her to stay at Saint-Denis, but the King's advisers had persuaded her to accompany the army to Paris, where she was immediately wounded.

Then comes another dangerous question.

Had not the assault on Paris taken place on a Church feast day?

Joan replied that she thought so.

Was that then a good thing?

She refused to answer. And we can understand her. Could the judge seriously pretend to believe that the English respected such conventions?

Here the session was adjourned for the second time.

After the examination, a clash occurred between Cauchon and the clerk Manchon. Cauchon wished to correct the latter's minutes. Manchon refused. It became necessary to go to Joan and repeat the question. It was shown that Manchon had understood her correctly. In other words, Cauchon had tried to falsify her testimony.

He repeated these attempts five days running, but each time Manchon was equally determined and in this displayed a highly courageous attitude in view of Cauchon's power and notorious ruthlessness.

During the night, Joan hears her "voices". They only tell her that she must hold out and show courage. In the course of the day, Cauchon is visited by an ecclesiastical jurist, Jean Lohier, whose opinion he values. He requests Lohier to go through the evidence and give him his opinion. Lohier promises to return when he has read through the reports.

February 24

On February 23, there was no examination. On the following day, sixty-three assessors are assembled in the courtroom as Cauchon makes his entrance. He repeats his customary tirade to Joan, bidding her tell

4 "*Dixit etiam quod nunquam requisivit a voce praefata aliud praemium finale, nisi salvationem animae suae.*"

the whole truth without reservations; she does not reply. He repeats his order three times. She remains silent. He cannot move her from her resolution.

Naïvely she tells him, "Take care, you who call yourself my judges! You take upon yourself a great responsibility if you put too great a burden upon me."[5]

What did she mean? First that sacred things are concerned which a bishop cannot violate. If God's voices have told her to be silent regarding the revelations, he must understand that this must be respected. Should he force her, he defies God himself and assumes a great responsibility. And he thereby also forces her to defy God.

If this were the hidden meaning of her words, we could ask ourselves, with the judges: What was it that she would not reveal? Nobody can know this, though Joan later, as we shall see, was forced to betray some of the truth. But in the history of other revelations and other saints, we have seen the same thing. There are revelations that should not and cannot be told, probably because they are of such a nature that they are bound to be misunderstood. Christ himself spoke of the necessity of spiritual maturity in order to understand the word of God. He said that he could only impart to his disciples fragments and elements of the truth—and yet it was too much for them, and they continually misunderstood him. Saint Paul says the same. To Joan it is clear, without any theological thought, that she cannot speak of unutterable things without the risk of great misunderstanding. In the end, it is because of this refusal that she is sentenced. She cannot act otherwise. She is graced with exceptional clarity, with a divine mission. But it is the extraordinary nature of her message that forbids it being spoken of. The only one who has understood her is the King, Charles VII. We must not object that he was a poorly endowed man, faint-hearted, possibly a wretched character. God often elects children and the feeble-minded. His standard is not that of humanism or of the universities.

A violent altercation now breaks out between Joan and Cauchon, who describes the perils to which she exposes herself. She tells him that she accepts all these perils and begs him to cease pestering her. Wearied by all his arguments, she says loudly in the silent courtroom: "I come

[5] "*Ego dico vobis, advertatis bene de hoc quod dicitis vos esse meum judicem, quia vos assumitis unum grande onus, et nimium oneratis me.*"

from God and have nothing to do here. Send me back to God from whom I have come."[6]

These are words blazing with power and inspiration. With what enormous confident authority this nineteen-year-old girl speaks to her learned judges! Saint Catherine must have silently nodded her approval in heaven at these confident and yet humble words. How is it possible that they did not move her hearers—experienced confessors trained in the study of the saints and Scriptures, well acquainted with the paths of mysticism?

Furious, Cauchon passes on the examination to Beaupère.

The latter is a far cleverer interrogator. He knows how to lead the examination on to dangerous ground by seemingly innocent questions. There comes an unforgettable exchange between the trained doctor and the inspired, clear-eyed girl.[7]

Beaupère: "When did you eat and drink last?"

Joan: "I have neither eaten nor drunk since yesterday at noon."

Beaupère: "When did you hear the 'voice' that spoke to you?"

Joan: "I have heard it yesterday and today."

Beaupère: "At which hour did you hear the 'voice' yesterday?"

Joan: "I heard it three times yesterday—in the morning, at the time of Vespers, and when Ave Maria was said in the evening. Often I hear it more times than I say."

Beaupère: "When the 'voice' came to you yesterday morning—what did you do then?"

Joan: "I slept; the 'voice' woke me."

Beaupère: "Did he touch your arm?"

Joan: "It woke me without touching me."

Beaupère: "Was the 'voice' in your room?"

Joan: "Not so far as I know. But it was in the castle."

Beaupère: "Did you thank it and bow down?"

Joan: "Yes, I thanked the 'voice'. I sat down on my bed and joined my hands in prayer. I had asked for its help before."

Beaupère: "What did the 'voice' say when you were awake?"

---

[6] "*Dixit ulterius quod venit ex parte Dei et non habet hic negotiari quidquam, petens ut remitteretur ad Deum a quo venerat.*"

[7] The Latin reports of the examinations are condensations where the questions are generally not included, and where Joan's replies are only in occasional cases reported in the first person. In the following Joan's words are unaltered but the advocate's generally added.

Joan: "I asked for advice concerning what I should answer here. I asked that it should ask God, and it answered me: 'Answer bravely. God will help you.'"

Beaupère: "Did the 'voice' say anything to you before you prayed?"

Joan: "It said something to me; I did not understand everything. But when I had awakened it told me to answer bravely."

Here Joan turns to Cauchon. One can see her stretching her hand out toward the bishop and gazing into his evasive eyes: "And you there, who say you are my judge: you are my enemy! Take care what you do, for I am in truth sent by God and you are placing yourself in great peril."[8]

Beaupère continues the examination: "Has the 'voice' ever changed its meaning?"

Joan: "I have never noticed that it contradicts itself. Last night it only told me to answer bravely."

Beaupère: "Has the 'voice' forbidden you to tell everything concerning the matters about which you are questioned?"

Joan: "That question I will not answer. I have revelations concerning the King of which I cannot speak."

Beaupère: "Has the 'voice' forbidden you to disclose your revelations?"

Joan: "I have not been advised about that. Give me a fortnight, and I will answer."

Beaupère: "Once more: Are you forbidden to tell the truth?"

Joan: "Do you believe that it is *men* who have forbidden this? Today I shall not answer. I do not know if I may say it or not before I have a revelation. I believe with as great certainty as I believe in the Christian Faith and as I believe that God has redeemed us from the tortures of hell that the 'voice' comes from God by his command."

Beaupère: "Is this God's own voice or is it that of an angel or a saint?"

Joan: "It comes from God. I do not believe that I can express clearly what I know. I am more afraid of saying things that would displease the 'voices' than I am not to answer you."[9]

Joan further tells that on the previous night she had had revelations concerning the King she could not disclose.

[8] "*Item, dixit nobis, episcopo praedicto: 'Vos dicitis quod estis judex meus; advertatis de hoc quod facitis, quia, in veritate, ego sum missa ex parte Dei, et ponitis vos ipsum in magno periculo'*"; gallice: "*en grant dangier*".

[9] "*Credo quod ego non dico vobis plane illud quod ego scio; et habeo majorem metum deficiendi, dicendo aliquid quod displiceat illis vocibus, quam ego habeam de respondendo vobis.*"

After further wearying questions she declared with great firmness: "The 'voice' is good and venerable, and I need not answer."

Beaupère asks if the "voice" has a face and eyes. Joan does not answer, but she says that according to a proverb people may be hanged for telling the truth.

Beaupère now tried to trap her with an innocent question, probably uttered in his gentlest voice: "Do you know if you are in a state of grace?"

This is going too far. One or two of the jurymen had not been able to listen to these clear honest replies without emotion. Jean Fabri calls out from his seat: "The girl must not be asked such questions."

Cauchon rises and shouts, red with anger: "Be silent."

But Joan answered calmly: "If I am not, I pray God to make me so, and if I am, may God keep me so."

These are precious words giving evidence of a wonderful balance and maturity.

Joan adds: "I should be the most unhappy person on earth if I knew that I were not in a state of divine grace."

She adds a thought that shows she had pondered over her problems: "If I were in a state of sin, I do not believe the 'voice' would come to me.... I would wish that everyone understood that as well as I do."[10]

Beaupère changes the slant of his examination. He begins to ask her about her youth, about the children in Domrémy and their political sympathies. Joan says that so far as she knows there was only one boy in her village whose sympathies were with Burgundy. She exclaims: "I would have wished that they had cut off his head."

She quickly added: "Of course if it were the will of God."

Beaupère feels that in this direction there is a chance of leading her into careless utterances. He asked if the "voice" had told her to hate the Burgundians, a cunning question, because the voice of God cannot inspire one person to hate another.

Joan is equal to the situation and answers: "When I realized that the 'voices' were for the King of France, I could not greatly love the Burgundians. They will get war if they do not act as they should. That I know from the 'voices'."

---

[10] In the original, "*et vellet quod quilibet intelligeret aeque bene sicut ipsa.*" The words can also be understood as a thrust at those present: she wished that they were as certain of being without sin as she was herself; at least that is how, for instance, Père Doncoeur interprets the text.

Beaupère continues the examination with extreme skill, and places one trap after another before her. He asked if the children fought each other for political reasons and received the answer that that was probably the case. He asked if as a child she went about wishing that she could drive the Burgundians out. Joan answered that her great wish was that the King should regain his kingdom.

He asked if she wished that she were a man when she was about to set out for France.

The question was dangerous as it touched on delicate matters.

Joan remained silent.

He alters his tactics and asks innocently if she used to guard the cattle at home. Joan knows that she has already answered this unnecessary question, but repeats that she probably did so in her youth, but that later she occupied herself with other matters.

And now came, in the friendliest manner, perhaps the most dangerous question of all: "What do you know about a certain tree near your village?"

Joan tells the facts we already know. Again and again he attempts to force her into an admission that she had herself shared this magical belief. She answered spontaneously "No." She had heard people say ... She had herself not believed ... She does not know what to think of such matters.... She has never seen any fairies herself so far as she knows.

But she relates touchingly that when the "voices" had at one time spoken to her she had lost the desire to dance under the tree with other children. In any case, she preferred to sing rather than dance.

Beaupère begins to speak about the mysterious oak wood—it is clear that he now wishes to show the connection between Joan and witchcraft and magic. She answered that she had never heard that there were any nature spirits to be met there. But she had heard it said that people believed that in this wood she had "*prit son fait*" ("dabbled in magic"), but that this was sheer nonsense.

But when she came to the King she must surely have been asked about this mysterious forest from which had come a miracle-performing Maid?

Yes, she had heard all that, but never believed in it.

Then comes the final question: Would she really not like to have feminine clothing?

Joan replies with spirit: "Give me a woman's dress, and I will put it on and go away. Otherwise I will not wear it but be satisfied with these clothes as God wishes me to wear them."

It is clear that for her two things cannot be separated: her special mission from God and her male attire.

And herewith the examination of the day ended.

For dinner Joan is served a large fish, an "alose", presented to her by Cauchon. What can have been the reason for this friendly gesture?

In the evening, Joan is taken ill. She vomits and has a high fever. Her warders become anxious—if she should die too soon. . . .

Doctors are called who examine her carefully. When the prosecutor, "Benedicite", who is present, grasps the situation, he is seized with fury, using the coarsest words to Joan and telling her that it is her own fault.[11]

Joan is weak but retains enough strength to answer back vigorously. She recovers.

Nobody knows if Cauchon had really attempted to poison her, but it scarcely seems to have been in his interest to do so.

Cauchon does not have an easy time either, for in the evening the learned jurist, Jean Lohier, comes up with his documents, and he is categorical. The trial is invalid, if only because of a number of errors in procedure. A trial must take place in conditions that permit all to give their real opinion freely; Joan is only an ignorant girl who cannot possibly answer satisfactorily all those learned questions.[12]

Cauchon is furious. As Jean Lohier is such a great jurist it will be best if he remains in Rouen to keep an eye on the proceedings. But Lohier is a wise man and announces that he is leaving—which may or may not be interpreted as a protest. In a state of perturbation, Cauchon seeks out his henchmen, Beaupère, Jacques de Touraine, Thomas de Courcelles, and the priest-spy Loiseleur, and tells them of Lohier's opinion. Is it really

---

[11] "Whore! You have eaten herring and other things that don't agree with you!"

[12] Lohier's own words are: "The trial is invalid because it does not follow the regular procedure of trials, because it is held *in camera* in the castle, where the assessors are not in full and complete freedom to declare their true and full opinion, because the honor of the King of France enters in, whose cause she is sponsoring, and who has not been asked to appear or been invited to send a representative, because no preparatory information has been made public to support the accusation, and finally because the accused is a simple and ignorant girl incapable of answering all these masters and doctors on matters of such eminence and particularly about her revelations."

necessary to take any notice of it? In that case the whole thing must be started again from the beginning.

It is decided to go on. Nobody guesses that Lohier's criticism will in due course see the light of day—at the Trial of Rehabilitation.

The following day, the first Sunday in Lent, Lohier encounters Manchon in Notre Dame de Rouen; the two lawyers proceed to discuss the trial. Lohier declares that he can quite well see how the thing is planned: "They can catch her on her own words, whenever they wish."

He adds that if only Joan had sense enough not to assert categorically that she had revelations, but only that it seemed to her as if she heard "voices", they would never be able to sentence her. But he realizes that the judges are actuated "more by a desire for revenge than by any other motive. They want her killed, and I do not want to remain here."

Filled with disgust, he too disappeared and traveled to Rome, where he seems to have remained until his death.

After that of Jean Lohier, the name of Nicolas de Houppeville should be mentioned, for it was he who had the courage to tell Cauchon at one of the preparatory meetings that neither he nor anyone else present could legally act as judge in this case; that the Bishop of Beauvais could not judge a woman whose case had already been decided by his superior, the Archbishop of Reims; and that it was quite apparent that this was a case of political opponents masquerading as judges in a question purely of faith.

This courageous attitude made Cauchon more furious than ever. When Houppeville presented himself as an assessor, he was turned away and had to leave the courtroom. Houppeville was a priest of Rouen and did not need to give way to the Bishop of Beauvais, and he calmly said so. A few days later he was arrested and thrown into prison. Just as Cauchon's henchmen were about to sentence him to be surrendered to the English, his friend the abbot of Fécamp managed to save him.

He disappears from history until the Trial of Rehabilitation.

Joan the Saint

Self-effacement lies at the very core of the Christian religion. The great psychological paradox maintained by Christianity pronounces: I am strong in my weakness; the only thing of which I can boast is my weakness; God's strength only manifests itself in a person who willingly admits his own helplessness and sacrifices his own will.

This view is in irreconcilable opposition to the view of man as self-determining, which—though more or less unexpressed—informs the essence of Western civilization. Neither naturalism nor humanism can accept the basic Christian attitude to man.

It is an attitude that presents many problems. One of these is that it is only with great difficulty that we can obtain genuine evidence of the state of soul of the "elect". This is partly because the meeting with God in its different forms cannot be adequately described; saints have frequently deplored the fact that to describe their experiences they have to use unsatisfactory symbols, often images borrowed from earthly love. But another reason is that it is of the nature of self-effacement that it cannot observe itself.

Along much of the road to holiness one can observe how the saints watch themselves with more or less anxiety, consciously working on themselves. Of course, these stages provide us with a certain evidence, but the farther the soul advances, the more anonymous it becomes, until it is so purified that it has almost forgotten itself. Its whole content is the will of God; the personal will remains only as a vague memory of vague temptations in a vague past. In such a soul, everything is divine presence and power. In such a soul, there is no self-observation unless it be to determine its own helplessness, its own anonymity. If one receives the grace to meet such persons in a religious house or in the world, one is struck by their indifference to self, their steady concentration upon God and his love, their anonymity.

Many holy men and women may irritate one because they seem to weigh themselves long and carefully and to speak about their forget-fulness of self. Sooner or later such souls are exposed to terrible trials. They have abandoned everything of the world and observe the sternest discipline, they are ready for any sacrifice, but in the very impulse itself, in the methods used, there are remnants of selfishness.

It is this obstinate love of self that explains Protestant criticism of the saints, particularly of saints of the highest order. But we find the same criticism, only more detailed and stern, in the writings of the saints themselves. In the striving toward sanctity, there remains a trace of self-ishness that must be eliminated; you love God not for his own sake but for your sake; you love God less than you love your love of God; you love God in spite of all, mostly because you expect to gain great happiness and peace for yourself from his Love.

In advanced spiritual literature, these are elementary matters that have been the subject of frequent discussion. They are mentioned here because they may help to throw a clearer light on the type of religious nature that Joan possessed.

It has been said that above all Joan was distinguished by her sound common sense, her realism, and activity. This is true, but none of these qualities touches the central secret of her religious life. Joan strikes one as so natural, so uncomplicated, so simple, that some people have wondered if she could seriously be put on the same plane as those saints whose infinitely painful, complicated, and subtle spiritual struggles we know of from so many biographies.

As a matter of fact, one is here the victim of a delusion. Joan appears so spontaneous, so simple, that one almost loses sight of her true religious quality. But the question may be asked whether the seemingly girlish love of and obedience to God Joan displayed during her short life is not something quite different from what it appears to be. Perhaps it is not the beginner's stage of rare freshness and beauty, but that final stage which the saints usually reach only after a lifelong struggle.

Joan knows so infinitely little about herself. She finds it difficult to formulate theories and opinions. To her, religious life is simplified to a few things: clarity of vision in her revelations; absolute obedience to the "voices"; love of the Savior who has sacrificed himself for her; and love of the suffering people round about her. It is as simple as that. And yet this is perhaps as high as man can attain.

As we have just seen, Joan tells her judges with authority that she is sent by God, and she demands respect for her mission. She warned one of her cruel judges that for his own sake he must be careful or he shall suffer. In vain we search in Joan for any expressions of pride or arrogance. Perhaps we can most clearly recognize her sincere and noble type of spirituality if we observe that she never compares herself with anybody else, never for a moment looks at herself, never gives a thought to that perfection which may one day be hers. Joan is one of the few examples of a soul that possesses holiness without being aware of it. She thinks herself an ordinary peasant girl, she energetically rejects all attempts to glorify or worship her; we remember how she smilingly said that anyone could bless a rosary as effectively as she could. She becomes vehement when she speaks about her duty to obey the "voices", but we never hear her set a value on herself. What is sublime in this young soul is that she appears through the grace of God to have attained purification without great suffering. There are here and there such cases in the history of the Church, particularly among people whom God elects to be the recipients of supernatural messages. Joan is perhaps the most pronounced case of this. In her we see Christian self-effacement to an exceptional degree. She is so pure that we are struck dumb with reverence and joy before her, but she herself knows nothing of this. If one wants a clear view of how far Joan had reached, one may imagine what she would have replied if she had been asked to write an account of her mystical life, of her sanctification. She would have remained silent, for she knew nothing of this. The only thing she knew about was the will of God and the aims he wished to realize through her.

The role of Joan of Arc as a national and moral example can hardly be exaggerated. But her greatest importance is of a different kind and less often observed—she realizes with simplicity and childlike candor the central and innermost emotion of the Christian soul, which to most of us is unattainable and which even the saints can reach only through a lifetime of sacrifice and suffering: self-effacement, the complete penetration of her own will by the will of God, the final extinction and disappearance of the ego.

A French physician[13] has attempted to establish the qualities that distinguish a genuine, healthy mysticism from a false and unsound one. To him the touchstone is spiritual balance. Among the qualities always found in the genuine mystic, he enumerates the following:

They are simple, childlike, spontaneous.

They are sincere, and they reject all forms of homage.

They are silent about their inner experiences; often their secret is not suspected. It was by an accident that Saint Francis' disciples discovered his stigmata.

They are calm, unhysterical, and show no trace of overwrought and emotional ecstasy.

They are unshakable in their conviction. They know through inner standards that which is genuine and that which is not. They are active in their love of mankind.

---

[13] Pierre Giscard, "Etat mental des mystiques", printed in *La Vie Spirituelle* (Nov. 8, 1949).

This simple table is valuable. Ecstasy, visions, even stigmata, may occur in many people who are not mystics and even less saints. The psychic and physical phenomena generally observable in the lives of saints can be met also in others, in pseudo-mystics. They display nearly all the outward signs that distinguish the saint: great piety, frequent penance, and spiritual exercises, ecstasy, pains, stigmata. And yet they are not true mystics. Why? Because they break the simple rules: they are not spontaneous but deliberate; they are not sincere but false; they love to observe themselves and to be observed; they are not silent about their spiritual experiences but speak of them; they have no spiritual balance but are hysterical.

The only way to determine if a person is a true mystic or not is to use this method. The commission in Poitiers had already done this when for the purpose of their investigations they emphasized not Joan's revelations but the analysis of her character, her moral state, her habits, and her piety. The Church also did this in due course when she canonized Joan: the Church did not enter into the nature or value of her revelations.

The records of the trial in Rouen are of extraordinary interest from many points of view: they reveal the decline of the Church, they give us an unrivaled picture of the times and with a broad brush paint a fresco of debasement and mendacity which has no equal. But above all they give a more complete and intimate picture of a medieval saint than is found anywhere else. As we see Joan imprisoned here in her iron cage, or frankly meeting the gaze of her judges, calm, clear-thinking, naïve, and confident, unconscious of her own worth, without understanding of her shattering greatness, we feel we see the entrancing picture of man as God wishes man to be.

The elevation of Joan's religious life is perhaps better understood if one adds to these points of view another. Despite the fact that Joan stands before her judges unconscious of her own sanctity, unconscious of the fact that she belongs to the host of those who are spotless, for whom the love of God is everything, in spite of all this, sacrifice awaits her—the death of a martyr.

We do not know why.

We only know that when a person to our eyes appears pure, she is still impure in the eyes of God. The love of God is so all-embracing that it accepts nothing less than that man himself, to use Christ's own words, becomes perfect as God. He places upon no one a greater burden than he can bear. But for the very pure, the very humble, those who stand stripped bare before him and who hunger to be absorbed in his love after ridding themselves of their own ego, for them he reserves the greatest grace of all—to die for his sake.

Chapter 12

On February 26, Joan was still exhausted after her poisoning, but thanks to her excellent constitution she was soon restored to health. She received a visit from Loiseleur, whom she still believed to be her friend. Confidingly she confessed to him, opening her heart.

At eight o'clock on February 27, she is summoned to a new examination before fifty-four assessors. Joan is astounded to see her good confessor among them. She does not understand; perhaps he is trying to help her.

As usual she is asked to swear to tell the whole truth and, as earlier, declines. She is prepared to tell the truth about everything that can conceivably affect the trial but not about other matters.

Beaupère, who leads the examination, observes that she has been ill and asks how she feels.

Joan replies, "You can see that for yourself. I feel as well as it is possible."

The questions now follow one another rapidly.

"Had she heard her 'voice' since the last examination?"

Joan: "Yes, several times."

Beaupère: "Did you hear the 'voice' on Saturday in the room where you were examined?"

Joan: "That has nothing to do with the trial. . . . Yes, I did. . . ."

Beaupère: "What did it say on Saturday?"

Joan: "I did not quite understand."

Beaupère: "And what did it say when you came back from prison?"

Joan: "It said that I should answer bravely. I asked it for advice concerning the questions you ask me. I will gladly tell you everything that

God gives me permission to reveal, but as to the revelations I had concerning the King of France I shall say nothing without the permission of my 'voice'."

Beaupère now presses her to give more detailed information about the nature of this inspiration. His tactics are clever but irreproachable.

"Was it an angel that spoke to you, or was it a saint—or was it God's voice direct?"

Joan: "It was the voices of Saint Catherine and Saint Margaret."

Beaupère: "What do they look like?"

Joan answers innocently, like the simple girl from Domrémy that she is: "They had beautiful crowns, precious and splendid.... That is a thing of which I may speak, as God has told me. If you doubt me you can send somebody to Poitiers where I was questioned earlier."

Perhaps unconsciously Joan here played her most important juridical card: she had already been examined and approved by an ecclesiastical court whose authority must be regarded as greater than the one before which she stood.

Beaupère bypasses this dangerous ground.

"How do you know that it is the two saints? Can you distinguish them from one another?"

Joan: "I am quite certain it is they, and I can very well tell them one from the other."

Beaupère: "In what way?"

Joan: "By the manner in which they greet me. It is now seven whole years since they took me under their protection. I also know them because they themselves give their names."

Beaupère: "Are they dressed alike?"

Joan: "I am not going to say anything more about this; I am not allowed to.... If you do not believe me go to Poitiers and inquire. These revelations concern the King of France and not you who sit and question me."

It is simple. It is disarming. Joan is so distant from this intriguing world of lawyers that she cannot understand its motives. To her it is obvious that if a man has had a revelation from God concerning a Christian king, it has nothing to do with anybody else. Besides, the highest authorities in Poitiers had given her their approval.

But Beaupère grinds on. "Were the saints of the same age?"

Joan: "I am not allowed to say."

Beaupère: "Do they speak at the same time or first one and then the other?"

Joan: "I may not tell, but I have always been advised by them both."

Beaupère: "Which one was revealed to you first?"

After some hesitation, Joan said that the first was the Archangel Michael. In the dialogue that follows there is a remarkable reply giving an insight into Joan's real experiences. Beaupère asks if a long time has elapsed since she first heard the Archangel's voice—a rather strange question. Joan replies, "I am not speaking about Saint Michael's voice. I am speaking of great help he gave me."[1]

Possibly this gives an indication of Joan's real problem. She experiences spiritual reality. She is in contact with a supernatural world. Quite naturally this world must reveal itself to her in the only form understood by her. Therefore she sees before her the saints as she knows them. At the same time she is conscious that these visions are not what is important. God speaks thus, but he could also speak in another way. What is important is spiritual reality. She therefore answers that that which is of importance is not so much the "voice" as the spiritual experience concerned.

But how can she convince the theologians of this? She herself cannot penetrate these mysteries.

Beaupère makes use of the opportunity and presses her with more questions. She is forced to say that the Archangel did not reveal himself alone but surrounded by angels, that is, as she had always heard him referred to in church.

Beaupère then asks her cynically, "Did you see Saint Michael and his angels physically and actually?"

"I saw them with the eyes of my body as plainly as I see you. And when they vanished I wept and would have wished that they had taken me with them."

How is it possible that such an answer could fail to move a man familiar with the experiences of the saints and whose education had taught him what difficulties are involved in the relationship between visions and inner experiences?

Beaupère knows that no saint could have answered these questions, but that does not concern him. Pitilessly, he continues: "What kind of body had Saint Michael?"

---

[1] *"Ego non nomino vobis vocem de sancto Michaele, sed loquor de magna confortatione."*

Desperate, Joan answers: "I will not answer your question. I have not yet permission to tell."

Every theologian in the courtroom must have known that no young peasant woman could be expected to answer such questions.

Beaupère asks what the Archangel had said first. Joan evades the question and refers to the examination in Poitiers. Beaupère asks what evidence she possesses that they were really the two saints.

Joan replies helplessly, "I have already told you that it is Saint Catherine and Saint Margaret. You can believe me if you want to."

How could she have answered in any other way? Every theologian knows that the question is unreasonable.

Beaupère goes on with new questions. Joan does not reply, but exclaims, "I would rather have been torn to pieces by four horses than to set out for France on my own without the will of God."

Beaupère returns to the question of her male attire. Does she think it seemly to appear in such clothes?

She answers that she has done nothing but what God and his angels have ordered her. If God tells her to wear other attire, she will do so immediately.

In answer to new questions, she replies in the same words: "All that I have done, I have done not of my own will but because God has ordered it." She can add nothing more.

And what could she have added? When has it been possible to prove the authenticity of a spiritual experience to people who lack the capacity for spiritual understanding?

Beaupère takes up another phenomenon, which he clearly wishes to interpret as evidence of demonic inspiration. What were the facts regarding that strange light Joan used to see in connection with her revelations?

Did she also perceive this light when she met the King?

Joan smiles and replies that there were certainly lights in that chamber: there were fifty men bearing torches along the walls, and in addition she saw the heavenly light.

Those who have studied the saints know how usual it is for them to speak of light phenomena. This must be understood thus; the physical apparatus of perception is blinded and a higher organ begins to function—an organ for the perception of the spiritual that is not developed among the majority of mankind. And before such men a girl of nineteen in a state of grace, without theoretical schooling, is asked to define the nature of the light she sees!

Beaupère turns the examination on to a number of concrete details. How about the sword she had sought for in Sainte-Catherine-de-Fierbois? Joan tells him. Beaupère then sets a trap: "What blessing did you read or cause to be read over the sword?"

He does not ask if she has read a blessing. He pretends to believe that the rumor is true and only wishes to know which blessing it was. His intention is to prove that Joan had read some magic formula over the sword.

Joan answers quickly: "I have never read, or caused to be read, any blessing of any kind over the sword. As far as I know, nobody has done so.... I only loved that sword because it was found in the Church of Saint Catherine; I have always loved her greatly."

Beaupère attempts to make her admit that she has performed witchcraft with her sword. She replies that she has never read any incantations but that she naturally wished that her sword should be successful.

Beaupère in a similar manner questions her about her banner. She gives him a fine answer: "When I attacked the enemy I always carried my banner so as not to kill anyone. I have never killed anyone."

The examination ended with a number of questions concerning details of the way Joan waged war.

After the examination a priest by the name of Eustache Turquetil asked his friend Jean Massieu, of whom we have already heard, what he really thought of it all. Massieu answered: "Till now I have only heard things which do honor to her, but I do not know how it will all end. God alone knows that."

Jean Massieu uttered these words in the Norman dialect, but on a later occasion did not hesitate to repeat his opinion in French. The matter came to the ears of Cauchon, who summoned him and gave him a terrible upbraiding. Had not Manchon intervened, the man would never have escaped with his life—or so Manchon thought, at least.

Thus among those present at the trial there are a few simple, unblinded individuals to whom the theological hair-splitting means nothing, but who spontaneously sense that this woman is honest and pure and that God speaks through her. They are of the same kind as the men and women who stood around Christ, outwardly powerless, able only to wipe his brow, help him bear his cross, and swathe him in his linen cloths, but who had a greater awareness than those who possessed merely learning.

In the evening Joan received a consoling visit from her good confessor.

March 1

The fifth examination took place on March 1. "Benedicite" sees to it that Joan is not allowed to bow before the chapel door on her way to the courtroom. This scene is memorable. A young woman has but one longing: to bow before the Blessed Sacrament, to receive Holy Communion, to meet her Redeemer. But this, of course, cannot be permitted by her priestly judges and executioners. All she can do is to kneel before a closed chapel door with aching limbs and bleeding from the night's fetters, praying in the direction of the Sacrament. A soldier who guards her day and night pulls her up and drags her into the courtroom.

When Joan as usual refuses to say anything, she happens to remark: "I will tell you exactly what I would say if I stood before the Holy Father in Rome."[2]

Possibly it is a mere heedless remark, but more probably it is a conscious argument, perhaps inspired by a well-disposed theologian. Joan has begun to understand the weakness of the men assembled to try her, who claim to represent the Church and speak in her name. Why then do they not respect the Poitiers commission, which with the same if not with much greater authority spoke in the name of the Church? And can it be possible that the Pope in Rome, the true Vicar of Christ, knows what is taking place here in the name of the Church?

Beaupère undoubtedly understands the point in her remark, but he is clever and knows how to avoid this dangerous ground.

At that time, the Papal See presented a problem. It is true that the great schism had been ended in 1429 by the abdication of Clement VIII, and there was now, therefore, only one Pope, but the problem was still being discussed, and in the background one glimpsed yet another schismatic Pope, Benedict XIV.

Beaupère asks, "What are you saying about our lord, the Pope, and which Pope do you think is the true one?"

Joan answers, "Is there more than one?"

<hr />

[2] "... et dicam vobis tantum quantum dicerem si ego essem corum Papa romano."

This means, or so it can be interpreted—what do I care about squabbles in the Church? There can be only one Pope. It is of him that I speak.

But Beaupère has a piece of evidence at hand. He knows that the Count of Armagnac had once written and asked Joan for advice concerning the Popes. Joan had received a letter in Compiègne on August 22. Joan's letter in reply is produced and read in court. In it, Joan says that she cannot just then answer which of the three competing Popes is the true one, but that she will answer when she has ended the campaign and entered Paris. She would receive this answer by turning to "the King of the whole earth".

Delighted, Cauchon intervenes: Has Joan really asserted that she had authority to decide this difficult question?

Joan answers in obvious confusion and denies that the letter is quite genuine. She says that she herself knows nothing about the matter except that she must be firm in her belief that the Pope must be the Pope in Rome.

They tried to make her admit that she had declared herself competent to decide in the question of the three Popes. Joan swears that the information she wanted to give the Count of Armagnac in Paris concerned an entirely different matter. Her answer is interesting because it shows that either she had often been misunderstood by her secretaries or that her entourage let her sign documents of which she did not know the exact meaning.

When the examination continues, Joan speaks openly about the catastrophes that await the English in the near future. Her "voices" have distinctly and clearly foretold their defeat. Now a new cross-examination of the most painful kind commences. The questions follow rapidly one after the other and reveal either the greatest mendacity or a profound ignorance of spiritual experiences.

Can Joan see the face of the saints?

Do they possess hair?

Is there anything between their hair and the crown?

Have they long, hanging hair?

Joan answers, "I know nothing about that. Nor do I know if they have arms and other limbs. But they speak to me distinctly and in a friendly manner, and I understand them very well."

More questions.

220

How can they talk if they have not got physical form?

Do they speak English or French?

Joan smiles, "How could they speak English when they are not on the side of the English?"

Do they have rings in their ears or anywhere else?

Has Joan herself got rings?

She replies that she has had rings, but Cauchon had taken one from her and the Burgundians the other.

Has she threatened anybody with her ring—with magic?

Has she met her saint under the magic tree?

Or at the spring?

Joan is at any cost to be forced to admit that she has dabbled in magic. Her revelations cannot be explained in any other way. Therefore: "What have you done with your mandrake?"

Joan: "I have not got one and never had one. I have heard it said that there was one in the neighborhood of the village, but I have never seen it myself. I was told that they are dangerous things one must be careful of. But I do not know what they are used for."

New question: "What did they say it could be used for?"

"I have heard people say that it could produce money, but I do not believe that in the least. My 'voices' have never said anything about it."

When this trap fails, the interrogation takes a new turn, equally distasteful. "In what form did Saint Michael appear to you?"

Joan: "I did not see that he had a crown, nor do I know anything about his clothes."

The judge: "Was he naked?"

Joan: "Do you imagine that God could not afford to dress him?"

The judge: "Did he possess hair?"

Joan: "Why should he have cut his hair?"

More questions: Did he have scales in his hand?

Wearied by all this, Joan says simply and clearly: "I know nothing about all that. I only know that when I see him I am always very happy and have a feeling that I am not in a state of sin."

New question: "Have you been guilty of mortal sin?"

Joan answers that she does not know.

"When you confess do you then think that you have committed a mortal sin?"

She answers that she cannot know this herself. She is not conscious of having committed a sin and hopes that she never has and never will. A hail of questions follow concerning the sign she made to gain the King's confidence in Chinon.

She refuses to answer.

The court is adjourned.

When one reads these questions one recollects the angry words of Sainte-Beuve—though he himself believed that Joan was the victim of pure hallucinations: "What particularly strikes one in these theologians is their stupidity and their materialistic attitude of mind: they understand nothing of Joan's living inspiration and with their questions ceaselessly try to degrade her sublime and naïve nature without ever succeeding in their design."

In that day's examination one can discern clearly the strategy of the judges. Their heads are filled with all the pious lies and inventions concerning Joan of Arc. They are firmly determined to nail her down on this point. She has dabbled in exorcism, performed magic with mandrakes, had contact with evil spirits under secret trees, and much else.

She denies all this with a clear conscience. She cannot understand this world of superstition, gossip, and pious nonsense that her admirers have created and that is now thrown back at her in the form of terrible accusations.

March 3

The sixth and last examination in the preparatory trial takes place on March 3 before forty-one assessors. Among them are several of the theologians who are to represent the French Church at the coming conference in Basel, where the Pope is to encounter energetic French opposition. Her reference to the Pope as the highest judge must be viewed against this background.

It began with the usual questions about the Archangel, the saints, and their appearances. Joan had to answer theological questions such as whether the Archangel and Saint Gabriel really possess the physical qualities that she believed she had observed.

She answered in the affirmative without really understanding the question.

Does she really believe that God has created them just like that?

She evades the question.

As Joan has so often appealed to the decision of the commission in Poitiers, the judge asks if the latter touched on the problem of Joan's male attire.

She answers that she does not remember.

Had they not asked in Poitiers if it was the "voices" that had ordered her to adopt male attire?

She cannot remember this.

The judge then asks her: "Do you think that you would have acted badly or been guilty of mortal sin if you had adopted female attire?"

Joan: "It is wisest for me to obey and serve my highest Lord who is God. If I had adopted female attire, I would sooner have done it at the request of the two ladies whom I have mentioned to you[3] than at the request of any other ladies in France with the exception of the Queen."

No result is reached, and the examination passes to other details that appear harmless but are to prove fatal enough to Joan. Has she had her banner sprinkled with holy water?

Joan denies that she has done so, nor does she know that anyone else has. The judge insists that she has performed magic under the guise of sprinkling holy water on her arms. He then leads the examination over to the dangerous Brother Richard, but this matter is only touched on; it is important enough that Joan admits that she has met him.

The pictures of Joan that are found in various parts of the country and the alleged worship of which she has been the object are then investigated. Joan knows nothing about this.

The judge asks if a special Mass had not been said in her honor. She replies that she had no knowledge of this. It had certainly not been done at her request, and if it really were so, that people prayed for her, there was surely nothing wrong in that....

Did her followers really believe that she had been sent by God?

She replied, "Yes."

"Did you really know the innermost heart of the people who kissed your hands and feet?" the judge asked.

[3] Jeanne de Luxembourg and la Dame de Beaurevoir.

He was making the suggestion that Joan had been the object of a godless cult by people who had never believed that she acted on divine inspiration.

Joan answered, "Many people liked to look at me, and if they kissed my hand I did everything I could to prevent it. But the poor creatures came to me because I did them no harm, but helped them as well as I could."

More questions:

Had not the suspect Brother Richard preached a sermon in connection with her arrival at Troyes?

Had she not held a child over the font in Troyes and Saint-Denis?

Did not the women touch Joan with their rings?

Had she not conjured up a glove that one of the knights had lost during the coronation at Reims?

Was it not Brother Richard who held her banner at Reims?

Had she not received the Sacrament dressed in male attire?

Did she herself believe that in Lagny she had brought the child back to life?

Was she not acquainted with the suspect Catherine de la Rochelle?

To all these questions she either replies in the negative or gives reasonable explanations. They then try to make her admit that she tried to take her own life—a deadly sin—by throwing herself from the tower in Beaurevoir. Had she not herself said that she would rather die than fall into the hands of the English?

Joan: "I said that I would sooner commit my soul to God than fall into the hands of the English."

The judge: "Have you not lost your temper and cursed the name of God?"

Joan: "I have never cursed any saint, and I have never used bad language."

The judge: "And the commandant in Soissons who surrendered—did you not swear that if you caught him you would cut him into four pieces?"

Joan denied this also.

With this the last examination of the preparatory trial ended, and Joan was removed from the courtroom. Cauchon then announced that a commission of ecclesiastical and lay assessors would be formed to prepare the evidence obtained. The other members of the jury should give their minds to the case and send the commission any suggestions they might have. Nobody was to be allowed to leave Rouen for the present.

In other words, everybody was to share the responsibility, but Cauchon and a small circle of his own choice were to prepare the evidence and formulate the accusations.

After this *procès d'office* came the real trial, the *procès ordinaire*, but before the latter commenced its sessions Joan was to be interrogated in her own prison by a smaller commission.

These examinations went on from March 4 to March 25.

CHAPTER 13

In Prison

The interrogations continued in Joan's prison. The English and French secretaries had found it difficult to agree as to what Joan had really said during the public examination, and it was considered that a number of important questions had not been investigated with sufficient thoroughness. The task was now, during these forced interrogations without witnesses, to obtain decisive evidence of Joan's guilt. The well-tried methods were employed—trying to tire Joan out by the endless repetition of questions already dealt with; laying traps for her to contradict herself. But there are two important questions to which the interrogators always return.

The first one of these has already been touched upon in the account of Joan's arrival at Chinon. It concerns her "sign". The judges are determined at all costs to force her to reveal her secret. She finally gives in, completely worn out we may assume, for it was during these days, while fettered, that she was beaten and exposed to attempted assaults by her guards, from which only her cries saved her. I have earlier suggested a possible interpretation of her words about the sign. We cannot assume that her statements recorded in the reports should be interpreted literally.

The "sign" will be found in the King's treasury; hundreds of people saw it in the King's chamber; an angel gave the King the "sign"; the "sign" was that which the angel explained to the King; around the angel were a large number of other angels; the crown, which was handed to the King, was a symbol of his reconquest of his country.

Much dispute is possible about the meaning of these mysterious words, which, however, were later partly denied. Perhaps it is wisest to narrow the explanations down to two.

In the first place, she speaks here in her helpless way of purely spiritual experiences that in her efforts to explain she seeks vainly to put into concrete pictures. In the second place, she is exhausted by her imprisonment and by her terror of soul and is tempted by the nature of the questions to build up her experiences into concrete images in a naïve way.

It cannot be sufficiently emphasized that all this is of secondary importance. Joan's visions are not essential to her greatness. Even if we accept them all, which is probably not possible, they are essentially of a patriotic and political nature and therefore lack any deep spiritual interest. Joan's real importance is of another kind.

This is seen in some answers she gave during these interrogations. She is censured by her judges because, in a way that they clearly look upon as unseemly, she ties her men's clothes tightly around her body. She replies that she has to do it in order not to be raped. It may be added that she appears not to have slept in a bed but upon the floor.

Despite her sufferings she speaks with dignity and calmness about the will of God. She is asked ironically if the "voices" must not have failed her as she had been so ignominiously captured. She rejects this: "As God willed it, I think it was the best that could happen to me to be taken prisoner."

Another time it is insisted that she behaved shamelessly when she departed from her parents without permission. It was the notoriously unscrupulous Cauchon who said this.

She replies: "As God ordered it, I had to obey. Even had I had a hundred fathers and a hundred mothers, and even if I had been the daughter of the King, I would have gone when God ordered it."

These two statements may appear very simple, but they show all that is essential about Joan's relations with God—her complete self-abnegation, her absolute obedience. Her understanding is insufficient, and it may even be said that during these interrogations she is driven to make some foolish remarks. But this is of little importance in comparison with her essential qualities. It is only during these days that Joan has begun to realize that God is preparing for her a new ordeal: that her task now will be simply to suffer.

She tells them that her "voices" have said to her: "Accept everything calmly. Do not fear your martyrdom. You shall nevertheless in the end reach Paradise."

She adds that by martyrdom she means her suffering in prison: "I do not know if I have to go through yet greater suffering. I leave that in the hands of God."

One divines her meaning: "I do not overestimate my sufferings; I do not count myself among the great martyrs, but if God will ask of me a great sacrifice, I will accept it."

This answer causes her judges serious reflection and causes her to reflect too. When the interrogators return the next day, she herself begins to speak: "As regards my certainty of being redeemed, of which we spoke yesterday, I mean that it is dependent on my promise to our Lord to preserve my virginity of body and soul."

The judge asks a cunning question: "Why is it necessary for you to confess, since you already know by the revelations of your 'voices' that you will be redeemed?"

Joan answers with dignity: "I do not know if I have committed any mortal sin.... But I believe that one cannot ever clear one's conscience too much."

The judge, sternly: "You assaulted Paris on a Church holiday; you have ridden a horse which belonged to the Bishop of Senlis; you have thrown yourself from a tower in Beaurevoir; you have worn male attire; you agreed to the killing of Franquet d'Arras—and still you do not think that you have been guilty of mortal sin."

Joan replies in detail to these charges. The other important point during these interrogations concerns Joan's relations to the Church.

Joan declares emphatically that if it can be proved that she has said anything against the Faith, then she will immediately withdraw it and recognize her error. Her judges then explain to her that she must distinguish between two Churches, between the *ecclesia triumphans* and the *ecclesia militans*. The former is the spiritual Church, in heaven. The latter is the Church that fights visibly upon earth. The question now is if she is willing to submit to the latter Church also.

Joan replies that everything that she has done she has done by the inspiration of God; she protests that she has never wished to act in opposition to the Christian Faith: "With all my strength I carry out the orders of God which are announced to me by my 'voices' so far as I believe that I can understand them, and they order me nothing without the approval of God."

It is easy now for the judges to corner her.

Does she, or does she not, wish to submit to the Church and recognize her authority?

She replies that she submits to God, who has sent to her the Blessed Virgin and all the saints of Paradise. "And I cannot understand otherwise than that it is the same thing, God and the Church, and that this cannot cause any difficulties. Why do you complicate it when it is the same thing?"

It is sublime and touching. A loyal theologian at her side could easily have helped her against her accusers and drawn the right distinction. What Joan by herself, with the limited intellectual resources at her disposal, cannot discern is to what degree these men really represent the Church of Christ; what authority a man like Cauchon really possesses; how it is that a bishop can say one thing and her "voices" another.

She does not suspect that he is deceiving her and usurping powers for himself and his court, powers that according to the laws of the Church they do not possess. Instead of being straightforward on this point, the judge does everything to confuse the issue. The Church Militant, Cauchon tells her, is represented by the Pope in Rome, the cardinals, the Church, the clergy, and all good Catholics. This "united" Church cannot be mistaken; she is guided by the Holy Ghost.

This is true, and it is untrue. It is untrue if it is interpreted to mean that an ecclesiastical court assembled in this manner by a bishop can with infallibility determine whether the visions of a Catholic are genuine or not.

Joan repeats that she is sent by the Triumphant Church and responsible to her. She would say no more.

They now attempt to confuse her by a number of stray questions.

Does she know if Saint Catherine and Saint Margaret hate the English?

Joan: "They love whom our Lord loves and hate whom our Lord hates."

Question: "Does God hate the English?"

Joan: "I know nothing about the love or the hate that God can feel toward the English or how he deals with their souls, but what I do know is that they will be thrown out of France."

She is then asked if God was for the English during the time when they were successful in France.

Joan: "I do not know if God hated the French then, but I believe that God allowed them to be vanquished because of their sins—if they had committed any."

The old question of her attire was again taken up. Would she be willing to change it if she were allowed to go to Holy Communion?

She replies that she will do so if she is given certain assurances. But in that case she will afterward return to her male attire, and she refuses to admit that it can be a sin to wear the clothes God has ordered.

The interrogation ends.

The Seventy Articles

The "ordinary trial" lasts from March 26 to March 31.

The first day is devoted to the preparation of the trial. It is Monday of Holy Week. During the following days, the Catholic Church celebrates the most moving feast of the year. The high prelates, who have witnessed how Joan in her prison has been forced to defend herself against brutal soldiers who beat her and try to violate her, every day say their Mass. They sit for hours in church listening to the familiar accounts of the Passion of Christ by the four Evangelists. They follow their Master to Gethsemane, they see him before the High Priest, they hear Peter deny him, they listen to his answer to Pilate, they follow him in the way of the Cross and witness his death. Is there no uneasiness in their hearts? Have they returned to their own trial with an easy conscience?

We do not know, but we must assume that strengthened and assured after Communion they left their churches and gathered for their meeting. They will serve the cause of our Savior and the Church by rendering a witch harmless. That is all. The thought apparently occurs to none of them that they themselves are playing the terrible part of the Jewish priests.

On Tuesday of Holy Week, the actual trial begins. Around Cauchon and the inquisitor are some thirty theologians and priests and with them at least three famous medical doctors. The courtroom is so crowded that two Dominicans, Jean Duval and Isambart de la Pierre, are seated close to Joan, besides Jean de la Fontaine.

On the basis of the accumulated evidence, "Benedicite" has compiled a tremendous Act of Accusation, which is now to be read. Before he speaks, he takes a solemn oath not to allow himself to be influenced by hatred or fear but to be actuated wholly by zeal for the Faith and truth. "Benedicite" takes the oath with a clear conscience. Nobody realizes that he is lying.

Then Cauchon rises, his hands folded over his episcopal cross, turns to Joan, and speaks to her in the kindliest way. He tells her that she has before her a gathering of learned, pious men who now, as before, will speak to her with great gentleness and wish her no harm. They are gathered there because she has committed great sins, but their motive is not revenge; they wish in the name of Christ to help her so that she may attain truth and salvation.

Joan is not hoodwinked. She thanks them for their kindness and their anxiety to assist her and also for their advice. But she cannot be untrue to God's clear commands. She is willing to take the oath to tell nothing but the truth.

It is Thomas de Courcelles who presents the great Act of Accusation in Latin. He reads it without interruption, and it takes a good hour. Joan does not understand a word of it.

Then Cauchon asks Thomas de Courcelles to translate the Act of Accusation paragraph by paragraph. Already in the preamble Joan is described as a magician, witch, false prophet, in conspiracy with evil spirits, full of superstition, unmasked as dabbling in magic, insubordinate to the true teaching, schismatic. . . .

In the first article it is established that the court possesses full competence.

Joan replies that she submits to the Holy Father in Rome but asks to be placed before him. She declares that she will never submit to her enemies.

At that moment, the Dominican Isambart leans over to her and whispers that she must submit to the General Church Council. Joan does not understand what this means, and he rapidly explains to her. She continues and asks to be taken before the Church Council in Basel.

Cauchon interrupts her furiously and shouts to the clerk, Manchon, to ignore this nonsense.

"Why do you put down that which is *against* me," asks Joan, "but not that which is *for* me?"

Article 2 says that Joan in a number of cases has been guilty of magic and witchcraft, that she has consorted with evil spirits, concluded an agreement with them, and asserted that this is permitted. She has allowed herself to be worshipped as an idol.

Article 3 says that Joan has been guilty of heretical statements.

Articles 4–6: Joan has from her earliest childhood engaged in magic and associated with fairies.

Article 7: Joan has by means of a mandrake attempted to acquire riches.

Article 8: Joan has left her home against the will of her parents and then resided with an innkeeper of evil repute, La Rousse, among harlots.

Articles 9–10: Joan has taken to court a decent man who refused to marry her because she associated with fallen women.

Articles 11–14: Joan has set out dressed as a man and carrying arms, which is against God's ordinances.

Article 15: Joan has declared that she would rather abstain from the sacraments than give up her male attire.

Article 16: Joan refused to live the simple life of a woman.

Article 17: Joan has by means of witchcraft predicted important military events.

Article 18: Joan has advised Charles VII against keeping the peace.

Article 19: Joan has with the help of demons found a sword in Fierbois, if indeed she had not first smuggled in the sword.

Article 20: Joan has bewitched her ring, her banner, and her sword.

Articles 21–23: Joan has addressed to the Duke of Bedford a letter inspired by demons.

Article 24: Joan has misused the names of Jesus and Mary.

Article 25: Joan has asserted that she had shed blood by the order of God.

Articles 26–30: Joan has in the question of the true Pope shown heresy.

Joan is permitted to reply to every article and at first does so, but every word of the indictment is a lie, and she soon sees that denials are useless.

The trial is adjourned, and Joan taken back to her cell.

It is the afternoon of Tuesday in Holy Week. She has not been allowed to attend Mass.

In the prison, she is visited by Jean de la Fontaine and the two Dominicans, Isambart de la Pierre and Jean Duval. They have come to warn her: she must not believe that this tribunal represents the Church Militant. The only correct forum for her would be the General Church Council, and the only person she need accept as authority, the Pope. But during this talk, Warwick enters the prison in a rage and throws himself on the Dominican Isambart. He had noticed that the latter had assisted Joan already that morning during the reading of the Act of Accusation. If he repeats this, he will be thrown into the Seine....

"Whereupon the two men who were with Isambart fled to their monastery in terror."

The following day was Wednesday of Holy Week, March 28. In church the judges have listened again to the story of the Passion told by another evangelist, but they have also heard Isaiah's mighty prophecy of him who was to come to carry the burden of man: "Surely he hath borne our infirmities, and carried our sorrows, and we have thought him as it were a leper, and as one struck by God and afflicted."

The Church mobilizes all her riches for humble men, to soften their hardness, to open their eyes to the greatest drama of history.

After a solemn Mass, the judges gather, with the hymns still echoing in their hearts, for the continued reading of the Act of Accusation.

Articles 31–37: False revelations, false prophecies, presumptuous claims to distinguish souls, angels, and saints from one another.

Articles 38–41: Joan's deadly sins, her insolent assertion that she is in a state of grace, her attempted suicide in Beaurevoir.

Articles 42–43: Joan has said that her "voices" were equipped with bodies, spoke French, and hated the English.

Articles 44–47: Joan has alleged that she is certain to be received in Paradise, to be redeemed; she has allowed the ordeal of Compiègne and has blasphemed against God before throwing herself from the tower.

Article 48: Joan has never wished to consult a bishop or a priest about her "voices".

Articles 49–50: Joan has worshipped evil spirits.

Articles 51–52: Joan has been in alliance with demons whom she has called angels.

Article 53: Joan has made herself a military leader.

Article 54: Joan has failed in her duties as a woman and led the life of a man.

(Here she answered: "Men were my guards, but when I was in bed I nearly always had a woman with me. But out-of-doors I always lay dressed and in arms unless I had a woman beside me.")

Article 55: Joan has profited by her false visions.

Article 56: A reference to the accusations of the witch, Catherine de la Rochelle.

Articles 57–58: Joan on the occasion of a Church holiday attacked Paris and misused her banner.

Article 59: Joan has placed her arms as relics in the church of Saint-Denis and has allowed wax to be dropped on the heads of small children in order to foretell their future.

Article 60: Joan refuses to reply to her judges.

Article 61: Joan refuses to submit to the Church Militant.

("No", Joan exclaimed. "My heart is filled with veneration and reverence for the Church Militant. I appeal to our Holy Father, the Pope, and to the Holy Church Council.")

Cauchon interrupts the indictment: Who was it who yesterday spoke to Joan in her prison? It is found that the Dominicans have disappeared, and he rages with fury.

Article 62: Joan has arrogantly defied the Church and scandalized the congregation.

Articles 63–65: Joan has lied before her judges; Joan has said that her sin in Beaurevoir had been forgiven; Joan has denied God.

Article 66: A summing-up of the accusations.

There is silence.

All eyes are directed at the girl.

Has she anything to say?

She answers calmly: "I am a good Christian. I will answer all these accusations before God."

Articles 67–70: Joan has not taken notice of the kindly explanations and directions given her; all the enumerated accusations the accused has admitted as true.

The indictment is concluded, and only the sentence remains to be announced.

Joan is returned to prison.

Ecce lignum crucis

In the afternoon: the Tenebrae of Maundy Thursday in the cathedral. The great psalms and the laments of Jeremiah: "*Jerusalem, Jerusalem! convertere ad Dominum Deum tuum!*" (Jerusalem, Jerusalem, turn to the Lord your God.)

Maundy Thursday: again the whole drama of the Passion passes in review: the judges and assessors spend long hours in church. Thomas' hymn, *Pange lingua*, is sung in procession, its notes capable of melting hearts of stone.... The short Vespers.... The bishop who after the example of Christ in the Mandatum washes the feet of the poor in the cathedral.

Good Friday, the most soul-stirring day of the Church year, when after Tenebrae, man cannot find peace, when the mind is challenged mightily by the prophecies and mysterious hints in the Scriptures, by images of visionaries, the words of prophets, the unbearable testimony of Holy Writ....

All that prophets and Church teachers, saints and apostles, have testified, seen, or sung about, is gathered together into an overwhelming masterpiece, the beauty of which has only one aim, to soften the heart, to melt self-will, to direct the eye to the mound with the three crosses and to him who is sacrificed for the sins of man.

Joan's judges do not fail in their churchly duties. Immobile and gripped by emotion they sit in their places.

How strange is the heart of man! These men are as we are, neither greater sinners nor greater saints. They are deeply perturbed, they pray sincerely, they see and recognize their own sins, and yet it is precisely at that moment that the judicial murder is being prepared in their hearts.

The finest brains of the country, theologians, learned men, pious abbots, experienced priors, trained priests, well acquainted with sin in all its guises—with intense concentration they sit gathered together and watch again the greatest trial and the greatest judicial murder of history; they are surrounded by the beauty of the cathedral, they are supported by the mightiest, the most moving testimony of Christian history, they are shaken by Jewish laments, prophetical visions, the realism of eyewitnesses, and the sublime silence of the Master. Despite this, they go from the cathedral with calm and measured paces to another judicial murder. Despite this, they burn with zeal to place an innocent girl on the stake of the martyr.

Ecce lignum crucis....

In her room Joan sits fettered, and in front of her are the English soldiery—they tear at her clothes, strike her face, and hurl coarse oaths and indecent words at her....

She understands that it is this that is God's new task for her: innocent, she must suffer and she must wish to suffer.

Where is Domrémy, where the church bells pealed so peacefully for Vespers? Where are the plains of the Loire where she rode under flowering trees at the side of her handsome Duke of Alençon? Where is her friend, the chivalrous Bastard of Orléans? Where are all the people who pressed around her calling her name, wishing to touch her clothes and hands? Where is the King himself, whom she guided to his coronation?

Her head whirls with questions, insults, misunderstandings. The prison stinks of uncleanliness.

She understands that she is now closer to the Redeemer she has loved than at any time during the moments of trial and battle.

So close to him that she can no longer distinguish his suffering from her own.

CHAPTER 14

The Twelve Articles

On Good Friday, Joan experiences her greatest degradation. The priest-spy visits her, and she is still unable to see through him but breaks into moans and tears. He consoles her in a fatherly manner.

As soon as he has left, the demons attack her.

Supposing, after all, these learned men should be right? Supposing she has misunderstood her "voices"? Perhaps she should have returned home after the coronation in Reims, for has not God since then abandoned her?

It is Good Friday; the fetters pain her sore wrists as she tries to dream her way back to the church at home.

Matins with the long psalms:

"O God, my God, look upon me: Why hast thou forsaken me?
Far from my salvation are the words of my sins.
O my God, I shall cry by day, and thou wilt not hear:
and by night, and it shall not be reputed as folly in me."

Out of the psalms emerge the familiar voices lamenting, abandoned, until in the end they are again filled with confidence and hope; God does not abandon those who stand fast....

It is dark in her prison. The hours become endless, and her body aches. Joan senses that she will soon be unable to offer any resistance, but it is with this very darkness that she is familiar: "There was darkness, while the Jews crucified Jesus, and about the ninth hour Jesus cried with a loud voice, saying: My God, my God, why hast thou forsaken me?"

He, too, had felt abandoned. "My soul is in anguish unto death ... and he became sad and in anguish." Yet he was the Son of God. Yet he knew his power and his anguish was not for himself but for the poor creatures he knew would soon torture him unto death. He was in anguish for his executioners. He himself was never abandoned. His human self could not recognize the nearness of the Father. He felt alone

237

and abandoned as Joan felt. Yet he knew that the silence was a voice. The very abandonment and anguish were signs that God was closer to him than ever. God is close to him who gives his life for others.

Joan raised herself on her aching elbow and drew a deep breath: Were not all these incomprehensible and cruel events full of meaning? Was this not the will of God? She had wanted to redeem her country. One does not redeem by arms, however, but by sacrifice. Was it really a sacrifice to leave Domrémy, to swear eternal chastity, to ride in shining armor from victory to victory? No. The great sacrifice demanded of her and that the redemption of the country required was that she should humble herself before the shamelessness and brutality of the coarse soldiers, the infamous cunning questions, the threatening death.

"*Illem autem tacebat....*" Jesus had remained silent. Silent and humble, he allowed the terrible things to happen, not so that evil should triumph, but because its power could not be broken in any other way.

Again Joan heard her "voices"; she lay smiling with her eyes closed. They were close to her, Saint Catherine and Saint Margaret.... Had they been abandoned by God because he allowed them to die? No, the contrary was true.

Could this mean that she herself must die?

She lies silent and knows that now Christ only remains: from her innermost being pours out a humble and uncomplaining acceptance of all God may send. How can one complain when one receives the grace of participating in Christ's suffering, when one knows that one's own suffering ransoms many sinners?

When the mysterious "voice" spoke to her for the first time it only gave her simple, moral advice. Then there came a time when it called her to action. This was followed by a period of uncertainty.... It was evidently not by martial deeds that she should serve her country. How many times had she not pondered over God's intention for her life? Now, during the silent Good Friday in the dark prison, her task became clear: *I am called to serve God and my country by dying for its sins.* I am willing.

The Saturday before Easter she receives a visit in her prison. It is Cauchon himself, with seven assessors and the chief of the prison. He asks her, "Will you submit to the Church on earth regarding all you have said and especially regarding the crimes of which you are accused and everything that concerns the trial?"

Joan: "In all that you speak of I submit to the Church Militant, but do not demand impossible things of me. What I have said and done, what I have told the court, the visions and revelations I have received, all this is of God, and I will at no price retract them."

Cauchon: "But if the Church Militant tells you that your revelations are delusions of satanic invention, pure superstition, or evil, will you then submit to the Church?"

Joan: "I will submit to our Lord whose commands I have always obeyed, but it would be impossible for me to retract all that I have told the court and I have done by the command of God, and if the Church Militant should order the contrary I would not give way to any being on earth—except to our Lord, whom I have always obeyed."

Cauchon: "You do not then believe that you are subordinate to the Church Militant, to our Holy Father the Pope, the cardinals, the archbishops, and the other prelates of the Church?"

Joan: "Yes, but first I must obey God."[1]

Cauchon senses that her stand is connected with her talk with the two vanished Dominicans and Jean de la Fontaine and decides that thereafter nobody, not even the inquisitor Jean Lemaître, shall be allowed to visit Joan without his permission.

Now his problem is how to proceed in order to reach the goal he has determined beforehand: the execution of Joan.

The situation is still delicate; there is the commission of Poitiers presided over by Cauchon's superior, the Archbishop of Reims, whose judgment had been the very reverse.

Cauchon realizes that the sentence must be backed by a large number of serious authorities. He cannot well dispatch copies of the actual proceedings, since these might awaken sympathies for Joan. He also knows very well that she has never admitted her guilt and that he cannot produce a single witness to back his assertions. The seventy articles have no substance.

He then decides to condense the seventy articles into twelve new articles that shall contain the definite and irrefutable evidence for the prosecution. Two experienced men, Midi and Touraine, work on this for three days. Copies are made and dispatched to all juridical and ecclesiastical authorities in the town for their opinion.

[1] *"Deo primitus servito...."*

Joan herself is never allowed to see these twelve articles, but the readers are given the impression that she has approved them. She does not even know of their existence. Nowhere is the nature of this cold-blooded judicial murder more evident than here.

But Cauchon has to wait a long time for the answers. It is whispered that the town thinks that Joan should have been allowed to have her say; the twelve articles do not seem to correspond with what has been actually heard at the trial. It is known that no less than five men have left the town, more or less driven out by Cauchon: Jean Lohier, Houppeville, Jean de la Fontaine, and the two Dominicans.

Cauchon realizes that he has made a wrong move: he should have turned to his friends in the University of Paris first, after which the Chapter of Rouen Cathedral would have fallen like a ripe fruit.

On April 12, he arranges for sixteen doctors of theology and six licentiates to meet and compose an address finding that Joan's guilt had been proved. But even in such a small assembly it is not easy to obtain unanimity.

No less than thirteen lawyers and five theologians make it known together that Joan was guilty unless she had acted following the commands of God. . . . One after another of the assembled experts shows hesitation. Dubois is of the opinion that the matter should be referred to the Pope. Ménier, Pigache, and Grouchet cannot see anything that suggests that Joan's revelations are inspired by the devil. The abbot of Jumièges counsels mercy. The Bishop of Avranches demolishes Cauchon's theses by quoting Thomas Aquinas: Cauchon becomes so furious that he does not permit the evidence to be entered in the proceedings. The Bishop of Coutances remarks that while he thinks that Joan's revelations are rather fantastic, he considers that they can be regarded as ordinary, petty lies. But the Bishop of Lisieux, the venerable and learned Zano de Castiglione, gives proof of his logical acuity by saying to his old friend Cauchon that "a woman of such humble origin can surely not be a messenger from God".

Cauchon sees with concern that when next the Chapter of Rouen meets on April 13, not enough members are present to constitute a quorum. On the following day, some thirty canons arrive, but announce their decision to wait until the University of Paris has expressed its opinion. They add to the irritation of Cauchon by demanding that under any circumstances the articles must first be submitted to the accused and explained to her in French, after which she must be lovingly exhorted to submit to the Church.

This Cauchon cannot very well refuse, but Joan is again ill and can only reply feebly to the new questions. Cauchon enters her prison in the company of the inquisitor, Jean Lemaître, and seven assessors, "learned and just men". Cauchon says that they have come to "lovingly console and support Joan". If Joan, who is an ignorant woman, requires a theological adviser to help her to understand the accusations, he will be happy to provide her with one. He adds movingly, "We are priests who by vocation, desire, and free will are striving to work for the salvation of your soul and your body by all means, as we should do for our neighbor and ourselves."

He exhorts Joan to avoid the perils that would follow a refusal of this gentle and paternal offer.

Joan is very ill, and the secretary finds it difficult to hear her answer. She is already far away from the world, exhausted by her fever and by all the threats, and filled with strange presentiments of the fate that awaits her: Is it a punishment or is she called by grace to a new mission?

She answers however, "I thank you for all you say about my salvation. I believe that being so ill as I am, I am in actual danger of death. If that is so and if God wishes to dispose of me according to his will, then I beg of you to let me confess and receive Communion and afterward to allow my body to rest in consecrated ground."

For Cauchon a lying witch is playing the part of a humble Christian, but he controls himself and replies with Christian forbearance: "If you wish to receive the sacraments of the Church you must confess like a good Catholic and submit to Holy Church, for otherwise we cannot give you the sacraments you desire—except the sacrament of penance, which we are always prepared to give you."

Joan answers feebly, incapable of continuing the discussion: "I cannot say more now...."

Cauchon: "The more you fear for your life in your sickness, the more you must think of living a better life. And if you do not submit to the Church you cannot enjoy the benefits of a Catholic."

Joan: "If my body dies in prison, I hope you will lay me in consecrated ground; if you do not I commend myself to our Lord."

Cauchon: "Once you said during the trial that if you had ever done or said anything that was not in accordance with our Christian Faith given us by our Lord, you would retract it."

Joan: "I repeat the answer that I then gave...."

Cauchon: "You have said several times that you had revelations from God through Saint Michael, Saint Catherine, and Saint Margaret. If a good person came to you and said that she had had a revelation from God, would you believe her?"

Joan: "There is no Christian person on earth of whom I would not recognize at once whether he spoke the truth, if he came to me and said that he had had revelations."

Cauchon: "How do you mean?"

Joan: "I should be told by Saint Catherine and Saint Margaret."

Cauchon: "You cannot then imagine that God could inspire a good person without your knowing about it?"

Joan: "Yes, of course. But without a sign I should believe neither man nor woman."

Cauchon: "Do you believe that Holy Scriptures are revealed by God?"

Joan: "You know very well that I believe that."

Cauchon: "I order you, I implore you to take the advice of priests and learned men and believe what they say—for the salvation of your own soul. Will you submit what you say and do to the Church Militant?"

Joan: "Whatever may happen to me, I shall never do or say anything other than I have said at the trial."

Cauchon has had enough and lets the others take it in turn to try to reason with Joan. She refuses to budge.

Cauchon has done his duty. Nobody can now accuse him of not having endeavored with fatherly love to enlighten the misguided girl.

He leaves her. She is feverish and tired. Now she must remain close to Christ, must have faith though she is not conscious of his support, must understand his silence as if he were present, understand that it is just by seemingly leaving her that he shows her his love.

She is alone as he once was upon his Cross.

If only the soldiers would leave her body in peace that night.

The Solemn Warning

The Chapter of Rouen refuses to give its opinions, but from different directions answers flow in. They are not all pleasant reading for Cauchon, although most of them agree with him from conviction or fear.

On April 29, Nicolas de Gémet and the abbot of Cormeilles, Guillaume, write that it seems to them that the whole case can be condensed into three salient points:

1. Joan must publicly and in a loving manner be enlightened and warned.
2. The revelations do not at first sight appear credible unless they can be confirmed by the holiness of her life and by miracles.
3. The question whether Joan is in a state of mortal sin can only be answered by God.

The two learned gentlemen add that as they were not present at the trial they cannot express themselves definitely.

Their statement is exemplary and exposes Cauchon completely. It establishes the standpoint that has always been that of the Church, that the genuineness of revelations can in themselves never be proved. They must be examined in relation to the personal life of the recipient. Actually the tribunal had completely failed to discredit the life of Joan. It had replaced truth by a tissue of lies.

Rodolphe Savage writes on April 12 to Cauchon that he is of the opinion that the case should be referred to the Holy See.

On May 2, Cauchon opens a solemn and public session, the purpose of which is to utter a final warning to Joan. No less than sixty-three savants are present. The archdeacon, Jean de Châtillon, has the first word. Cauchon recommends him to show the greatest possible love and kindness. The archdeacon begins an oration about the duties of a Christian but is interrupted by Joan, who says, "You read your manuscript, after which I shall answer that I leave everything to God my Creator, whom I love with my whole heart."

Jean de Châtillon: "Will you have faith and keep the article *Unam sanctam Ecclesiam* and submit to the Church Militant?"

Joan: "I believe in the Church Militant but refer my deeds and words to God. I do not believe that the Church Militant can be mistaken, but as regards my deeds and words I refer them to God who has himself compelled me to act as I have done."

Jean de Châtillon: "Does that mean that you do not admit that you have a judge on earth and that you do not see our Holy Father, the Pope, as your judge?"

Joan: "I have nothing more to say about the matter."

243

Jean de Châtillon: "If you refuse to believe in the Church and in the Article *Unam sanctam Ecclesiam catholicam*, then you are a heretic and shall be ordered by other judges to be sentenced to death by burning."

Joan: "I have nothing to add; if I saw the stake before me, I would say exactly the same to you as I say now and nothing more."

Jean de Châtillon: "If the General Council of the Church, if the Holy Father, the cardinals and the other prelates of the Church were present, would you then submit?"

Joan: "You cannot make me say more than I have said."

Jean de Châtillon: "Will you submit to our Holy Father, the Pope?"

Joan: "Take me to him, and I will answer you."

After a few words concerning Joan's male attire, Jean de Châtillon asserts that Joan's revelations are pure imagination, which Joan vigorously denies. If Joan does not alter her views, she will suffer from the eternal fire, which shall devour her soul, and an earthly fire, which shall destroy her body. Angrily she replies, "You cannot do that which you say you will do without your own body and soul suffering badly."

It is her last defiant answer. When a number of other theologians attempt to persuade her she remains silent.

In the Torture Chamber

On May 9, the day before Ascension Day, the executioner, Mauger le Parmentier, received orders to have his instruments of torture in readiness.

Cauchon, accompanied by eight of his colleagues, is waiting in the torture chamber when Joan is brought in.

Cauchon: "If you do not tell the truth, you shall be tortured so that you can be brought back to the path of truth, for the salvation of your soul and your body, which you expose to great dangers by your lying tricks."

Joan looks at the instruments of torture. She has had time to get used to the idea and thinks of her saints, who also struggled with learned men obstinately possessed by their learning, and who were tortured.

"Even if you were to tear me limb from limb, I would not tell you more than I have. And even if I should say something later, I would always insist that they were things you have forced me to say."

She relates that she has had a visit from a new saint, the Angel Gabriel. Through her "voices", she knew it was he. She had also asked her "voices" if she should submit to the Church and they had answered her: "If you wish that your Lord shall help you, confide everything to him."[2]

She knows that God has always been behind everything she has done and that the devil has never inspired her. She also tells them that she asked her "voices" if she was really to be burned alive, and they had answered her: "Turn to God. He will help you."

Until the end Cauchon is afraid of Regnault, Archbishop of Reims, and he therefore asks Joan if she would submit to the opinion of the Archbishop regarding the sign she asserts that she has seen.

Joan realizes that this is all empty talk, and replies, "Bring him here and let me hear him speak, and then I shall answer. He will never dare to say the contrary to what I have said."

Cauchon then has her led away.

He is, however, very much in favor of her being tortured, and therefore, on the evening of May 12, he assembles thirteen savants to obtain their opinion.

It is a warm spring night. Through the open window comes the song of birds. The Seine flows past bordered by flowering fruit trees. The scent of flowers is wafted in; the learned gentlemen lean back comfortably in their chairs and debate, as is seemly for Christian authorities, with prayer and humility.

Should Joan be tortured or not?

Cauchon pretends to await submissively the decision of his learned brothers.

Rodolphe Roussel: "No, because that might spoil the effect of such an admirably conducted trial."

Nicolas de Vendères: "No, at the moment it does not seem to me desirable to torture her."

André Marguerite: "No, not now."

Guillaume Érard: "What would be the use of handing her over to the torturer when we have obtained such excellent evidence without torture?"

Robert Barberin: "I share this opinion. We must lovingly enlighten her once for all; if she does not then submit, we must carry the matter further."

---

[2] "... *et illae voces dixerunt sibi quod, si velit quod Deus adjuvet eam, ipsa se exspectet ad eum de omnibus factis suis. . . .*"

Denis Gastinel: "It will serve no purpose to torture her."

Aubert Morel: "I think it would be quite a good idea to torture her so as to obtain the truth about her lies."

Thomas de Courcelles: "It would be correct to torture her. She must be asked if she will submit to the sentence of the Church."

Nicolas Couppequesne: "It is undesirable to torture her. Instead we should urge her to submit to the decision of the Church."

Jean Ledoux: "That, too, is my opinion."

Nicolas Loiseleur, the priest-spy: "For the sake of her soul I think it would be beneficial if she were tortured. But I bow before that which has already been said."

Guillaume Hector: "No torture."

Cauchon did not get his way.

The University of Paris Takes a Stand

In Paris decision hung fire, but this was not due to lack of interest, rather the contrary. As soon as Cauchon's letter containing the evidence of the trial arrived, the rector of the University, a Dutchman by the name of Pierre de Gonda, gathered the different "Nations", or faculties, together. Cauchon had sent four of his most loyal men to Paris to assist in the discussion. The theological and juridical faculties worked on the matter from April 29 to May 14, when the case was taken up at the meeting of representatives of the faculties. The two opinions were read. Both the theological and the juridical faculties considered that Joan was an obvious heretic. The faculties separated, each to debate the matter on their own and then to meet again for a corporate vote. The University drafted two letters, one to the King of England and the other to Bishop Cauchon.

In their subservient letter to the King of England, it was stated that the case should soon be brought to its correct conclusion, that is, Joan's execution. A delay would entail great dangers, and it was of importance that the French people, who had been so badly misled by the witch, be brought back as quickly as possible to the true Faith.

The letter was signed "Your most humble daughter, the University of Paris".

This is perhaps the darkest page in the history of the University of Paris.

The letter to Cauchon is no less shameful. "Your sincere and burning zeal has manifested itself in a virile, grandiose struggle, thanks to which, by the grace of Christ, the unceasing efforts of your righteousness have delivered into your just hands a woman called the Maid, whose poisonous influence has spread so far that nearly the whole of the Christian flock of the west has been infected...."

The University declared itself deeply grateful for Cauchon's manful struggle, his zeal, his energy, his tried wisdom, his vigilance, his perspicacity, all serving the glorification of God's name, the integrity of orthodox faith, of honor, of the edification of the faithful.

The well-considered view of the University regarding this dangerous case was to receive further comment from the three theologians Beaupère, Touraine, and Midi, who had brought the letter.

Obviously Cauchon was delighted.

On May 19, he assembled the members of his jury in a great meeting, at which the letter was read, and he announced that Joan would once more be exhorted in the most paternal spirit, after which the trial could be regarded as concluded and sentence be pronounced.

The theological faculty commented on the twelve articles, to which Joan had never agreed and which were not supported by any kind of evidence.

Among the details of this commentary, the following may be mentioned:

Joan's revelations are false and derive from evil and diabolical spirits, Belial, Satan, and Behemoth.

Joan has turned from the true Faith.

Joan has blasphemed and must be regarded as an idolator who imitates the customs of pagans.

Joan is a traitress who desires to see human blood shed.

Joan betrays her parents.

Joan has by her attempted suicide shown that she has a mistaken view of human free will.

Joan is consciously mendacious.

Joan offends Saint Catherine and Saint Margaret and fails in her duty to love her neighbor.

Joan conjures up evil spirits.

Joan is schismatic.

The six paragraphs of the juridical faculty can compete with those of the theological faculty.

Cauchon now allowed those present to express themselves individually on the matter. The minutes of this meeting make horrifying reading. Theologians, jurists, priests, monks, pious and learned men all stand up and declare their adherence to the verdict of the University of Paris: Joan is a witch, a heretic, and must be dealt with accordingly.

After the last speaker had sat down, Cauchon pronounced: "Venerable Fathers, I thank you. It is our intention to exhort Joan to return to the way of truth and of physical and spiritual salvation. In accordance with your freely given decision and your wise counsel, I shall move over to the next stage and herewith declare the examination concluded. We shall decide the day when the judgment will be pronounced."

On May 23, at Pentecost, Joan again meets Cauchon, who with nine members of his jury awaits her in a room adjoining her prison. We know nothing about what she had gone through in the interval, but her answers provide some indication.

Pierre Maurice has condensed her atrocious crime under twelve headings. These cover Joan's whole life, touch on nearly all the important events she has experienced, and describe them all as of satanic inspiration.

After having determined—and according to his own opinion proved— that Joan is the most dangerous heretic, the most insolent witch that can be imagined, Pierre Maurice speaks to her in a fatherly manner: "Joan, dear friend, your trial is coming to an end, and it is now time that you consider what is said to you."

Joan has over and over again been admonished in private as well as in public but has never yielded. Now, in addition to all that, the University of Paris, "the light of all doctors and the antagonist of all heresies", has pronounced its opinion.

> After having received its advice, your judges have decided for the purpose just mentioned to make another attempt to persuade you, while emphasizing the mistakes, scandalous doings and other misdeeds committed by you, that, before the body of our Lord Jesus Christ who chose to suffer such a cruel death to redeem mankind, you should take back your words and submit to the judgment of the Church, which is the duty of every true Christian; that you should not wish to be separated from our Lord Jesus Christ who has created you so that you shall share in his glory; nor choose the road to eternal damnation together with the enemies of God

who daily seek to disturb men by claiming to be Christ, or an angel or a saint....

Pierre Maurice ends eloquently:

> I exhort you to abandon this attitude if you love God, your Creator, your precious Bridegroom and Savior. Obey the Church, accept her judgment, and know that if you do not, if you adhere to your mistake, your soul will be condemned to eternal punishment, and, as regards your body, I fear that that too will be destroyed. Do not be held back by fear of the opinions of your fellow men, nor by false shame. Place before all things the honor of God and the salvation of your body and soul. That will be altogether lost if you do not do as I tell you, because you will then cut yourself off from the Church and the Faith into which you have been received by baptism; you deny that the Church owes her authority to God, though he leads, governs and guides her with the authority of his Spirit. God has also said to the priests of the Church, "Those who hear you, hear me. Those who reject you, reject me." If you do not submit to the Church, you do not submit to God and you sin against the article *Unam sanctam Ecclesiam*....

The whole of contemporary theological authority is mobilized against the nineteen-year-old girl. She does not falter, but declares that she will adhere to what she has said at the trial: "Even if I were sentenced, even if I saw the burning stake, the faggots, the executioner lighting the fire, yes if I stood in the middle of it, I would not say anything else, and I should until death adhere to what I said at the trial."[3]

After months of imprisonment, with her body broken by sickness and chains, beaten, flogged, and maltreated, exposed to ceaseless spiritual torture, Joan is still able to answer with energy.

In the Churchyard of Saint-Ouen

On May 24, Joan is taken from her prison by Jean Beaupère, who exhorts her to submit. She is placed in a cart, which takes her to Saint-Ouen. The streets are filled with spectators.

Joan is made to descend outside the churchyard and to enter through a little gateway in the wall. Here she finds her friend, the priest-spy, Loiseleur. He whispers to her that she will be spared if she will only do as

---

[3] "*Responsio superba*" remarks the scribe in the margin.

the priests tell her and accept female attire. Above all, if she obeys, she will be released from the English prison and surrendered to the Church. In the churchyard, there is a great assembly of people. Two stands have been erected for the notables. On one of them is seen Guillaume Érard with two secretaries. On the other is the Cardinal of Winchester, who has not been present at the trial. By his side are the Bishop of Beauvais, the Bishop of Norwich, the Bishop of Noyon, the Bishop of Thérouanne, the abbot of Mont-Saint-Michel, several other abbots, two priors, twenty-seven men from the University, and many others. In his hand, Cauchon holds a paper containing the two alternative sentences he has prepared. One is to be used if Joan retracts and the other one if she persists.

English soldiers swarm around the stands. The procedure opens with a sermon by Guillaume Érard. He begins it with the parable of the branch, which cannot bear fruit of itself except it abide in the vine (John 15). Joan is the broken branch. He enlarges about her pride and charges her with defying God and the Catholic Faith and with having seduced her people. He also attacks Charles VII. Finally, he turns to Joan and says, "I am speaking to you, Joan. I say to you that your king is a heretic and a schismatic."

Joan rises before the assembled spectators and answers, "Preacher, you do not speak the truth. Do not mention my king. He is the noblest of all Christians, and none loves the Faith and the Church more than he. He is not what you say. Speak to me instead."

Shouts are heard that she must be silenced, but she again obtains a hearing: "As regards submission to the Church, I have already said that all I have done and said should be sent to Rome and submitted to the Holy Father, the Pope, to whom after God I submit. What I have done and said is of God. I do not lay the blame for what I have done and said upon anyone else, neither on my king nor on anyone; if there have been faults, they are mine and nobody else's."

When Joan refuses to submit, Cauchon reads the sentence. In the meanwhile, the priest-spy, Loiseleur, comes up to her and tries to persuade her by fatherly advice: "Joan, do as I have told you. Put on female attire."

Joan does not answer, but seeing the executioner's cart before her, she murmurs that she has always been an obedient daughter of the Church.

Cauchon has not yet finished reading out the sentence when he is suddenly interrupted by an English priest, Laurent Calot. It is not clear what he says, but he rages against Cauchon. He probably thinks, as do the English soldiers, that Cauchon is going to let Joan off too easily. "Traitor", he shouts to the French bishop.

Cauchon is so annoyed that he throws the manuscript on the ground and shouts that he will have nothing more to do with the matter. The Cardinal of England has to intervene and order Calot to be silent.

Joan makes a pathetic remark: "How you wear yourself out trying to get me to give in."

When Cauchon had calmed down, he asked the English Cardinal what he was to do.

"Ask her to do penance" is the reply.

The version of the judgment that had just been read seems to have been abandoned, and instead Guillaume Érard reads out a document containing the articles Joan must recant.

"I do not know what is meant by recant", she says. "I want it explained to me."

"Tell her about it", says Érard to his friend Massieu.

The latter at first tries to evade the task, but finally says to Joan: "It means that if you act against any of these articles, you will be burned. But I advise you to appeal to the Catholic Church as to whether you should accept these articles or not."

At a much later day Massieu gave evidence that he observed that Joan understood nothing and had no suspicion of the mortal danger she was in.[4]

Joan obeyed him to the best of her ability and said loudly to Érard: "I appeal to the Holy Catholic Church as to whether I should recant or not. I request that the document be given to the priests to whom I shall be surrendered, and if they afterward advise me to sign it, I shall do so."

One can see how Joan is trying to escape from the English in the certain conviction that placed before an exclusively ecclesiastical tribunal she will not be sentenced.

Érard roars at her that she must recant immediately, or she will be burned.

But he adds immediately after in a friendly tone: "Do as you are advised, and you will be released from prison."

---

[4] "The witness saw very well that Joan did not understand the aforesaid paper nor the peril that threatened her. He pointed out to Joan the danger and the meaning of the aforesaid document."

Before this definite promise, Joan replies that she will gladly do as they tell her. Witnesses report that she was surrounded by numerous persons who implored her to obey.

We do not know precisely what her words meant, how much she had understood of all she had heard during the last hour, or whether the meaning of the recantation was clear to her. In any case, her words roused great anger among the English soldiers, who were anxious to be present at such a popular event as the burning of a witch. Stones are hurled toward the stands, which must mean that there is a serious difference of opinion between the French, who want to spare Joan, and the English, who at any price want to kill the young woman who has defeated them so ignominiously in one battle after another.

In the middle of all this tumult, Érard hands Massieu a document for Joan's signature. It was the Form of Recantation, a brief document of about seven lines, written in French. It appears to have been a promise on the part of Joan that she would no longer bear arms, dress as a man, or wear her hair short. On the other hand, her "voices" are not mentioned nor anything about her mission.

Massieu reads this out, and Joan repeats it after him.

After the document has been read and approved by Joan, a very curious incident occurred, according to the testimony of many eyewitnesses. The English cleric Laurent Calot, who has just been mentioned, comes up to Joan's stand, crumples up the document Massieu has just read, draws another one out of his sleeve and lays it before Joan.[5]

"But I can neither read nor write", she says.

Calot nevertheless hands her a pen with which she smilingly draws a ring on the paper. Calot then takes her hand and guides it to form a cross and a signature at the foot of this new retractation, in which it is expressly said that Joan rejects her revelations and "voices".

Joan appears to understand nothing. She is happy in the thought that she will soon be free of the soldiers and surrendered to the Church, which will deal justly with her.[6]

---

[5] "Another than the witness had read in the acts of the trial ...", says Massieu.

[6] The Bishop of Noyon, who was an eyewitness, writes: "*Ut videtur, ipsa Johanna de illa abjuratione nun multum curabat, nec faciebat de eadem compotum, et illud quod fecit in hujusmodi abjuratione, fecit precibus adstantium devicta.*" (It appeared that Joan paid little attention to the recantation and did not understand it; what she did in making this recantation she did at the urging of those around her.)

Many of those present maintained that the document was of no importance. Joan herself only laughed.

Cauchon read out the prepared sentence. It ends:

> You have sinned seriously by mendaciously asserting that you have had revelations and divine visions, by seducing others, by engaging in witchcraft and magic, by blaspheming against God and the saints, by defying the law, Holy Scriptures and the canonical orders.
>
> But as you have, after being lovingly enlightened and given long time for reflection, at last thanks to God's grace returned to Holy Mother Church and publicly retracted your heresies with a sorrowing heart and in complete sincerity; as your heresies have been made clear in the public sermon; as you have with your own voice loudly forsworn all heresy, we free you from the bonds of excommunication in which you have been fettered, though on the condition that you return to the Church with a contrite heart and honest faith and that you will do that which we will tell you.
>
> But as you have according to that which has here been laid down deliberately sinned against God and the Holy Church, in order that you may make suitable penance, we sentence you to imprisonment for life in the bread of pain and waters of sorrow, and that there imprisoned you may weep over your evil acts and never repeat them.

When Cauchon had finished his reading the priest-spy, Loiseleur, exclaimed: "Joan, what a great day! If God grants it, you have now saved your soul."

Joan replies that she wants to be surrendered to the Church immediately and freed from the English.

But then an astounding thing happens. Cauchon orders Massieu to take her back to her old prison. Joan is placed in the cart that had brought her from the castle. Some of the English soldiers shout jeeringly to Cauchon and accuse him of having attempted by treachery to save her from a just sentence.

Frightened, the judges withdraw, but they are pursued by the enraged Englishmen, who cry that the King has spent money unnecessarily on them.[7]

---

[7] *"Dicentes quod rex male expenderat pecunias suas ergo eos."* If this report is true, the soldiers must have known the proven fact that the judges had to a large extent received money from the English king. This hardly seems likely.

Warwick especially is furious. He openly blames Cauchon for permitting Joan to escape with her life, of which the King will not approve.

Cauchon answers: "Do not worry. We will get her."

This version is the traditional one. Even a modern scholar like Calmette agrees with it in the main. As usual, Cordier is more critical. He considers simply that advantage was taken of Joan's exhaustion—her laughter on the sinister occasion must have been hysterical—and that they made her sign a short résumé of the Form of Recantation, which was also at hand but in Latin. That the documents should have been exchanged in such a way as to deceive Joan, Cordier regards as unlikely.

What supports Cordier's view is the fact that Joan later repeated her recantation in considerably calmer conditions, which she could hardly have done if she had been completely deceived. This happened the same afternoon, when she was visited by the inquisitor, Jean Lemaître, and six priests wanting to explain to her what extraordinary mercy God had shown her.

Joan is then supposed to have answered that she would willingly put on female attire and that she would obey and submit to the Church in everything.

She was given female clothing, in which she at once dressed herself, and her hair was done in a different way.

She then said: "Let me now have women around me, and send me to the Church's prison so that I can be guarded by priests."

But her judges leave her in the same prison, probably still fettered and still exposed to the brutalities of the English soldiers.

Already on May 27, there was a rumor in Rouen that she had withdrawn her recantation.

CHAPTER 15

Joan Retracts

Joan had confessed her errors and submitted to the Church. This produced the greatest anger in the English camp, for an immediate execution had been expected. The soldiery made the streets unsafe, and Cauchon and his followers were continually subjected to abuse and treated like traitors; it was thought that they had tried to save Joan from her just punishment.

Joan had hoped to be placed in an ecclesiastical prison, to be free from her English warders, and to be allowed to attend Mass; one has the definite impression that this was the decisive motive for her action. She was, however, taken back to her old prison. The only difference was that now she wore feminine clothing in the presence of the English warders and that her hair was completely cropped.

Until the end she thought this was a passing phase and that she would be taken away. Instead the warders' brutality increased. She was beaten until blood flowed, and she related afterward that an English "milord" attempted to rape her.

Then a rumor was spread that Joan had reverted to male clothing.

It is not known for certain why or how this happened.

Without doubt, Joan had found that she had betrayed her mission and failed her "voices". But what concrete facts lay behind the reports of her withdrawal of her recantation is difficult to know. It is easiest to assume that after pondering the matter for a few days she realized that she had been duped and the promises would never be kept, and that she then regretted what she had done. But there are a number of other accounts. For instance, it is said that one night when Joan was asleep the warders took her female clothing away. Instead they offered her her old male clothing, which had meanwhile been in a sack in a corner of the prison. She refused and said that this was not allowed. She did not give way until about noon, when she was compelled to put on her old clothing.

This had been interpreted to mean that Cauchon had been so severely criticized by the English for having saved Joan that he ordered the warders to steal her female clothing, thereby forcing her to break her word. He was supposed to have told the English that there was no need to worry, he would know how to get her....

However, these are all unsubstantiated reports. The one thing that is certain is that after Joan's recantation, Cauchon read out a sentence prepared beforehand by which Joan was condemned to imprisonment for life, and that soon after that she assumed male attire, which made it necessary for her case to be taken up anew.

The Archdeacon of Rouen, Margueri, was one of the first to visit Joan. He stated that it was not enough to know that she had exchanged her clothing, but that it was also necessary to know why she had done so. He evidently had his suspicions. This made some of the English furious: one of them called Margueri "Armagnac traitor" and tried to cut him down.

When a number of judges sought out Cauchon to discuss the new situation with him, they barely escaped being massacred by the English soldiery. These incidents seemed to confirm the theory that the tribunal was satisfied with the sentence, but that the English pressure was so strong that it had to be revised in one way or another. Either Joan was forced to resume male attire or she did so of her own free will, but whichever was the case, it provided the opportunity for a new trial.

On the first day, Cauchon appear not to have dared to show himself out of doors for fear of the enraged Englishmen. But on the following day, May 28, he gave orders that a special commission was to visit Joan. Manchon replied that he refused to take part in it as he would not risk his life. He would come, but only if Warwick in person escorted him and guaranteed him against attacks.

When the commission entered Joan's prison, they found her almost unrecognizable. She had been beaten bloody, her face ravaged by weeping, her hair close-cropped, and she was wearing her old male clothing. Her woman's clothing lay on the floor. It has been believed that her warders laid it there to make it appear as if she had changed her clothing of her own free will. One can only wonder in that case why she did not immediately change again.

Cauchon asked her why she had changed her clothing.

If the report about the warders' trick were correct, Joan would have replied that her female clothing had been stolen. Instead she replies, and there is every reason to believe her: "I prefer male clothing to a woman's."

Cauchon: "But you have promised and sworn never again to wear male clothing."

Joan: "I have never done so."

Cauchon: "Why have you done this?"

Joan: "Because the promises made to me have not been kept, that I should be allowed to attend Mass, that I should be allowed to receive Communion, that I should be freed from my fetters. Have you not yourselves, my judges, promised that I should be handed over to the care of the Church? And that I should be allowed to have a woman with me? I have put on male attire again because I want to guard my virtue, because I cannot feel safe in female clothing with warders who are always throwing themselves on me trying to violate me. Have I not complained about this to you, my Lord Bishop?"

Cauchon: "Have you not recanted, and have you not clearly promised not to dress as a man again?"

Joan: "I would rather die than remain in prison. But if I am promised to be allowed to attend Mass, to be released from my fetters, and to be taken to a decent prison and given a woman, I shall do what the Church asks."

Cauchon then asks: "Have you heard your 'voices' since Thursday?"

Joan: "Yes."

Cauchon: "And what did they say?"

Joan: "God told me by Saint Catherine and Saint Margaret that I had committed a serious act of treachery in agreeing to recant in order to save my life. Before Thursday my 'voices' had foretold what I should do and what I have today done. When I was on the stand, my 'voices' told me to answer bravely the priest who made the sermon. He is a false preacher. He told of many things that I have never done. If I should say that God had not sent me, I would condemn myself to eternal damnation. The truth is that God has sent me.

"Ever since Thursday my 'voices' have said to me that I did something very despicable when I confessed that I should not have done what I have done. What I said or retracted was only because of my fear of the stake."

She added that now she would rather die than remain in the prison. What was read to her from the paper she had been asked to sign she never understood. She had clearly stated that she would never withdraw anything if it were not the will of God.

Should the judges wish it, she would resume female attire. But that is the only thing to which she will agree.

When Cauchon left the castle, he encountered a group of eagerly waiting Englishmen, among whom was Warwick. Cauchon is said to have cried out in delight: "Farewell, farewell! Have no fear; she is ours."

On the 29th, Cauchon assembled forty-two theologians and learned men for new discussions. He informed them that after solemnly retracting her heresies Joan had again heard her demoniac "voices", and as soon as she could had resumed male attire.

He naturally did not mention that Joan had been beaten and had been the object of attempted rape, and that she had found no other way of protecting herself than by wearing male clothing tightly bound around her body.

Full of indignation those present made their declaration one after the other. They were agreed that Joan had relapsed into sin and quickly decided that she should now be handed over to the temporal authorities. There is no indication that any of the judges asked for an explanation. Cauchon's word was accepted.

On the Stake: "Consummatum est"

On March 1, Cauchon had asked Joan, "Have your 'voices' told you that you will be released from your prison where you now are?"

Joan answered: "Ask me in three months, and I will reply."

To the day three months later, May 30, 1431, Joan was released, though in a different way than she had thought.

At half past seven in the morning, Massieu entered Joan's prison and informed her that at eight o'clock she must present herself before her judges in the square of the Vieux-Marché to receive her new sentence.

After Massieu had left, two monks, Martin Ladvenu and Jean Toutmouillé, arrived to prepare Joan for her death. Toutmouillé has told of this talk. He raised the question of her "voices", and she told him that she heard them most often when the church bells pealed for Compline and Matins.

The monks asked Joan if she did not now realize that the "voices" had deceived her.

She is said to have answered: "Yes, now I really see that they cheated me."

Asked whether she thought the "voices" were evil or good spirits, she is said to have answered: "That I do not know. I submit to the Church."

Or—the informants themselves hesitate—"... you who are men of the Church...."

They add that Joan seemed quite clear in her head. Afterward she is said to have confessed.

Martin Ladvenu relates that Joan admitted that the angel that appeared before Charles VII in Chinon was herself, that the King had never received any crown, and that everything she had told in this connection was invention.

One can well believe that the tortured girl might have agreed to everything without the strength to resist.

When Martin Ladvenu informed Joan that she was to be burned alive she burst into tears. Her words have been reported as follows: "Oh, that I should be treated so cruelly! Oh, that my whole body, which has never been defiled, should today be consumed and become ashes! Oh, I would sooner have my head cut off seven times than be burned in this manner! Oh, if I had only been in the hands of the Church instead of in those of my enemy, I would never have come to this terrible end! Before God the highest judge I appeal against these assaults and acts of violence to which I am exposed by my warders and the people they allow to come in to me."

At that moment Cauchon entered. To this executioner of hers, she cried, "My Lord Bishop, it is you who murder me."

Cauchon replied that she must die because she had not kept her promises but returned to her heresies.

Joan replied, weeping, that if she had only been placed in an ecclesiastic prison this would never have happened. By this she must have meant that she was quite willing to dress as a woman, but that in order to protect herself against the warders she had been compelled to wear male attire.

When Joan saw Pierre Maurice behind Cauchon, she asked him, "Where will I be tonight?"

He answered, "Dare you not put your faith in the Lord?"

Joan answered, "By the grace of God I shall be in Paradise."

She then confessed and afterward received Holy Communion. Jacques le Camus relates that as Martin Ladvenu was about to hand her the Host he asked her, "Do you believe that this is the Body of our Lord?"

Joan answered, "Yes" and added that it is the only thing which could save her and that she wished to receive Him.

Immediately afterward the monk asked her, "Do you still believe in those 'voices'?"

"I believe in nothing but God: I do not wish any longer to believe in the 'voices' as they have deceived me."

According to one report, a priest had come with the Sacrament but without stole or candle, whereupon the monk had angrily sent him back. The Sacrament was then carried to Joan in a great procession with many burning candles and amid prayers: "*Orate pro ea....*"

As the hour struck eight, she was released from her fetters and dressed in a long linen garment. On her head was placed a cap in the shape of a mitre on which were written the words: "Heretic, Relapsed, Apostate, Idolater".

She mounted a cart, and Martin Ladvenu and Massieu seated themselves at her side. Before and after the cart marched eight hundred fully armed English troops. The priest-spy, Loiseleur, stood in the crowd watching the procession. Suddenly he elbowed his way up to the cart and, weeping, begged Joan to forgive him. The English abused him as a traitor and hurled him to the ground—he would have been killed if Warwick had not intervened.

Nicolas de Houppeville, who had earlier described the trial as invalid, relates that he had a glimpse of Joan's tear-stained face from the castle gate. He refused to follow the excited crowd and went away by himself.

On the way Joan cried out, "Rouen, Rouen—is it here that I am to die?"

The two priests sitting by her side wept.

It was nine o'clock, and the cart arrived at the square. The whole population of the town was, of course, present, and many clung to the roofs to obtain a better view.

Three stands were erected on the square.

On one were seated the churchmen, Cauchon, Jean Lemaître, the English Cardinal, and many others.

On the second sat the city counselors and lay jurists.

On the third stand, the theologian of the University of Paris, Nicolas Midi, stood awaiting Joan. He was to give her a final admonition. In front of this stand was erected a board with the words: "Joan, who calls herself the Maid, liar, evildoer, seducer of the people, sorceress, witch, blasphemer of God, denier of the Faith of Jesus Christ, idolater, fallen, evoker of evil spirits, apostate, schismatic, heretic."

The stake was unusually high in order that all should be able to see the witch die, and perhaps also so that the executioner should not be able to reach up to give her the *coup de grâce* and cut short her suffering.

Nicolas Midi's sermon was based on the words of Saint Paul: "And whether one member suffer, all the members suffer with it." Joan is the rotten member that must be cut off in order that other members shall not be infected....

He ended with the words: "Joan, go in peace. The Church can no longer defend you but surrenders you into the hands of the secular authorities."

Cauchon rises. Referring to the Fathers of the Church, he explains that an infected limb must be severed. The Church removes her hand from her, rejects her from her community, and surrenders her to the secular authorities in the hope that they will treat her with gentleness and if she shows signs of sincere repentance, permit her the sacrament of penitence.

Joan prays without ceasing, and witnesses present thought that they could distinguish the words:

"Holy Trinity, have mercy upon me.

"Jesus, have mercy upon me.

"Holy Mother, have mercy upon me.

"O saints of Paradise, pray for me.

"Saint Michael, pray for me.

"Saint Catherine and Saint Margaret, help me."

She is also said to have chivalrously defended her king for the last time: "All that I have done for good or evil, I have done of my own; my king has not forced me to do it."

Turning to the crowd, she says, "All of you who stand there, I beg you to forgive the harm I have done you as I forgive you the harm you have done me, and I beg you to pray for me."

261

When she sees several priests with tears in their eyes, she says, "All you priests who are here, I beg you to say a Mass for me, every one of you."

For half an hour Joan prays in this manner before her waiting executioners. There is evidence that Cauchon and most of the English judges shed tears. Sobs are heard all around.

Joan now asks for a crucifix, and strangely enough, it is an English soldier who makes a cross from two twigs and hands it to her. She presses it to her breast, prays to God, and thrusts it between her garment and her body.

Now she says to those nearest to her: "I beg of you go into that church there and bring the crucifix. Hold it just before my eyes until I die. I wish to see the cross upon which God was nailed as long as I remain in life."

Massieu does as she asks. She grasps this cross too and presses it long to her lips. Around her are several priests who try to console her.

But the English are becoming impatient. The soldiers ask if they are to wait here till noon. Two officers mount the stand and seizing Joan take her to the other stand where the town counselors are seated, for it is they who are to pronounce judgment. The only words one hears from the stand are "Take her to the stake."

The two Englishmen lead Joan to the executioner, who awaits her at the foot of the stake, and say, "Do your duty."

A number of the priests depart, unable to bear the sight.

Joan steps onto the faggots, and the two priests follow. When from the top of the stake she sees the crowd, she exclaims, "Oh, Rouen—I shudder when I think what you will suffer from my death."

She kisses the crucifix.

The executioner lashes her to the pole in the middle of the stake, while she cries, "Saint Michael, Saint Michael."

When she is fastened firmly the executioner steps down and lights the faggots. Joan says to the priests, who are still at her side, "Hurry, get down."

And she repeats, "Hold up the crucifix in front of me so that I can see it the whole time."

When the flames reach her she calls for holy water.... She is not heard to cry out or groan.

But she repeats that her "voices" are true, she calls to her saints and cries that her revelations are no invention, and repeats several times, "Jesus, Jesus...."

"We are lost, we have burned a saint"

Joan's death made a deep impression. One cannot escape the suspicion that many of the French judges really wished her well, and that the death sentence was to a great extent due to political pressure by the English. Cauchon can, without doubt, be condemned as a traitor, and he was a pretty bad character. It is nonetheless possible that his tears before the dying Joan were in their way genuine. One of the secretaries of the English king, John Tressart, was particularly moved. According to the evidence of contemporary witnesses, he stood there sad and despairing, and said, "We are lost. It is a saint we have burned; her soul is certainly in the hands of God, for in the midst of the flames she continually uttered the name of Jesus."

We see a repetition of what happened after the death of Jesus at Golgotha, when the Roman captain understood that an innocent man had been killed. The executioner himself visited the Dominican monastery in the town the same evening and told Martin Ladvenu that he was mortally afraid of eternal damnation for having burned a holy woman. He added that she had been killed in a "tyrannical" manner. He also related that when the body had been burned the heart had remained filled with blood untouched by the fire. He had thrown oil, sulphur, and wood over the heart and intestines, but in spite of this had been unable to destroy them. He regarded this as being "a clear miracle".

Another strange story that gained great circulation was the following:

An English soldier related that he had come up to the stake with a faggot just at the moment when Joan had loudly cried the name of Jesus. The Englishman had then observed a white dove rise from the flames. He remained rooted to the ground "as if in ecstasy" and had to be led away by his comrades. In the evening he went to the Dominican monastery and confessed to Isambart de la Pierre that he had assisted at something terrible and that he repented of what he had done to Joan. "She was a good woman."

One of Joan's judges, the canon Jean Alespée, had watched her die and had cried all the time: "God permit that my soul be where her soul is."

A man whose evidence was of great importance in the Trial of Rehabilitation was Manchon, who related that Joan prayed so piously and sincerely that many of those present were moved to tears. Manchon's own repentance has already been described.

The prior of the Benedictine monastery of Saint-Michel later related that he had heard several witnesses testify that the name of Jesus could be clearly heard from the actual flames and added that if the English had had such a woman on their side, they would have "covered her with honors and not treated her in this manner".

Joan's ashes were gathered together and thrown into the Seine. Every year, even up to our own day, a beautiful ceremony takes place in Rouen.

On the anniversary of Joan's death, young girls garbed in white assemble on the spot where her ashes were cast into the river. In memory of her, the girls strew white flowers on the water, which gently carries them out of the town toward the sea.

CHAPTER 16

The Trial of Rehabilitation

After the fall of La Trémoille, the favorite of Charles VII, the High Constable de Richemont, assumed the command, and it was not long before the situation had changed completely.

In 1449, Rouen was recaptured; in the following year, the High Constable with three thousand men gained an overwhelming victory over six thousand Englishmen at Formigny. Then fell Honfleur, Caen, Falaise, Cherbourg—all the large Norman cities. Guyenne was still occupied by the English, and it took two more years of fighting before it could be conquered. The decisive battle was fought at Castillon in the Périgord in the summer of 1452, where six thousand Englishmen under Talbot suffered a crushing defeat.

This was really the end of the Hundred Years' War, and the English were thrown out of France.

Eighteen years had gone by since Joan was burned. She was not forgotten, her memory lived on, and one of the King's first measures was to take up her case anew. He began this in 1449, when he gave orders to Guillaume Bouillé, an eminent theologian who was also his counselor, to make a preparatory investigation. The King wrote that he wished "to know the truth about this trial and the manner in which it had been conducted".

Bouillé began his task immediately and first examined seven witnesses: Jean Toutmouillé, Isambart de la Pierre, and Martin Ladvenu, who had all assisted Joan in her last hour; Guillaume Duval, one of the judges; Manchon and Massieu; and finally the examiner at the trial, Jean Beaupère.

Toutmouillé, who was a Dominican, did everything in his power to free his order from responsibility and to place this on Cauchon.

Isambart de la Pierre had been Joan's friend and had advised her to appeal to the Church Council. He related a number of compromising facts regarding Cauchon's attitude.

Martin Ladvenu, also a Dominican, spoke in the same spirit and described the judgment as invalid.

Manchon's and Massieu's testimonies have already been related. Guillaume Duval had nothing of importance to contribute.

Jean Beaupère did his best to evade responsibility and pointed out that he was not present when sentence was pronounced. He was asked for his personal opinion of Joan—he was then a man in his seventies—to which he replied nervously that Joan had answered very cunningly, with typical feminine trickiness, but that he had never concluded from her answers that she was a bad woman.

In his summary, Bouillé considered that the trial must be regarded as null and void, that it was a disgrace that the name of the King of France should be associated with a person who had been sentenced as a witch, and that the revision must be undertaken as soon as possible.

It is to be observed that this new trial also had a political background. It is evident that nobody who had testified against Joan now had the smallest prospects. What mattered was that the victorious King should be cleansed of the shame that attached to him because of Joan's sentence. This does not, however, alter the fact that in the course of the Trial of Rehabilitation much evidence saw the light of day that clearly proved the illegality of the first trial and the many errors in procedure committed by Cauchon.

Just then the papal legate, Cardinal d'Estouteville, later (in 1453) Archbishop of Rouen, arrived in France. The King instructed him to continue the revision of the sentence. But the real object of the Cardinal's mission was to reconcile France and England and if possible to unite the two countries in a war against the Turks, and he was therefore disinclined to undertake anything that would irritate the English. The King and his counselors then hit upon the idea of letting Joan's own family make the first move and demand a re-hearing. Joan's mother, now an aged widow, took up the matter and pursued it with astonishing energy. The Pope, Nicholas V, died in 1455 before having taken a definite stand, but his successor, Calixtus III, intervened and nominated three commissioners: Guillaume Chartier; Richard de Longueil, Bishop of Coutances; and Jean Jouvenel des Ursins, Archbishop of Reims.

The new trial was opened in Notre Dame in Paris on November 7, 1455. The Archbishop of Reims, the Bishop of Paris, and the Inquisitor, Jean Bréhal, were the presidents. Joan's mother appeared—"with many sobs and groans"—and formally demanded that the matter should be examined anew. Her advocate, Maugier, expounded the juridical side. It is interesting to note that both in this address and in the address of the Pope when he gave authority for the case to be taken up anew, the names of those judges who were still living were avoided. Cauchon, who had died in the meantime, is mentioned in the most courteous way ("of happy memory"). Ample time was given to those involved to make their defense, but neither they nor any advocates representing them appeared. Four great examinations were held in Domrémy, Rouen, Orléans, and Paris. One hundred and fifty witnesses were heard, and the evidence obtained was prepared and embodied in ninety-two articles. The arguments of the tribunal may be summarized thus:

1. The Rouen trial was invalid on the grounds of procedure; Joan did not belong to the diocese of Beauvais. The question of visions and revelations can only be judged by the Pope; Joan's appeal to the Pope had been ignored; Joan was a minor and had not been provided with counsel; the twelve articles were inaccurate; the paper Joan had been induced to sign was not identical with the record in the trial.

2. The judges had lacked impartiality; here the brutal treatment Joan had undergone was examined, as well as all the questions intended to trap her and take her unawares, and much other material.

3. Joan's whole manner had been irreproachable; backed by an enormous amount of fresh evidence, it was proved that Joan had been an example of piety, that she had never acted in opposition to the Church, that her "voices" could not possibly have been satanic, that her male attire was necessary in the situation in which she found herself, and that her statements about the sign in Chinon must be taken in an allegorical sense.

Of course, most of the examination is convincing, but it is clear that the most dangerous questions were evaded. For how could it be known with certainty that Joan had been sent by God, and why did she refuse to submit to the decision of the Church in Rouen? If the outcome of the Rouen trial was obvious from the start, the same is true of the later trial; it could only end in one way.

The most interesting moment of this reexamination has been pointed out by Lucien Fabre.

Among the documents Manchon produced was a copy of the twelve articles, made by one of his collaborators, Jacques de Touraine. In the margin of this copy were a number of alterations, all of them in Joan's favor. The new judges also discovered a marginal note to the effect that the twelve articles did not correspond with Joan's own evidence. This annotation had been made by Manchon.

Manchon was interrogated.

The summary of the accusations under twelve articles was a convenience in accordance with the usage of the times and not in itself remarkable. But what was remarkable was that the sentence had been based on the twelve articles and not on the original records. Why had the judges not had recourse to the records?

Manchon: "They had at that time not yet been recorded in their present form, that is, in Latin; this was only done after the death of Joan."

"On what evidence did the judges then base the sentence? On Joan's French evidence?"

"No."

"On what then?"

"On the twelve articles."

"Had these been read and approved by Joan?"

"No."

"Was there then not a corrected copy of the twelve articles?"

"Yes. During a secret conference, certain of the articles were altered at the suggestion of some of the judges."

"And yet the judges were provided with copies without any alterations?"

"Yes."

"Why?"

"I had received my orders. The judges thought it best to do it this way."

The last meeting took place in Rouen in the large hall of the episcopal palace.

The necessary formalities were completed during the first week of July, and on July 7 the verdict was announced. Jean Jouvenel des Ursins was the president, the two bishops were judges, Joan's brother represented the family. Among those present were a number of priests, among them Martin Ladvenu, the same monk who had remained at Joan's side until the end.

The Archbishop of Reims read out the judgment.

On the spot where Joan had been burned, a cross was raised in expiation.

The news was celebrated with great festivities all over the country, but the joy was especially great in Orléans.

Charles VII defrayed all the costs of the trial.

Joan the Saint

In 1869, Bishop Dupanloup of Orléans had the inspiration to invite to the annual commemoration of Joan of Arc the bishops of all the towns through which Joan had marched on the way to Reims or before she had been taken prisoner.

On this occasion the bishop made his now famous speech about Joan's importance as a patriot and as a Catholic. Then all the bishops present addressed a solemn appeal to Pope Pius IX, from which we quote:

> Not only Orléans and France but the whole world venerate God's acts through Joan of Arc, the piety and enthusiasm of this young girl, the purity and unbending self-abnegation with which she always carried out the will of God, as well as the reputation for holiness which crowned her life both in Domrémy, where she tended her father's cattle as a modest peasant girl, on the battlefield where she showed the skill and courage of a great captain, and at the stake where she displayed her unalterable loyalty to the Christian Faith and the Apostolic See.
>
> The Roman Popes have already defended, shielded, and praised this admirable heroine, and it is the general wish that Your Holiness now honor and exalt her memory. This would constitute a just tribute to Joan, who in freeing her country also saved it from the heresy which might have become a danger in the future. It would also constitute a title of honor to the French people, who have done so much for religion and for the Throne of Saint Peter, and who also have deserved the name of "God's soldier".

The Congregation of Rites in Rome began its work and in 1894 took up Joan's case—"*la cause de la vénérable servante de Dieu Jeanne d'Arc, vierge*".

The beatification was pronounced by Pope Pius X, and the canonization by Benedict XV on May 9, 1920.

Joan thus became the national saint of France. Her picture is to be found in most French churches. In processions in Orléans, Catholics and freemasons march side by side to honor her memory; commemorative tablets and statues keep alive her rides through France.

However, it is only since her real personality has begun to appear through the editions of Quichérat and Champion of the documents of her trial that she has aroused the interest and love of the great Catholic poets. Paul Claudel has described her death. Georges Bernanos has paid tribute to her Catholic loyalty and courage. Charles Péguy has probed the mystery of her vocation in *Le Mystère de la Charité de Jeanne d'Arc*. In strange fragments filled with deep insight, Léon Bloy has endeavored to fit her story into his Christian interpretation of history.

For Bloy, history and all its sufferings is nothing but a continuation of the Incarnation of Christ and his suffering on the Cross. The deep inner meaning of history is that Christ became man for the sins of mankind. "All centuries are Christ's centuries ... are of the same infinitely deep nature, literally of the same eternity", says Péguy. That means that the events of history are not only symbols of deeper truths, they are actually moments in a divine process of redemption and re-creation in which mankind takes part. In history, God writes his own revelation. According to Léon Bloy, our history corresponds to the history told in the Old and New Testaments. Nothing happens that is not the "figure" of one and the same event. God becomes man and dies for our sins. History is not just a repetition or a copy of the drama of redemption. It is the *same* drama, conceived by us as a succession of events in time. The thirty-three years of the life of Christ and all other events in time occur in the same moment of eternity. The suffering of the world is the same suffering as the death agony of Christ, which in this manner is prolonged until the end of time in his Mystical Body. Without end we experience the Passion, and through it we are contemporaneous with all suffering mankind, all who have suffered and all who shall suffer. All of our suffering is universal suffering—there is only one suffering, the agony of Christ. Christ is therefore the center of everything. Every blow that is struck is received by him.

God has spoken twice: in Holy Writ and in history. But his language is always the same: love—which sacrifices itself for those who have no love.

Joan used to ask to be allowed to communicate not with the congregation but with the poor children whom the Dominicans brought up and educated. She is as humble as a child. Yes, she is a child, not only in years. She is not aware of her humility, for she knows no other state of mind. From the beginning she has that total trust, that faith to which it is self-evident that God is behind everything that happens—a faith to which grown Christians usually attain only after much suffering and many trials. The public activity of this girl took place between her seventeenth and eighteenth years. Her visions are psychologically interesting, but they cannot be compared to the meetings with the supernatural experienced by more developed saints. Joan is never allowed to obtain an insight into the planning of great spiritual events. She only gets clear orders how to act. When she was canonized, the Church therefore placed no emphasis upon her visions and did not base her sainthood on these experiences. Her mission was of another kind. It was to suffer for the sins of mankind. At first she believed, like her contemporaries, that her mission was as a soldier to free France and crown the King, and there is no reason why we should not accept her view. But her mission became more profound in the same degree as her own loyalty proved equal to her task. She is found worthy of the greatest task of all—to be cut off from the help of man, from all spiritual support—to suffer alone the death of a martyr. This task is high above the human sphere. It is beyond reason and appears to be injustice and sheer cruelty to anyone who does not see mankind as a single whole and the suffering of Christ as the profoundest content of history. Joan is human, she is young, and the sacrifice appears to her terrifyingly hard when she recognizes it. She weeps, she sorrows because her pure body is to be destroyed. But as soon as she discovers that she has weakened or has been tricked into denying her life's deepest purpose, she acts quickly and purposefully and takes back what she has said. She knows then that she faces death. She is not capable of theoretically expounding her mission, but she knows that it is as simple as to carry a sword and ride a charger in a battle for a French town. She must adhere to her "voices" and take all the consequences, for God is reality and his will, which is love, lies behind even the greatest suffering.

It is by this courage, this willingness, that Joan of Arc has her place in history as one of the greatest figures of mankind. Too long she has been conceived principally as the glorious patriot, the dashing amazon at the head of France's armies, and it is true that history can show no one who can compare with her in this respect. But the patriotic side of Joan must not be allowed to obscure her deepest mission, which is to follow the example of Christ and to give her life for mankind.

Better than anyone else Georges Bernanos has evoked the first part of Joan's mission.

He speaks of her joy in the twelve beautiful chargers she had at her disposal. He speaks of the hundred banners beating in the wind during the assaults. Calmly she rode her horse against a wall of spears fifteen feet in length while the arrows rained against her armor and the sinews of the great bows clanged as they discharged their missiles. He understood that she experienced not fear but genuine joy at the sound of the hoofbeats of all the horses of her personal staff who followed behind.

It is a glorious picture almost unique in history; it comes to us from the world of myth and chivalry. Yet neither myth nor the epic poems of chivalry have produced a figure nobler and purer than the eighteen-year-old Joan of Arc riding over the plains of France, where the cathedrals are dimly seen on the misty horizon, where the heaths are golden with broom and the forests are streaked by white acacia blossoms, while the sun pursues its royal road over her head.

And yet it is the other part of her mission that is the greater: the times when she who has been followed by armored hosts, who with a movement of the hand could let loose a rain of arrows or a charge by a thousand horsemen, sits fettered in an iron cage and is dragged out only to be maltreated and insulted by coarse and drunken warders; when she bravely and clearly withdraws her recantation and declares herself ready to die; when in the hour of her anguish she is never once tempted to accuse God or question his love.

Joan's real greatness is her willingness to die as shameful a death as the Savior upon the Cross.

Human reason raises a protest against such an interpretation.

How can the death of an innocent girl have such a value? How can it cause gain or relief for a tortured mankind? How can we others reap any other benefit than a great example of submission and courage through the death of this girl?

To such questions there is no answer. Historians and poets have for centuries attempted unsuccessfully to convey this secret in words. And yet we are here close to the deepest meaning of history. We do not know how sacrifice freely and humbly given can become a blessing and gain for others; for reason alone can never make us understand that fallen and redeemed mankind is one single, living unit. We understand it as little as we can really understand why God's Son had to be sacrificed to redeem a world created by an Almighty God. But if instruments more delicate than human reason have once made us grasp the immensity of love that lies behind Jesus' voluntary death, then we may also understand Joan's place in the plan of God. So terrible was the fall of man that the Son of God had to be sacrificed. So appalling is the continued blindness of redeemed mankind that, as a sacrifice for all the cowardly, the cold-hearted, and the arrogant, God must call upon the purest and bravest souls to suffer innocently and to die.

POSTSCRIPT

This book is based on old and modern literature, but not on the study of archives.

From what has been said in the body of the text, it will be clear that, mainly through Jacques Cordier's revolutionary work *Jeanne d'Arc, sa Personnalité, son Rôle* (1948), the study of Joan of Arc has entered upon a crisis; for Cordier relegates to legend a very large number of the accepted reports concerning Joan of Arc, reduces her revelations to hysterical phenomena, rejects most of the accounts of her miracles as later inventions, and in general attempts to show that Joan's military and political contribution has been exaggerated.

To a great extent I have agreed with this treatment of the material for a biography of Joan, but I differ radically from Cordier concerning the basic view of Joan's person. My book may be said to be an attempt to create a picture of Joan of Arc as a mystic out of the material left by Cordier and others. Thus I use Cordier's conclusions, with certain reservations, but I use them in a manner of which he would highly disapprove.

The older works written by more or less Christian students of Joan of Arc all build on unreliable material, especially the dangerous *Chronique de la Pucelle*, and appear to me to sentimentalize and cheapen her.

The most important sources for Joan's biography are still Jules Quicherat's five volumes of documentary collections. P. Champion's book about the trial deals only with the examinations and conclusions, not with the evidence in the Trial of Rehabilitation, which is most important. One can read with advantage about the Trial of Rehabilitation in Belon and Balme's enormous opus *Jean Bréhal, Grand Inquisiteur de France, et la Réhabilitation de Jeanne d'Arc* (1893); Siméon Luce's *Jeanne d'Arc à Domrémy* (1886) is still essential. The *Chronique de la Pucelle* exists in an edition of 1859, published by Vallet de Viniville. Anatole France's book is extremely readable and supported by an imposing erudition; it gives picturesque details and clever conclusions and often poetically delicate vignettes, but is flawed by the author's inability to comprehend any of Joan's mysticism. G. Hanotaux' *Jeanne d'Arc* (1911), though a brilliant work, has been superseded by more recent research. Joseph Calmette's *Jeanne d'Arc* (1946) is exemplary, and his great work, *Les grands ducs de Bourgogne* (1949), also is important. Lucien Fabre's *Jeanne d'Arc* (1947) throws a clear light especially on Cauchon's role in the tragedy and is written with genuine enthusiasm. Important essays have been contributed by Stanislas Fumet (*Sainte Jeanne d'Arc*, 1929), Hilaire Belloc (*Joan of Arc*), and Georges Bernanos (*Jeanne, relapse et Sainte*, 1934). The works of the Jesuit P. Doncoeur are insignificant and tendentious. Various special studies have been mentioned in the text of this book.

Most of all I have learned from the few pages Léon Bloy devoted to Joan of Arc and from the Christian interpretation of history and of the doctrine of suffering propounded in his works.